Study Guide

for use with

Financial Accounting

Tenth Edition

Robert F. Meigs
San Diego State University, Emeritus

Jan R. Williams
University of Tennessee

Susan F. Haka
Michigan State University

Mark S. Bettner
Bucknell University

Prepared by
Mark S. Bettner
Bucknell University

**Irwin
McGraw-Hill**

**Boston   Burr Ridge, IL   Dubuque, IA   Madison, WI   New York   San Francisco   St. Louis
Bangkok   Bogotá   Caracas   Lisbon   London   Madrid
Mexico City   Milan   New Delhi   Seoul   Singapore   Sydney   Taipei   Toronto**

Irwin/McGraw-Hill

A Division of The McGraw·Hill Companies

Study Guide for use with
FINANCIAL ACCOUNTING

1 2 3 4 5 6 7 8 9 0 CUS/CUS 0 9 8 7 6 5 4 3 2 1 0

ISBN 0-07-240413-2

http://www.mhhe.com

CONTENTS

TO THE STUDENT

This self-study guide is designed for your use as a student taking your first course in accounting at either the undergraduate or the graduate level. It is prepared to accompany *Financial Accounting,* tenth edition. However, it can be used effectively with other introductory accounting texts. The key purposes of this study guide are:

1. To help you in *mastering the material* as you initially study each chapter.

2. To *summarize the essential points* in each chapter and to *test your knowledge* with a series of objective questions and exercises, thus making it possible for you to *review the material quickly* from time to time, particularly before examinations.

3. To make the study of accounting *more enjoyable and more efficient* for you. This is accomplished by presenting an informal and concise summary of each chapter, followed by three groups of objective questions and some short exercises. The answers to these questions and exercises are provided at the end of each chapter in order *to give you immediate feedback and to point out areas that need additional attention.*

The manner in which each student uses this study guide may differ. However, we recommend the following approach:

1. Study the chapter in your textbook.

2. Read the *Highlights of the Chapter* section of the study guide. If you encounter any statements that you do not understand, refer to the textbook for a more detailed discussion of the topic.

3. Work the questions and exercises in the *Test Yourself* section of the study guide and compare your answers and solutions with those provided at the end of the chapter. This will show you how well you really understand the material contained in the related chapter in your textbook. Again, if you find something you do not understand, refer to your text for a thorough discussion of the subject.

4. Work the problems assigned as homework in your text.

Once you have mastered the material in this manner, rereading the *Highlights of the Chapter* section of the study guide will assist you in quickly reviewing the material before examinations.

Robert F. Meigs
Mark S. Bettner
Susan Haka
Jan Williams

ACCOUNTING INFORMATION FOR DECISION MAKING

Highlights of the Chapter

1. The primary purpose of accounting information is to enhance financial decision making. Because accounting information is so widely used in business activities, it is sometimes called *the language of business*

2. Accounting is a means by which economic events are measured. Users of accounting information must understand the general characteristics of economic activities, be familiar with the assumptions and techniques used in measuring economic activities, and correctly identify relevant information for each decision they make.

3. Just as there are many types of economic decisions, there are many types of accounting information. Three types of accounting information that are widely used in the business community are: (a) *financial accounting* information (b) *managerial accounting* information, and (c) *general-purpose* information.

4. *Financial accounting* refers to information describing the financial resources, obligations, and activities of an economic entity. Financial accounting information is used primarily by investors and creditors to help them assess an entity's financial position, its results of operations, and its ability to generate cash flow. Financial accounting information is so widely used that it is often called *general-purpose* information.

5. *Managerial accounting* involves the development and interpretation of accounting information intended *specifically to aid management*. Managers use accounting information in virtually every decision they make, including the setting of company goals, performance evaluation, and decisions whether to launch a new product line. Of course, managers must also consider many *nonfinancial* factors relevant to decision making, such as political and environmental considerations, product quality, customer satisfactions, and legal issues.

6. *Tax accounting* is a specialized field within the accounting profession. Tax accounting involves both the preparation of income tax returns and the planning of business activities to minimize the income tax burden. To a large extent, tax returns are based upon financial accounting information; however, the information is often adjusted or reorganized to comply with income tax regulations.

7. *Accounting systems* consist of the personnel, procedures, devices, and records used to develop accounting information and to communicate this information to decisions makers. Accounting systems can take many forms depending upon an organization's needs and the resources it has available for the operation of the system.

8. The design, installation, and maintenance of an accounting system may involve accountants, experts in management information systems, computer programmers, and many other individuals with specialized talents. Regardless of its complexity, an accounting system should be *cost effective*. In other words, the value of the information it provides should exceed the cost of producing the information.

9. *External users* of accounting system information have a financial interest in an enterprise, but are not involved it its day-to-day operations. These parties may include owners, creditors, regulatory agencies, suppliers, customers, and the general public. External parties are most interested in *financial accounting information*. However, providing financial accounting information to such a diverse group of users in a single format would be nearly impossible. Therefore, financial accounting reports are directed primarily to the information needs of *investors* and *creditors*.

10. *Investors* actually "own" the reporting enterprise. Examples of investors include stockholders of a giant corporation, the partners in a law firm, or the sole operator of a snow removal service. *Creditors*, on the other hand, are those parties that have provided resources to the enterprise in the form of credit, but have no ownership interest in the enterprise. Banks or individuals that have "loaned" money to a business, for example, are examples of creditors.

11. Investors and creditors share some common interests. Both are concerned about the future cash flow prospects of the company in which they have invested or loaned resources. Specifically, they want information about the company's ability to: (a) eventually *payback* the amount invested or loaned at a future date, and (b) provide adequate *additional payments* for the use of the resources invested or loaned.

12. The repayment of the initial amount invested or loaned to an organization is commonly referred to as the *return of investment*. The additional amount earned for the use of these resources is often referred to as the *return on investment*. Providing information to investors about potential return of, and return on, investment is essentially what financial accounting is all about.

13. Meeting the objectives of investors requires that financial accounting reports provide: (a) information about economic resources, claims to resources, and changes in resources and claims, (b) information useful in assessing the amount, timing, and uncertainty of future cash flows, and (c) information useful in making investment and credit decisions. This information is provided via a "set" of *primary financial statements*.

14. The primary financial statements (reports) include: (a) *the balance sheet* (or *statement of financial position*), (b) *the income statement*, and (c) *the statement of cash* flows. A balance sheet reports a company's resources, and the claims to those resources at a particular point in time. An income statement reports detailed results of a company's profit-related activities for a specific period of time, such as a month or year. A statement of cash flows reports all cash received, and all cash disbursed for a specific period of time.

15. The information reported to external parties via the primary financial statements is *historical* in nature. That is, it looks back in time, as opposed to forward in time. However, we will discover in later chapters of this text that much of the information reported to external parties is based, in large part, upon certain *estimates and assumptions* pertaining to future performance.

16. *Internal users* of accounting systems are interested in *managerial accounting* information. Internal users of managerial accounting information include plant managers, supervisors, chief executive officers, vice presidents, controllers, and members of the Board of Directors. Each of these users requires information specifically designed to help them achieve unique financial *goals and objectives*.

17. Enterprises design and use management accounting information in three primary ways: (a) to help them achieve their *goals and objectives*, (b) to help support *decision making activities* among a variety of internal users, and (c) to *evaluate the effectiveness* of the decision making process.

18. Managerial accounting information must possess the following general characteristics in order for it to be useful: (a) it must be *timely*, (b) it must clearly establish who within the organization has *decision making authority*, (c) it must be *oriented toward the future*, (d) it must provide measures of *efficiency and effectiveness*, and (e) it must be viewed as a means of helping an organization *accomplish its goals and objectives*.

19. The accounting information used by both external and internal parties must have *integrity*. That is it must be reliable, complete, and honest. The integrity of accounting information is enhanced in three primary ways: (a) through *compliance with generally accepted accounting principles*, (b) through *sound systems of internal control*, (c) through the *support of several organizations concerned with maintaining ethical responsibility and integrity throughout the profession*, such as the *AICPA,* the *IMA,* the *IIA,* and the *AAA,* and (d) by requiring professional accounts to *be competent and to demonstrate sound judgment and ethical behavior*.

20. The accounting information communicated externally to investors and creditors must be prepared in accordance with *generally accepted accounting principles* (GAAP). Two organizations are particularly important in establishing GAAP: (a) the *Financial Accounting Standards Board* (FASB), and (b) the *Securities and Exchange Commission* (SEC).

21. *The FASB* issues authoritative statements addressing the principles of financial reporting. The FASB's official statements are intended to resolve accounting problems in a logical consistent manner. The FASB is part of the private sector of our economy – *it is not a governmental agency.*

22. *The SEC* is a governmental agency with the legal power to establish accounting principles and reporting requirements for publicly owned corporations. In the past, however, the SEC has generally adopted the recommendations of the FASB. The GAAP developed by the FASB are given the *force of law* when they are adopted by the SEC.

23. A company's *internal control structure* includes all measures used by an organization to (a) guard against errors, waste, and fraud, (b) assure the reliability of accounting information, (c) promote compliance with management with management policies, and (d) evaluate the performance of the entire organization. *Audits* help to ensure that adequate systems of entrant control are in place. An audit is an *investigation* of a company's financial statements performed by independent certified public accountants (CPAs). The intent of the audit is to provide reasonable assurance of the integrity of the information reported. Auditors do not guarantee accuracy of financial statements. They do, however, express an *opinion* on the statements' *fairness of presentation*.

24. Various organizations issue professional accounting designations in the form of licenses and certifications. Examples include: (a) *Certified Public Accountant* (or CPA license), (b) *Certificate in Management Accounting* (CMA), and (c) *Certificate in Internal Auditing* (CIA).

25. Beginning in the year 2000, the *American Institute of Certified Public Accountants* (AICPA) will require its new members to have completed 150 semester hours of college work. This represents about one additional year beyond a bachelor's degree. One can be a CPA without belonging to the AICPA. Therefore, in some states it may be possible to be licensed as a CPA without having a 150 semester hours of college education. However, many states are changing (or have already changed) their licensing requirements to make the 150 hour requirement mandatory.

26. Careers in accounting may be divided into four broad areas: (a) public accounting careers, (b) managerial accounting careers, (c) governmental accounting careers, and (d) careers in accounting education.

27. *Public accountants* (often CPAs) engage in audit services, tax services, and management advisory services.

28. *Management accountants* are employed by business and are often involved in financial reporting, system design, budgeting, cost accounting, income tax reporting, and internal audit processes.

29. *Governmental accountants* provide services at the federal, state, and local levels. Many governmental accounts are employed by the General Accounting Office (GAO), the Internal Revenue Service (IRS), and the Federal Bureau of Investigation (FBI).

30. *Accounting education* also provides many rewarding career opportunities. At many institutions, accounting faculty must have an earned doctorate to be considered for a full-time teaching position. A career as a faculty member allows an individual great freedom to pursue his or her specific professional interests.

TEST YOURSELF ON ACCOUNTING INFORMATION

True or False

For each of the following statements, circle the T or the F to indicate whether the statement is true or false.

T F 1. Bookkeeping is often referred to as the language of business.

T F 2. Financial accounting information is the term used to describe the reports used by an organization's investors and creditors.

T F 3. Accounting systems may be defined as the computer software used to store, retrieve, and communicate accounting information to internal and external parties.

T F 4. The primary external users of financial accounting information include the Board of Directors, regulatory agencies, and the Securities and Exchange Commission (SEC).

T F 5. Investors and creditors learn about the financial condition of an enterprise from a variety of sources other than the enterprise's financial statements.

T F 6. The financial statements issued to external parties lack an "historical" focus.

T F 7. Externally reported financial information contains very little, if any, approximations or inexact measures.

T F 8. Internal users of accounting information depend heavily upon general-purpose financial statements in making day-to-day decisions.

T F 9. Virtually all managerial accounting information is oriented toward historical events and performance.

T F 10. Information integrity is important only to external users of accounting information.

T F 11. The Securities and Exchange Commission (SEC) is primarily responsible for developing generally accepted accounting principles (GAAP) and other authoritative accounting pronouncements.

T F 12. The Financial Accounting Standards Board (FASB) does not require the support of the SEC in developing new accounting standards.

T F 13. A company's internal control structure is intended to ensure that the entire organization operates according to the plans of management.

T F 14. Managerial accountants are required to earn a Certificate in Management Accounting (CMA) in order to be licensed in a particular state.

T F 15. By the year 2000, only a few states will make 150 semester hours of college course work a mandatory requirement for becoming a licensed CPA.

T F 16. The American Institute of Certified Public Accountants (AICPA) does not have a "formal" code of ethics for its members.

T F 17. Public accounting is often referred to as governmental accounting.

T F 18. Bookkeepers are often responsible for evaluating efficiency of operations, resolving complex financial reporting issues, forecasting the results of future operations, tax planning, auditing, and for designing accounting information systems.

Completion Statements

Fill in the necessary word to complete the following statements:

1. Accounting is not an _____, but rather a _____ to an end.

2. Because accounting is widely used to describe all types of business activity, it is sometimes referred to as ____ _____ __ _____.

3. _____ accounting information is used primarily by external decision-makers, whereas _____ accounting is used primarily by internal decision-makers.

4. An _____ _____ consists of the personnel, procedures, devices, and records used by an organization to (a) develop accounting information, and (b) communicate this information to decisions makers.

5. Investors and creditors are concerned about an enterprise's ability to generate both a _____ ____ investment and an adequate _____ ____ investment.

6. External financial reporting is directed primarily toward the information needs of _____ and _____.

7. Management accounting information is used primarily for _____ and _____ purposes.

8. The _____ of accounting information is often enhanced by strong systems of internal control, compliance with accounting principles, involvement by professional organizations, and ethical professional behavior.

9. Certified Public Accountants (CPAs) are _____ by the states in which they practice.

10. Working as an accountant for the FBI is an example of a _____ accounting career.

Multiple Choice

Choose the best answer for each of the following questions and enter the identifying letter in the space provided.

___ 1.   An accountant licensed by a state after meeting rigorous education, experience, and examination requirements is referred to as:

    a.   Managerial accountant.

    b.   Governmental accountant

    c.   Certified public accountant.

    d.   Internal auditor.

___ 2.   The private-sector organization responsible for establishing generally accepted accounting principles (GAAP) is called the:

    a.   AICPA.

    b.   SEC.

    c.   IMA.

    d.   FASB.

___ 3.   Which of the following is *not* an example of an external user of accounting information?

    a.   The company's Board of Directors.

    b.   The company's creditors.

    c.   The company's labor union.

    d.   The company's suppliers.

___ 4.   Which of the following is *not* considered a general-purpose financial report used by the investors and creditors of an organization?

    a.   A statement of cash flows.

    b.   A production budget.

    c.   A balance sheet.

    d.   An income statement.

___ 5.   The repayment to an investor of the amount originally invested in the enterprise is referred to as:

    a.   Return on investment.

    b.   Return of investment.

    c.   Profit.

    d.   Interest.

___ 6.   The government organization with the legal power to establish accounting principles for publicly owned companies in the United States is called the:

    a.   AICPA.

    b.   SEC.

    c.   IMA.

    d.   FASB.

_____ 7. The clerical dimension of accounting that includes recording routine daily transactions is called:

     a. Internal auditing.

     b. Managerial accounting.

     c. Bookkeeping.

     d. Accounting information systems.

_____ 8. The professional designation granted by the Institute of Management Accounting (IMA) is the:

     a. CMA.

     b. CIA.

     c. CPA.

     d. CIMA.

_____ 9. The career path in accounting that deals primarily with the independent audit of financial statements is referred to as:

     a. Internal auditing.

     b. Governmental accounting.

     c. Managerial accounting.

     d. Public accounting.

_____ 10. Which of the following is *not* an example of an internal user of accounting information?

     a. The company's Board of Directors.

     b. The company's labor union.

     c. The company's senior management.

     d. The company's Chief Executive Officer.

_____ 11. A plan of financial operations for some future period is referred to as:

     a. A financial forecast.

     b. An income statement.

     c. A balance sheet.

     d. A statement of cash flows.

_____ 12. The formulation and analysis of the costs associated with certain business activities is referred to as:

     a. Financial accounting.

     b. An independent audit.

     c. Cost accounting.

     d. An internal audit.

Exercises

1. Listed below are eight technical accounting terms emphasized in this chapter.

Audit	*General purpose information*
Bookkeeping	*Return on investment*
Public accounting	*Statement of financial position*
Income statement	*Financial accounting*

    Each of the following statements may (or may not) describe one of these technical terms. In the space provided below each statement, indicate the accounting term described, or answer "None" if the statement does not correctly describe any of the terms.

    a. A financial statement that shows detailed results of a company's profit-related activities for a particular period of time.

    _____

    b. Principles that provide the framework for determining what information is to be included in financial statements and how that information is to be presented.

    _____

    c. An independent investigation of financial statements for the purpose of determining their fairness in relation to generally accepted accounting principles.

    _____

    d. A projected plan of financial operations for a specified period in the future.

    _____

    e. The clerical dimension of accounting that includes the recording of routine daily transactions.

    _____

    f. The repayment to investors of the amounts they originally invested in a particular enterprise.

    _____

    g. Another term for balance sheet.

    _____

2. Assuming that you wish to open your own small business shortly after graduating from college. Unfortunately, you do not have the cash necessary to get you started. Your father is willing to lend you $50,000, provided that you agree to pay the entire amount back in one year, plus interest at 15%.

   a. Your father's anticipated return of investment is: $_____.
   b. Your father's anticipated return on investment is: $_____.

3. In the space provided, indicate whether each of the following parties should be considered an internal user of accounting information or an external user.

   I = Internal User
   E = External User

   _____ a. Bankers.

   _____ b. The Board of Directors.

   _____ c. The Vice President of Human Resources.

   _____ d. Labor unions.

   _____ e. Suppliers.

   _____ f. Trade associations.

   _____ g. Factory supervisors.

   _____ h. Stockholders of a corporation.

SOLUTIONS TO CHAPTER 1 SELF-TEST

1. **F** The term *accounting* is often referred to as the language of business. Bookkeeping is a routine subset of accounting involving the routine recording of daily transactions.

2. **T** Financial accounting information is designed specifically for external decisions makers. Management (or managerial) accounting is the term used for internal decision-makers.

3. **F** Accounting systems are not limited to software. They include all personnel, procedures, devices, and records used by organizations to develop and communicate information to decision-makers.

4. **F** The primary users of financial accounting information are investors and creditors .

5. **T** Investors and creditors learn about the financial condition of an enterprise from financial statements, the financial press, newsletters, the Internet, etc.

6. **F** The financial statement used by investors and creditors lack a focus toward the *future*.

7. **F** External reported financial statements rely heavily upon estimates and inexact measures.

8. **F** Internal users of financial information depend heavily on accounting reports uniquely designed for their special decision making needs.

9. **F** Managerial accounting information is oriented primarily toward the future.

10. **F** Integrity is important to all users of accounting information.

11.   **F** The Financial Accounting Standards Board is primarily responsible for developing GAAP.

12.   **F** The FASB needs the support of the SEC to make GAAP legally binding.

13.   **T** The broad object of an internal control system is to help ensure that an enterprise accomplishes its goals and objectives.

14.   **F** Managerial accountants are not required to become CMAs. Those that do earn the CMA designation are *not* licensed by any state.

15.   **F** By the year 2000, *most* states will make 150 semester hours of college course work a mandatory requirement for becoming a licensed CPA.

16.   **F** The AICPA has a very detailed code of ethics for its members.

17.   **F** Public accounting and governmental accounting are two separate career paths within the accounting profession.

18.   **F** Bookkeepers are usually responsible only for recording the daily transactions of an enterprise.

Completion Statements

1. end, means. 2. the language of business. 3. Financial, managerial (or management). 4. accounting system. 5. return of, return on. 6. investors, creditors. 7. planning, control. 8. integrity. 9. licensed. 10. governmental.

Multiple Choice

1.   Answer **c** – only certified public accountants (CPAs) are licensed by states as accounting professionals. Other accounting professionals may receive designation of a particular specialty, but these specialties do not require licensing.

2.   Answer **d** – the Financial Accounting Standards Board (FASB) is responsible for establishing GAAP. The FASB needs the support of the Securities and Exchange Commission (SEC) is not directly involved in the development of GAAP.

3.   Answer **a** – creditors and suppliers are clearly external users of accounting information. Although labor union members are internal users of accounting information, labor union themselves are separate, external, entities.

4.   Answer **b** – a production budget is a custom report used by production managers to plan for manufacturing operations.

5.   Answer **b** – the return to an investor of the amount originally invested is the return of investment. Profit and interest represent additional returns referred to as the return *on* investment.

6.   Answer **b** – the Securities and Exchange Commission (SEC) has the legal power to establish accounting principles. However, it rarely uses this power. Rather it relies upon the FASB to establish GAAP for publicly traded companies.

7.   Answer **c** – bookkeeping is the clerical subset of accounting that involves the daily recording of routine transactions.

8.   Answer **a** – the CMA is awarded by the Institute of Management Accounting (IMA) to members who have passed a rigorous examination and who have fulfilled certain education and experience requirements.

9.   Answer **d** –public accountants perform independent audits of financial statements. Unlike internal auditors, public accountants are *external* to the enterprises that they audit.

10.   Answer **b** – the members of labor unions are internal users of accounting information. However, labor union themselves are separate and external entities.

11.   Answer **a** – only a financial forecast looks forward toward future operations. The income statement, balance sheet, and the statement of cash flows have *historical* orientations.

12. Answer **c** – cost accounting is that area of expertise within the accounting profession that is directly involved in the formulation and analysis of cost data.

Solutions to Exercises

1.

a.   Income statement

b.   None (This statement describes *generally accepted accounting principles, or GAAP*.)

c.   Audit

d.   None (This statement describes a *financial forecast*.)

e.   Bookkeeping

f.   None (This statement describes *return of investment*.)

g.   Statement of financial position

2.

a.   <u>$50,000</u> (the original amount of the loan)

b.   <u>$ 7,500</u> ($50,000 x 15%)

3.

a.	E
b.	I
c.	I
d.	E
e.	E
f.	E
g.	I
h.	E

BASIC FINANCIAL STATEMENTS

HIGHLIGHTS OF THE CHAPTER

1. To really understand "accounting," you must understand three things:

   a. The nature of the economic activities described in accounting reports.

   b. The assumptions and measurement techniques involved in the accounting process.

   c. How the accounting information relates to specific decisions.

2. For example, let us apply this "three perspectives" approach to the presentation of assets in a balance sheet. What should you understand about assets? First, know what they represent *future economic benefits* that have been purchased by the business. Next, know that current accounting practice is to value most assets at cost. Thus, a balance sheet provides information about the *nature and dollar amount* (cost) of *financial resources* owned. This information is useful in evaluating the company's ability to pay its debts, and also in determining whether its resources are being used efficiently.

3. The process of providing financial information about a business to decision makers other than management and employees is termed *financial reporting*. These "outsiders" may include investors, creditors, financial analysts, government regulators, and in some cases, even the general public (including the company's competitors).

4. *Financial statements* provide a means of reporting financial information about an enterprise to parties outside the enterprise itself. The three primary financial statements include:

   a. A *balance sheet* showing the financial position of the company at a given date.

   b. An *income statement* indicating profitability of the business over a specific time period.

   c. A *statement of cash flows* summarizing cash receipts and cash payments over the same period covered by the income statement.

   These statements are prepared by the company's accounting department; management is primarily responsible for the statements' reliability.

5. Regardless of whether an accounting system is operated manually or makes use of a computer, the system performs three basis functions. First, the company's economic activities are *recorded* in accounting records. Next, the recorded data are *classified* to accumulate subtotals for various types of activities. Finally, the classified data are *summarized* in accounting reports designed to meet the needs of decision makers.

6. The *transactions approach* to recording economic activities focuses upon completed transactions, that is events that (1) cause an *immediate change* in the financial position of the business, and (2) can be *measured objectively* in monetary terms. The primary strength of this approach is that the information is reliable and can be measured objectively. A weakness is that some nonfinancial events may not be recorded.

7. Accounting information is gathered for specific business entities. A business *entity* is any economic unit which enters into business transactions. The business entity is regarded as separate from its owners; the entity owns its own property and has its own debts. In preparing a balance sheet, the *same* definition of the "business entity" must be used in identifying the assets, liabilities, and owner's equity of the business.

8. *Assets* are economic resources owned by a business, such as land, buildings, and cash. Assets are valued in a balance sheet at their cost, rather than at current market prices because cost is more

factual and can be more *objectively determined* than current market value. Another reason for valuing assets at cost is that a business is assumed to be a *going concern* that will keep and use such assets as land and buildings rather than sell them.

9. Adhering to the cost basis of accounting implies that the dollar is a *stable* unit of measurement, as is a gallon, or an inch. The cost principle works well in periods of stable prices. Severe inflation, however, weakens the usefulness of cost as a basis for asset valuation. In recent years, the FASB has required large corporations to experiment with disclosures of "price-level adjusted" accounting data. However, the cost of developing this information was found to exceed the benefits. Thus, at present, the *cost principle* and the *stable dollar assumption* remain generally accepted accounting principles in this country.

10. Liabilities are debts. Either borrowing money or buying on credit will create a liability. Liabilities represent the claims of *creditors* to the resources of the business. Example of liabilities are accounts payable and notes payable.

11. Owners' equity represents the stockholders' investment in the business; it is equal to total assets minus total liabilities. Owners' equity in a corporation is called *stockholders' equity*. The equity of the stockholders is a residual amount. It is the claim to all resources (assets) of the business *after* the claims of the creditors have been satisfied. If a loss occurs, it is the owners' equity rather than the creditors' claims which must absorb the loss. Thus, creditors view the owner's equity as a "buffer" which protects the safety of their claims to the resources of the business.

12. Increases in owners' equity result from (a) the stockholders investing cash or other assets in the business and (b) profitable operation of the business. Owners' equity is decreased by (a) dividends distributed to stockholders, and (b) unprofitable operation of the business.

13. The "accounting equation" is *Assets = Liabilities + Owners' Equity*. The listing of assets shows us what things the business owns; the listing of liabilities and owners' equity tells us who supplied these resources to the business and how much each group supplies.

14. *Revenue* represents increases in an enterprise's assets as result of profit-oriented activities. The increased profits resulting from the earning of revenue cause owners' equity to increase, as well. *Expenses* represent resources consumed in the past, present, or future in the process of generating revenue. Expenses decrease profits and, therefore, cause owners' equity to decrease, as well.

15. Profits (or net losses) are reported in detail in the *income statement*. The income statement shows all revenue earned during the period, less all expenses incurred during the period. Revenue, less the expenses, is often termed *net income*, or a *net loss*.

16. The *statement of cash flows* reports all inflows and outflows of cash for the same time period covered by the income statement. Revenue and expenses reported in the income statement *are not* necessarily the same as cash flows reported in the statement of cash flows. We will address this issue frequently in later chapters. The statement of cash flows reports three types of cash flows: (a) cash flow from *operating activities* – the cash flows related to revenue and expense transactions, (b) cash flow from *investing activities* – the cash flows resulting from the sale and purchase of property and equipment, and (c) cash flow from *financing activities* – the cash flows resulting from financing transactions with the creditors and the owners of the enterprise.

17. The three most common forms of business entities are sole proprietorships, partnerships, and corporations. Accounting principles and concepts apply to all three forms of organizations. A sole proprietorship is an unincorporated business owned by one individual. A partnership is an unincorporated business owned by two or more people who have agreed to act as partners. A corporation is a business granted a charter by the state and owned by *stockholders.* Ownership of a corporation is evidenced by *shares of capital stock* that may be sold to investors.

18. A corporation is legally an entity separate from its owners. Thus, the stockholders' liability for the losses incurred by an unsuccessful corporation is limited to the amount they have invested in the business. Nearly all large businesses, and many small ones, are organized as corporations.

19. Financial statements are used by outsiders in making investment decisions; hence financial statements are designed to provide information useful to these decision-makers. Two factors of concern to outsiders are the *solvency* and *profitability* of business organizations. Being solvent means having the liquid resources to pay debts on time. One key indicator of short-term solvency is to compare a company's liquid resources with the liabilities requiring payment in the near future. Profitable operations increase the value of the owner's equity in the business.

20. A transaction that causes a change in one of the primary financial statements (e.g., the balance sheet) often changes either or both of the other primary financial statements, as well (e.g., the income statement and the statement of cash flows). This close relationship among the financial statements is referred to as *articulation.*

TEST YOURSELF ON BASIC FINANCIAL STATEMENTS

True or False

For each of the following statements, circle the T or the F to indicate whether the statement is true or false.

T   F   1. The basic purpose of accounting is to provide financial information to economic decision-makers.

T   F   2. Financial statements are confidential documents made available only to the top management of a business enterprise.

T   F   3. The most useful financial statement would be a detailed list of every business transaction in which the business enterprise has been involved.

T   F   4. By using the transaction approach, one will be assured that all important events that happen in the firm are reflected in the financial statements of the company.

T   F   5. One characteristic of a corporation is that its owners are personally liable for any losses incurred by the business.

T   F   6. Assets are valued in the balance sheet at current liquidation values to show how much cash would be realized if the business went broke.

T   F   7. The cost principle of asset valuation is no longer widely used in the United States.

T   F   8. Losses from unprofitable operations cause the owners' equity in a business enterprise to decrease.

T   F   9. The purchase of a building for cash will cause total assets to increase.

T   F   10. The payment of a liability will not affect total assets, but will cause total liabilities to decrease.

T F 11. In the balance sheet of a sole proprietorship, any increase in capital earned through profitable operations and retained in the business is added to the capital originally invested, and a single figure is shown for the owner's capital.

T F 12. The cash flow reported in the statement of cash flows will probably differ from the revenue and expenses reported in the income statement.

T F 13. Meshing is the term used to describe the close "mechanical" relationship among the primary financial statements.

T F 14. Corporations are required to show capital stock and retained earnings separately in the balance sheet.

T F 15. A business that is unable to pay its own debts is said to be *insolvent*

T F 16. A business can become insolvent even though it is operating profitably.

Completion Statements

Fill in the necessary word to complete the following statements:

1. The three primary financial statements are the: (a) _____ _____, (b) _____ _____, and (c) _____ ____ _____ _____.

2. The three common forms of business organizations are (a) _____ _____,(b) _____, and (c) _____.

3. The accounting equation states that _____ = _____ + _____ _____.

4. Land advertised for sale at $90,000 was purchased for $80,000 cash by a development company. For property tax purposes, the property was assessed by the county at $25,000. The development firm intended to sell the property in parcels for a total of $150,000. The land would appear in the balance sheet of the development company among the _____ at a value of $_____.

5. On December 15, Shadow Mountain Golf Course had a contractor install a $90,000 sprinkler system. Since no payment to the contractor was required until the following month, the transaction was not recorded in December and was not reflected in any way in the December 31 balance sheet. Indicate for each of the following elements of the balance sheet whether the amounts were overstated, understated, or correct. Total assets _____, total liabilities _____, owners' equity _____.

6. The owners' equity in a business comes form two sources: (a) _____ by owner and (b) _____ operations.

7. A transaction that causes total liabilities to increase but that has no effect on owners' equity must cause total assets to _____.

16

8. The types of cash flows activities reported in the statement of cash flows are: (a) _____ _____, (b) _____ _____, and (c) _____ _____

9. _____ is the term used to describe the close "mechanical" relationship among the primary financial statements.

10. The concept of _____ _____ requires providing with financial statements any financial facts necessary for proper interpretation of those financial statements.

Multiple Choice

Choose the best answer for each of the following questions and enter the identifying letter in the space provided.

___ 1. Which of the following best describes the nature of an *asset*?

    a. Something with a ready market value.

    b. An economic resource which will provide some future benefits.

    c. Tangible property (something with physical form) owned by a business.

    d. The amount of the owner's investment in a business.

___ 2. The *owners' equity* in a business may best be described as:

    a. An economic resource that is owned by a business and is expected to benefit future operations.

    b. An obligation of the business entity.

    c. Profits that have been retained in the business rather than being distributed to the Stockholders.

    d. Assets minus liabilities.

___ 3. In this chapter, several accounting principles relating to the valuation of assets are discussed. Which of the following is not one of these principles?

    a. The cost principle – assets generally are recorded at cost rather than at estimated market values.

    b. Objectivity – accountants prefer to use values that can be objectively verified.

    c. Going-concern assumption – accountants assume that a business acquires assets such as land, buildings and equipment for use and not for resale.

    d. The safety principle – assets are recorded in the accounting records at the lower of cost or insured value.

___ 4. Which of the following equations cannot be derived from the basic accounting equation (Assets = Liabilities + Owners' Equity)?

    a. Assets – Liabilities = Owners' Equity.

    b. Liabilities = Assets –Owners' Equity

    c. Owners' Equity = Liabilities – Assets

    d. Assets – Owners' Equity = Liabilities.

___ 5. Which of the following transactions causes *total assets to increase by $10,000?*

    a. Purchasing an automobile for $10,000 cash.

    b. Purchasing $10,000 of office furniture on account.

    c. Collecting a $10,000 account receivable

    d. Paying a $10,000 liability.

___ 6. Magic Forest Land Development Company sold a parcel of land at a profit. This will cause:

    a. A decrease in assets and liabilities.

    b. An increase in assets and owners' equity.

    c. An increase in assets and liabilities.

    d. A decrease in liabilities and owners' equity.

___ 7. Lake Arrowhead Boat Shop bought a $700 electric hoist to lift engines out of boats. The boat shop paid $200 in cash for the hoist and signed a note to pay the balance in 60 days. This transaction will cause:

    a. The boat shop's assets to increase by $700 and liabilities to increase by $500.

    b. Assets to increase by $500 and owners' equity to decrease.

    c. No change in total assets, but a $500 increase in liabilities and a similar decrease in owners' equity.

    d. No change in owners' equity, but a $500 increase in both assets and liabilities.

___ 8. Which of the following is an example of a cash inflow from operating activities?

    a. The purchase of a delivery truck.

    b. The sale of an old delivery truck that is no longer being used.

    c. Receiving a bank loan to purchase a new delivery truck.

    d. The cash received from selling the products delivered to customers by the delivery truck.

_ 9. Which of the following is an example of a cash inflow from investing activities?

   a.   The purchase of a delivery truck.

   b.   The sale of an old delivery truck that is no longer being used.

   c.   Receiving a bank loan to purchase a new delivery truck.

   d.   The cash received from selling the products delivered to customers by the delivery truck.

_ 10. Which of the following is an example of a cash inflow from financing activities?

   a.   The purchase of a delivery truck.

   b.   The sale of an old delivery truck that is no longer being used.

   c.   Receiving a bank loan to purchase a new delivery truck.

   d.   The cash received from selling the products delivered to customers by the delivery truck.

Exercises

1.   Listed below are eight technical accounting terms emphasized in this chapter.

Solvent   *Objectivity principle*
Owners' equity   *Balance sheet*
Income statement   *Accounting equation*
Business entity   *Statement of cash flows*

Each of the following statements may (or may not) describe one of these technical terms. In the space provided below each statement, indicate the accounting term described, or answer "None" if the statement does not correctly describe any of the terms.

a.   A financial statement that shows detailed results of a company's profited-related activities for a particular period of time.

   _____

b.   An economic unit which enters into business transactions.

   _____

c.   Assets minus liabilities.

   _____

d.   Able to pay debts as they come due.

   _____

e.   An accounting assumption that a business will operate in the foreseeable future unless evidence suggests otherwise.

   _____

f.   A financial statement that reports the financial position of an enterprise.

_____

g.   Assets minus the sum of liabilities and owners' equity.

_____

2.   In the space provided below, prepare a balance sheet for the Titan Company at
December 31, 20_, from the following alphabetical list of accounts

Accounts payable	$38,000	Capital Stock......................	100,000
Accounts receivable	37,000	Retained Earnings..............	30,000
Automobiles	8,000	Land	35,000
Buildings	60,000	Office equipment	16,000
Cash	14,000	Property taxes payable	2,000

(Hint: The sum of the Capital Stock and Retained Earnings equals the owners'
equity.)

TITAN COMPANY
Balance Sheet
December 31, 20_

Assets		Liabilities & Owners' Equity	
	$		$
	$		$

3.   Use the following information to complete the balance sheet of the Unitrex
Company on December 31, 20_.

  a. The company was organized on January 1, 20_. and has operated for a full year.

  b. The land and building were purchased for a total price of $350,000 on December
      30, 20_.

  c.   The seller was asking $390,000 and the appraisal by the insurance company was
      $360,000. Cash and Accounts Receivable together amount to three times as much
      as Accounts Payable.

The company's partial balance sheet is shown at the top of the following page.

Determine the missing figures in the Company's balance sheet shown below:

UNITREX COMPANY
Balance Sheet
December 31, 20–

Assets		Liabilities & Owners' Equity	
Cash..	$42,000	Liabilities:	
Accounts receivable		Notes payable.............	$
Land..	90,000	Accounts payable	
Building..		Total liabilities	$112,000
Office equipment..............................	56,000		
		Owner's equity:	
Total assets	$_____	Capital Stock	400,000
		Retained Earning................	
		Total liabilities & owners'	
		equity..........................	$592,000

4.   The Billiard Den was organized as a corporation by the family of Robert Neal on July 1 of the current year. In the table on the following page, indicate the effect of each of the following transactions on the various balance sheet items of the Billiard Den. Indicate the new balance for every item after the July 3 transaction and each subsequent transaction. The effects of the July 1 transaction are already filled in to provide you with an example.

July 1   Robert Neal began the business by depositing $20,000 cash in a bank account in the name of the business. The money was raised by selling shares of capital stock to himself and other family members.

    3   Purchased an existing pool hall at a price of $21,000 for the land and $30,000 for the building. Billiard Den paid the former owner $10,000 in cash and issued a short-term note payable for the balance of the purchase price.

  10   Purchased 10 pool tables for $1,000 each, paying $6,000 cash and agreeing to pay the balance within 30 days.

  14   Sold one pool table to a friend for $1,000. The friend paid $500 cash to the Billiard Den and promised to pay the balance within 30 days.

  20   Paid $2,000 of the amount owed on the pool tables.

  24   Collected $200 from the friend who has bought the pool table.

  29   Purchased one used pool table from another pool hall, paying $600 cash.

  31   Cash revenue earned in July amounted to $5,000. Cash expenses incurred for the month totaled $3,500.

	Assets					=	Liabilities		Owners' Equity	
	Cash	Accounts Receivable	Land	Building	Pool Tables		Notes Payable	Accounts Payable	Capital Stock	Retained Earnings
July 1	+20,000								+$20,000	
3										
Balance										
10										
Balance										
14										
Balance										
20										
Balance										
24										
Balance										
29										
Balance										
31										
Balance										

SOLUTIONS TO CHAPTER 2 SELF-TEST

1. **T** Economic decision makers include the executives and managers of the business as well as outsiders such as business owners, bankers, creditors, potential investors, labor unions, the government, etc. Information about the financial position and operating results of a business is vital in making decisions about the future.

2. **F** Financial statements are the main source of financial information to persons outside the business organization; they are also of great importance to management.

3. **F** Financial statements *summarize* information contained in the hundreds or thousands of pages comprising the detailed accounting records of a business. A detailed list of *every* business transaction would be too cumbersome to be useful to decision makers.

4. **F** The transactions approach records only completed transactions that cause an immediate change in the financial position of the business, and which can be measured objectively in monetary terms. Consequently, many important events are not recorded in the accounting records because they do not meet this definition of a "transaction."

5. **F** A corporation is a legal entity *separate* from its owners, unlike a sole proprietorship or partnership. In a sole proprietorship or partnership, the owner(s) are personally liable for all debts incurred by the business.

6. **F** An asset is shown in a balance sheet at its historical cost – the dollar amount originally paid by the business to acquire the asset.

7. **F** As of the current time, the cost basis is still the generally accepted method of reporting assets in the United States.

8. **T** Also, distribution of cash or other assets by the business to the owners (such as payment of dividends) causes a decrease in owner's equity.

9. **F** There is no change in total assets; cash was decreased by the amount paid out, but a new asset (Building) was acquired.

10. **F** Payment of a liability causes a decrease in cash (asset) and an equal decrease in liabilities.

11. **T** A sole proprietorship is not required to maintain a distinction between invested capital and earned capital.

12. **T** Revenue earned and expenses incurred do not always correspond to cash inflows and outflows.

13. **F** *Articulation* is the term used to describe the close "mechanical" relationship among the primary financial statements.

14. **T** The state laws which govern the incorporation of businesses require that the owners' equity of a corporation be separated into categories of *earned* capital (retained earnings) and *invested* capital (such as capital stock).

15. **T** To be solvent is to have cash on hand sufficient to pay debts as they fall due.

16. **T** Many of the assets of a profitable business may consist of real estate or machinery or accounts receivable from customers. If *cash* is not available to pay debts promptly, the business is insolvent.

Completion Statements

1. (a) balance sheet, (b) income statement, (c) statement of cash flows. 2 (a) sole proprietorships, (b) partnerships, and (c) corporations. 3. Assets, Liabilities, Owners' Equity. 4. assets $80,000. 5. understated, understated, correct. 6 (a) investments, (b) profitable. 7. increase. 8(a) operating activities, (b) investing activities, (c) financing activities 9. Articulation. 10. adequate disclosure.

Multiple Choice

1.   Answer **b** – assets are economic resources that will provide future benefits. Answers **a** and **c** are incorrect, because assets may benefit the current owner even though they have no ready market value (a special-purpose machine that cannot be moved), or are not tangible (an account receivable). Answer **d** describes owners' equity, not an asset.

2.   Answer **d** – owners' equity is a residual amount, defined as total assets minus total liabilities. Answer **a** describes assets, answer **b** describes liabilities, and answer **c** describes only one component of owners' equity. (Investments by owner are also part of owners' equity.)

3.   Answer **d** – the "safety principle, " is not an accepted accounting principle. One obvious shortcoming of this fictitious "principle" is that all uninsured assets would be valued in the accounting records at zero. Answers **a** through **c** are basic principles of accounting affecting the valuation of assets.

4.   Answer **c** – Owners' Equity = Assets – Liabilities, not Liabilities – Assets.

5.   Answer **b** – purchasing a $10,000 assets on account increases both total assets and total liabilities by $10,000. Answers **a** and **c** involve the conversion of one asset into another; this type of transaction causes no change in total assets. Answer **d** paying a liability, decreases total assets.

6.   Answer **b** – one asset (land) will decrease but another asset (say, cash) will increase by a larger amount due to this transaction. The net increase in total assets is the profit on the sale, which increases owners' equity.

7.   Answer **d** – one asset (hoist or equipment) increases by $700, but another assets (cash) decreases by $200 as a result of this transaction. This net increase of $500 in total assets is accompanied by a $500 increase in liabilities (a note payable due in 60 days for $500).

8.   Answer **d** – operating activities are primarily the day-to-day transactions related to earning revenue and incurring expenses.

9.   Answer **b** – investing activities involve the sale and purchase of major plant assets, such as land and equipment.

10.   Answer **c** – financing activities involve financing transactions with creditors (e.g., banks) and the owners of the enterprise.

Solutions to Exercises

1.

a.   Income statement

b.   Business entity

c.   Owners' equity

d.   Solvent

e.   None (This statement describes the going concern assumption.)

f.   Balance sheet

g.   Accounting equation

2.

TITAN COMPANY
Balance Sheet
December 31, 20_

Assets		Liabilities & Owners' Equity	
Cash....................................	$ 14,000	Liabilities:	
Accounts receivable..........	37,000	Accounts payable..............	$38,000
Land.................................	35,000	Property taxes payable	2,000
Buildings...........................	60,000	Total liabilities..........	$ 40,000
Office equipment..............	16,000		
Automobiles......................	8,000		
		Owners' equity..................	130,000
		Total liabilities & owners'	
Total assets......................	$170,000	equity.........................	$170,000

3.

UNITREX COMPANY
Balance Sheet
December 31, 20_

Assets			Liabilities & Owners' Equity		
Cash....................................	$42,000		Liabilities:		
Accounts receivable..........	$144,000	c	Notes payable.............	$ 50,000	e
Land.................................	90,000		Accounts payable.......	62,000	d
Building.............................	260,000	b	Total liabilities......	$112,000	
Office equipment..............	56,000				
			Owners' equity:		
Total assets......................	$592,000	a	Capital Stock..............	400,000	
			Retained Earnings......	80,000	f
			Total liabilities &owners'		
			equity.........................	$592,000	

[a]Total assets must be $592,000 to agree with the total of liabilities and owners' equity.

[b]Total cost of land and building ($350,000) minus amount shown for land ($90,000) equals $260,000 allocated to building.

[c] Accounts receivable must be $144,000 to achieve a total asset figure of $592,000.

[d]Cash, $42,000, plus accounts receivable, $144,000. equals $186,000. Accounts payable are stated to be one-third of the combined total of cash accounts receivable; that is, $186,000 ÷ 3 = $62,000

[e]Notes payable must be $50,000 to achieve a total liability amount of $112,000.

[f] Retained Earnings must be $80,000 to achieve total liabilities plus owners' equity of $592,000.

4.

	Assets					=	**Liabilities**		**Owners' Equity**	
	Cash	Accounts Receivable	Land	Building	Pool Tables		Notes Payable	Accounts Payable	Capital Stock	Retained Earnings
July 1	+20,000								+$20,000	
3	-$10,000		+$21,000	+$30,000			+$41,000			
Balances	$10,000		$21,000	$30,000			$41,000		$20,0000	
10	-$ 6,000				+$10,000			+$4,000		
Balances	$ 4,000		$21,000	$30,000	$10,000		$41,000	$4,000	$20,0000	
14	+$ 500	+$ 500			-$ 1,000					
Balances	$ 4,500	$ 500	$21,000	$30,000	$ 9,000		$41,000	$4,000	$20,0000	
20	-$ 2,000							-$2,000		
Balances	$ 2,500	$ 500	$21,000	$30,000	$ 9,000		$41,000	$2,000	$20,0000	
24	+$ 200	-$ 200								
Balances	$ 2,700	$ 300	$21,000	$30,000	$ 9,000		$41,000	$2,000	$20,0000	
29	-$ 600				$ 600					
Balances	$ 2,100	$ 300	$21,000	$30,000	$ 9,600		$41,000	$2,000	$20,0000	
31	$ 1,500 *									$1,500*
Balances	$ 3,600	$ 300	$21,000	$30,000	$ 9,600		$41,000	$2,000	$20,0000	$1,500

*Cash Revenue $5,000
- Cash Expenses (3,500)
  Net Increase $1,500

26

THE ACCOUNTING CYLCE:CAPTURING ECONOMIC EVENTS

HIGHLIGHTS OF THE CHAPTER

1. The effects of business transactions are recorded in accounting records called *journals* and *ledgers*. The recorded data then are used to prepare financial statements and other accounting reports at periodic intervals.

2. Transactions are recorded first in a journal, and the data is later transferred to the ledger. We can best illustrate the nature of these accounting records if we discuss the ledger first.

3. A *ledger account* may be viewed as the smallest unit of storage in an accounting system. In a manual system, each ledger account is represented by a separate page in a binder. In a computerized system, of course, each unit of storage is maintained electronically using general ledger software. But each general ledger account can still be viewed separately.

4. Each ledger account lists all of the increases and decreases in a particular financial statement account, and also indicates the account's current "balance."

5. In its simplest form a ledger account may be viewed as having two sides. The left side of the account is called the *debit* side; the right side is called the *credit* side.

6. Information entered on the left side of a ledger account are called *debit entries.* Information entered on the right side of a ledger account are called *credit entries*.

7. For all *asset* accounts, increases are recorded by debit entries, and decreases are recorded by credit entries.

8. For all *liability* accounts and *owners' equity* accounts, increases are recorded by credits, and decreases are recorded by debits.

9. The debit and credit rules for recording revenue and expenses are based upon the changes they cause in owners' equity. Revenue *increases* owners' equity; therefore, revenue is recorded by *credit* entries. Expenses *decrease* owners' equity and are recorded *debits*.

10. The double-entry system of accounting requires that *equal dollar amounts of debits and credits* be recorded for *every* transaction.

11. Virtually every business maintains a *journal* as a record of "original" entry. A journal is a chronological listing of all transactions in the order they occur.

12. The journal shows all information about each transaction: (a) the date of the transaction, (b) the accounts debited and credited, and (c) a brief explanation of the transaction.

13. After a transaction has first been recorded in the journal, each debit and credit is later transferred to the appropriate ledger accounts. This transfer is called *posting*.

14. Two things can cause changes in owners' equity: (a) owner investments and dividends, and (b) profits or losses resulting from the operation of the business.

15. Profits increase owners' equity, and may either be distributed to the owners or reinvested in the business to help finance expansion and growth. Losses, however, reduce owners' equity, making the owners worse off, economically.

16. *Net income* is the term most often used to describe increases in owners' equity resulting from profitable operations. *Net loss* is the term used to describe decreases in owners' equity resulting from unprofitable operations.

17. Net income is computed by deducting *expenses* incurred during the accounting period from *revenue* earned during the period. Net income for each accounting period is reported in a financial statement called an *income statement*.

18. An income statement covers *a span of time*, whereas a balance sheet shows a company's financial position at *one particular date*. The need to relate net income to a period of time is called the *time period principle*.

19. *Revenue* is the price charged to customers for goods sold and services rendered during the accounting period. Revenue is not necessarily "cash" flowing into a business. Rather, it is the amount "earned" during the period. Recognizing revenue as it is "earned" illustrates the *realization principle*. Cash received from customers may be received by a business *before* revenue is earned, *after* revenue is earned, or at the *same time* that revenue is earned.

20. *Expenses* are the cost of goods and services incurred in the effort to generate revenue. Expenses are typically recorded as "resources" are *used up*, regardless of when payment for the resources is made. Thus, cash may be paid *before* resources are used up, *after* resources are used up, or at the *same time* that resources are used up.

21. An income statement shows the revenue earned during the period and the expenses incurred during the period in generating that revenue. This policy of offsetting revenue with related expenses is called *the matching principle*.

22. Businesses often purchase assets that will be "used up" over two or more accounting periods. The matching principle requires that an effort be made to allocate an appropriate portion of the asset's cost as an expense in each period that the asset helps the business to earn revenue.

23. At the end of the accounting period, when all entries in the journal have been posted to the ledger, the debit or credit balance of each account is computed. These balances are listed in a *trial balance*.

24. The trial balance is a two-column schedule listing all of the accounts in the order they appear in the ledger. Debit account balances are shown in the left column and credit account balances are shown in the right column. Since the total of the debit balances should equal the total of the credit balances, the two columns *will be equal* if the ledger is in balance. However, the amounts shown are not necessarily the correct amounts.

25. The trial balance is not a formal financial statement, but merely a preliminary step to preparing financial statements.

26. The accounting procedures covered in this chapter were part of what is referred to collectively as *the accounting cycle*. The accounting cycle involves eight steps: (a) journalizing transactions (b) posting journal entries to ledger accounts, (c) preparing a trial balance, (d) making adjusting entries, (e) preparing an adjusted trial balance (f) preparing financial statements from the adjusted trial balance figures, (g) closing appropriate accounts, and (h) preparing an after-closing trial balance. In this chapter we have illustrationd steps a-c of the accounting cycle. In Chapter 4, the remaining steps will be addressed.

TEST YOURSELF ON THE ACCOUNTING CYCLE

True or False

For each of the following statements, circle the T or the F to indicate whether the statement is true or false.

T F 1.   In a prosperous and solvent business the accounts with credit balances will normally exceed in total dollar amount the accounts with debit balances.

T F 2.   The term *debit* may signify either an increase or a decrease; the same is true of the term *credit*.

T F 3.   A business transaction is always recorded in the ledger by entries to two or more different ledger accounts.

T F 4.   An entry on the left side of a ledger account is called a debit entry and an entry on the right side is called a credit entry, regardless of whether the account represents an asset, a liability, or owners' equity.

T F 5.   Accounts representing items which appear on the left-hand side of the balance sheet usually have credit balances.

T F 6.   A trial balance with equal debit and credit totals proves that all transactions have been correctly journalized and posted to the proper ledger accounts.

T F 7.   The sequence of the account titles in a trial balance depends upon the size of the account balances.

T F 8.   A journal entry may include debits to more than one account and credits to more than one account but the total of the debits must always equal the total of the credits.

T F 9.   If a business transaction is recorded correctly, it cannot possibly upset the equality of debits and credits in the ledger.

T F 10. In a journal entry recording the purchase of a desk for $275.80, both the debit and credit were recorded and posted as $257.80. This *transposition error* would *not* be disclosed by the preparation of a trial balance.

T F 11. The double-entry accounting system means that transactions are recorded both in the journal and in the ledger.

T F 12. An income statement relates to a specified period time whereas a balance sheet shows the financial position of a business at a particular date.

T F 13. The realization principle states that a business should never record revenue until cash is collected from the customer.

T F 14. Expenses cause a decrease in owners' equity and are recorded by debits.

T F 15. If cash receipts are $10,000 greater than total expenses for a given period, the business will earn a net income of $10,000 or more.

T F 16. The journal entry to recognize a revenue or an expense usually affects an asset or liability account as well.

T   F   17.   Under accrual basis accounting, revenue is recognized when cash is received, and expenses are recognized when cash is paid.

T   F   18.   An expense may be recognized and recorded even though no cash outlay has been made.

T   F   19.   Buying a building for cash is just exchanging one asset for another and will not result in an expense even in future.

T   F   20.   Revenue increases owners' equity and is recorded by a credit.

Completion Statements

Fill in the necessary word to complete the following statements:

1.   Increases in assets are recorded by _____, and decreases in assets are recorded by credits; increases in accounts appearing on the right side of a balance sheet are recorded by _____, while decreases in those accounts are recorded by _____.

2.   In accounting, the term *debit* refers to the _____ side of a _____ _____, while the term *credit* refers to the _____ side.

3.   Asset accounts appear on the _____ side of the balance sheet and normally have _____ balances. Liability and owners' equity accounts appear on the _____ side of the balance sheet and normally have _____ balances.

4.   When a company borrows from a bank, two accounts immediately affected are _____ and _____ _____. The journal entry to record the transaction requires a _____ to the first account and a _____ to the second one.

5.   A _____ _____ is prepared from the ledger accounts at the end of the month (or other accounting period) in order to prove that the total accounts with _____ _____ is equal to the total accounts with _____ _____.

6.   The _____ principle of accounting states that revenue should be recognized in the period that it is earned. The _____ principle indicates that expenses should be recognized in the period in which they help produce _____.

7.   The principle distinction between expenses and dividends is that expenses are incurred for the purpose of _____ _____.

Multiple Choice

Choose the best answer for each of the following questions and enter the identifying letter in the space provided.

___ 1. A *ledger* contains a separate "account" for each:

    a. Business transaction.

    b. Business day.

    c. Asset, liability, and element of owners' equity.

    d. Journal entry.

___ 2. Which of the following statements about the rules for debiting and crediting balance sheet accounts is *not true*?

    a. Liability accounts are reduced by debit entries.

    b. Accounts on the left side of the balance sheet are reduced by credit entries.

    c. Each transaction is recorded by equal dollar amounts of debits and credits.

    d. Owners' equity accounts and asset accounts are increased by the debit entries.

___ 3. The key point of *double-entry accounting* is that every transaction:

    a. Is recorded by equal dollar amounts of debit and credit entries.

    b. Is recorded in both the journal and the ledger.

    c. Affects both sides of the balance sheet.

    d. Is both recorded and posted.

___ 4. A *journal* consists of:

    a. A listing of the balances of the accounts in the ledger.

    b. A storage center of information within a computer-based system.

    c. A chronological record of individual business transactions.

    d. a separate "account" for each asset, liability, and element of owners' equity.

___ 5. The purpose of a *trial balance* is:

    a.   To determine that journal entries are in balance before posting those entries to the ledger.

    b.   To indicate the effects of business transactions.

    c.   To prove the equality of debits and credits in the ledger.

    d.   To determine that the number of ledger accounts with debit balances is equal to the number of credit balances.

___ 6. Red Hill Vineyards completes a transaction which causes an asset account to decrease. Which of the following *related effects* may also occur?

    a.   An increase of equal amount in a liability account.

    b.   An increase of an equal amount in owners' equity.

    c.   An increase of an equal amount in another asset account.

    d.   None of the above.

___ 7. The *time-period principle*:

    a.   Requires that all companies prepare monthly, quarterly, and annual financial statements.

    b.   Involves dividing the life of a business entity into accounting periods of equal length.

    c.   Requires all companies to use a fiscal year ending December 31.

    d.   Stems from the Internal Revenue Service requirement that taxable income be reported on an annual basis.

___ 8. The *realization principle*:

    a.   Indicates that a business should record revenue when services are rendered or merchandise sold is delivered to customers, even if cash has not yet been received.

    b.   Indicates that revenue should be recognized in the accounting period when cash is received, even if the business has not yet performed all the required services.

    c.   Indicates that revenue should be recorded only after two conditions have been met: (1) the earning process is complete, and (2) the cash has been collected.

    d.   Provides guidelines as to when expenses should be recognized.

___ 9. A produce supplier enters into a contract with a supermarket chain on September 8 to deliver pumpkins in October. The pumpkins are delivered on October 14 at a price of $4,000, $2,000 payable on November 1, and $2,000 December 1. When should the produce supplier record the $4,000 as revenue?

    a.   September 8.

    b.   October 14.

    c. $2,000 November 1, and $2,000 December 1.

    d.   When the supermarket sells the pumpkins.

___ 10. The *matching principle* implies that expenses:

    a. Should be deducted from revenue in the period which the suppliers of the goods or services are paid.

    b. For a period should be equal in amount to the revenue recognized during the period.

    c. Should be deducted in the period in which use of the related goods or services help to produce revenue.

    d. Should be equal to the cash payments made during the period.

___ 11. On April 1, Hudson Company received and paid a $700 bill for advertising done in March. In addition to this bill, the company paid $6,100 during April for expenses incurred in that month. On May 2, Hudson Company paid a $4,600 payroll to employees for work done in April. Based on these facts, total expenses for the month of April were:

    a. $ 6,100.

    b. $ 6,800.

    c. $10,700.

    d. $11,400.

___ 12. If a journal entry recognizes an expense, the entry might also:

    a. Increase an asset account.

    b. Decrease the Capital Stock account.

    c. Decrease a liability account.

    d. Increase a liability account.

Exercises

1. Listed below are eight technical accounting terms emphasized in this chapter.

   Trial Balance   *Accounting Cycle*
   Debit   *Realization principle*
   Revenue   *Accrual accounting*
   Net income   *Credit*

   Each of the following statements may (or may not) describe one of these technical terms. In the space provided below each statement, indicate the accounting term described, or answer "None" if the statement does not correctly describe any of the terms.

   a. An eight-step process by which economic events are initially captured and transformed into financial statements.

   _____

   b. The price of goods sold and services rendered during the period.

   _____

   c. Revenue earned less expenses incurred during the period.

   _____

   d. A two-column schedule listing all of the accounts in the general ledger and their respective balances.

   _____

   e. The generally accepted accounting principle that expenses are to be recognized in the period that the related expenditure helps to produce revenue.

   _____

   f. The right-hand side of a ledger account.

   _____

   g. The technique of recognizing revenue when it is earned and expenses when the related goods and services are used, without regard to when cash is received or paid.

   _____

2. Show the change in total assets, total liabilities, and total owners' equity that will be caused by posting each amount in the following journal entries. In the effect of transaction row, show the total change in assets, liabilities, and owners' equity that has occurred after all parts of the transaction have been posted. Hint: The effect of each transaction should be that the total change on the left side of the balance sheet (change in assets) should equal the change on the right side (change in liabilities + change in owners' equity). Explanations have been omitted from journal entries to conserve space.

Journal Entry	Dr	Cr	Assets	=	Liabilities	+	Owners' Equity
Example:							
Office Equipment	600		+600				
Cash		150	-150				
Accounts Payable		450			+450		
Effect of transaction			+450	=	+450	+	0
a. Cash	1,230						
Accounts Receivable		1,230					
Effect of transaction				=		+	
b. Cash	5,000						
Capital Stock		5,000					
Effect of transaction							
c. Cash	3,800						
Notes Payable		3,800					
Effect of transaction				=		+	
d. Accounts Payable	350						
Cash		350					
Effect of transaction				=		+	
e. Land	9,000						
Cash		1,000					
Notes Payable		8,000					
Effect of transaction				=		+	

35

3. A list of accounts for Jones Company is given below followed by a series of transactions. Indicate the accounts that would be debited and credited in recording each transaction by placing the appropriate account number(s) in the space provided

1.   Cash
2.   Accounts Receivable
3.   Office Equipment
4.   Accumulated Depreciation: Office Equipment
21. Notes Payable
22. Accounts Payable
31. Capital Stock
35. Retained Earnings
41. All Revenue Accounts
51. All Expense Accounts
99. Dividends

Transactions	Accounts(s) Debited	Accounts(s) Credited
Example Purchased office equipment, paying part cash and issuing a note payable for the balance	3	1,21
a. Paid creditor amount due on open account		
b. Collected from customer for services performed by Jones Company in previous period		
c. Utility bill is received; payment will be made in 10 days		
d. Performed services for a customer; $50 cash received and the balance due in 30 days		
e. Office equipment purchased giving note payable		
f. Made a Cash distribution to the stockholders.		

36

4. Indicate the effects that each of these transactions will have upon the following six *total amounts* in the company's financial statements for the month of May. Use the code letters *I* for Increase, *D* for Decrease, and *NE* for No Effect.

| | Income Statement | | | | | | Balance Sheet | | | |
Error	Total Revenue	-	Total Expenses	=	Net Income	=	Total Assets	Total Liabilities	+	Owners' Equity
Example: Rendered services to a customer and received immediate payment in cash but made no record of the transaction	U		NE		U		U	NE		U
a. Payment for repairs erroneously debited to Building account										
b. Recorded collection of an account receivable by debiting Cash and crediting a revenue account.										
c. Recorded twice revenue earned on account.										
d. Recorded twice a purchase of offices supplies on credit										
e. Recorded the purchase of office equipment for cash as a debit to Office expense and a credit to cash.										
f. Recorded cash payment for advertising by debiting Repairs Expense and crediting Accounts Payable.										

37

SOLUTIONS TO CHAPTER 3 SELF-TEST

True or False

1. **F** Regardless of whether a business is solvent or profitable, the sum of accounts with credit balances (normally Liabilities and Owners' Equity) will always equal the sum of accounts with debit balances (assets).

2. **T** The term *debit* means an entry on the left-hand side of an account, and *credit* means an entry on the right-hand side of an account. Whether the entry results in an increase or decrease depends upon the type of account affected.

3. **T** Equal dollar amounts of debit and credit entries are needed to record each transaction. Although more than two accounts may be affected, a transaction would never involve just a single account.

4. **T** By definition, a *debit* is an amount recorded on the left-hand side of an account and a *credit* is an amount recorded on the right-hand side of an account.

5. **F** Liability and owners' equity accounts normally have credit balances. These accounts appear on the right-hand side of the balance sheets illustrated in your text.

6. **F** A "balancing" trial balance only gives assurance that (a) equal debits and credits have been recorded, (b) the balance of each account has been computed correctly, and (c) the addition of account balances in the trial balance has been done accurately.

7. **F** Accounts appear in the trial balance in the order in which they appear in the ledger, which is in financial statement order (assets, followed by liabilities, owner's equity, revenue, and expenses).

8. **T** An entry which includes more than one debit or more than one credit is called a *compound journal entry*.

9. **T** Every transaction is to be recorded by an equal dollar amount of debits and credits; recording a transaction properly will maintain equality of debits and credits.

10. **T** Since both debit and credit of the original journal entry were equal, the trial balance would still show equality of debits and credits.

11. **F** The premise of double-entry accounting means that equal dollar amounts of debits and credits are used to record each business transaction.

12. **T** Net income cannot be evaluated unless it is associated with a specific time period.

13. **F** The realization principle states that revenue should be recognized when services are rendered or goods are delivered.

14. **T** Expenses offset revenue in determining net income and therefore reduce owner's equity.

15. **F** Net income equals revenue minus expenses; cash receipts and revenue are not the same.

16. **T** To record an expense, the expense account is debited and cash or a liability is credited; to record revenue, the asset received is debited and revenue is credited.

17. **F** Revenue is recognized when *earned*; expenses are recognized in the period in which the cost helps to produce revenue.

18. **T** The cash payment for an expense may occur before, after, or in the same period that an expense helps to produce revenue.

19. **F** A portion of the cost of the building will be recognized as depreciation expense each period over the building's useful life.

20. **T** Revenue is the gross increase in owner's equity resulting from business activities; all increases in owner's equity are recorded by credits.

Completion Statements

1. Debits, credits, debits. 2. Left, ledger account, right. 3. Left, debit, right, credit. 4. Cash, Notes Payable, debit, credit. 5. Trial balance, debit balances, credit balances. 6. Realization, matching, revenue. 7. producing revenue.

Multiple Choice

1. Answer **c** – a separate ledger account is maintained to record the changes in each asset, liability, and element of owners' equity. Answers **a**, **b**, and **d** all relate to the journal, which consists of a chronological record of business transactions.

2. Answer **d** is false. Owners' equity accounts appear on the right-hand side of the balance sheet and are increase by credit entries.

3. Answer **a** – double-entry accounting means that equal dollar amounts of debits and credits are needed to record any business transaction.

4. Answer **c** describes a journal. Answer **a** describes a trial balance; answer **b**, a database; and answer **d**, a ledger.

5. Answer **c** – a trial balance is a listing of the balances of the accounts in the ledger. Answers **a** and **b** are incorrect because they relate to data not yet posted into the ledger. Answer **d** is incorrect because it is the total dollar amount of debit and credit balances that must be equal, not the number of accounts with each type of balance.

6. Answer **c** – a decrease in one asset account must be accompanied by an increase in another asset account, or by a *decrease* in either a liability or an owners' equity account.

7. Answer **b** – for accounting information to be useful, it must be available on a frequent periodic basis. This requires dividing the overall life of the business entity into equal "accounting periods." Answer **a** is incorrect because the principle does not require monthly statements. Answer **c** is incorrect because a company's fiscal year need not end on December 31. Answer **d** is incorrect because generally accepted accounting principles are not governed by income tax laws.

8. Answer **a** – under the realization principles revenue is recognized when it is earned regardless of when the cash is collected. Answers **b** and **c** are incorrect because they tie the recognition of revenue to the collection of cash. Answer **d** describes the matching principle, not the realization principle.

9. Answer **b** – the realization principle indicates that revenue should be recognized when it is earned – that is, when services are rendered or when goods sold are delivered to customers.

10. Answer **c** – expenses should be offset against the revenue produced by these expenditures. Answers **a** and **d** are incorrect because the period in which expenses are recognized may differ from the period in which the related cash payments are made. Answer **b** is incorrect because expenses may differ from revenue by the amount of any net income or net loss.

11. Answer **c** – $6,100 + $4,600. Answer **a** excludes the $4,600 in salaries expense for April. Answer **b** excludes the salaries and improperly includes $700 in advertising expense for the month of March. Answer **d** improperly includes the $700 in advertising expense applicable to March.

12. Answer **d** – the debit entry to record an expense is always accompanied by either a credit (decrease) in an asset account, or a credit (increase) in a liability account.

Solutions to Exercises

1.

a. Accounting Cycle

b. Revenue

c. Net income

d. Trial Balance

e. None (The statement describes the *matching principle*.)

f. Credit

g. Accrual accounting

2.

Journal Entry	Dr	Cr	Assets	=	Liabilities	+	Owners' Equity
a. Cash	1,230		+1,230				
Accounts Receivable		1,230	-1,230				
Effect of transaction			0	=	0	+	0
b. Cash	5,000		+5,000				
Capital Stock		5,000					+5,000
Effect of transaction			+5,000	=	0	+	+5,000
c. Cash	3,800		+3,800				
Notes Payable		3,800			+3,800		
Effect of transaction			+3,800	=	+3,800	+	0
d. Accounts Payable	350				-350		
Cash		350	-350				
Effect of transaction			-350	=	-350	+	0
e. Land	9,000		+9,000				
Cash		1,000	-1,000				
Notes Payable		8,000			+8,000		
Effect of transaction			+8,000	=	+8,000	+	0

3.

Transactions	Accounts(s) Debited	Accounts(s) Credited
a	22	1
b	1	2
c	51	22
d	1,2	41
e	3	21
f	99	1

4.

Error	Income Statement Total Revenue	-	Total Expenses	=	Net Income	=	Balance Sheet Total Assets	Total Liabilities	+	Owners' Equity
a	NE	-	U	=	O	=	O	NE	+	O
b	O		NE		O		O	NE		O
c	O		NE		O		O	NE		O
d	NE		NE		NE		O	O		NE
e	NE		O		U		U	N		U
f	NE		NE		NE		O	O		NE

THE ACCOUNTING CYCLE: PREPARING AN ANNUAL REPORT

HIGHLIGHTS OF THE CHAPTER

1. There is much more to year-end than adjusting and closing the accounts. Accountants also prepare financial statements, income tax returns, annual reports, and budgets for the coming year. Meanwhile, CPAs may be auditing the financial statements, requiring constant access to accounting records and explanations of past transactions. That's why accountants call year-end their "busy season."

2. In this chapter, we focus upon adjusting entries and the preparation of financial statements. Some businesses may *adjust* and close their accounts monthly; however, most companies adjust their accounts every month but make *closing* entries only at year-end. (Preparation of interim financial statements by a business that closes its accounts only at year-end is discussed in Highlight **21**.)

3. Annual financial statements cover the company's *fiscal year*. Most companies use the calendar year ending at December 31 as their fiscal year, but others end their fiscal year at the seasonal "low point" in their business activities. Many retailers, for example, end their fiscal year in early January.

4. Some transactions involve revenue or expenses relating to several accounting periods. In such cases, *adjusting entries* are needed at the end of each period to recognize the appropriate amount of revenue or expense. Thus, adjusting entries help accountants to achieve the goals of *accrual accounting*—recognizing revenue when it is earned, and recognizing expenses as the related goods and services are used.

5.   There are four basic types of adjusting entries. Entries to: (1) apportion costs already recorded in the accounting records *(recorded costs)*, (2) apportion *unearned revenue*, (3) record expenses *not yet* recorded in the accounting records *(unrecorded expenses),* and (4) record *unrecorded revenue.*

6.   Each type of adjusting entry affects both an income statement account (revenue or expense) and a balance sheet account (asset or liability). Thus, adjusting entries serve two purposes: (1) they recognize revenue or expenses relating to the accounting period, and (2) bring various asset and liability accounts up-to-date. We will now discuss the four basic types of adjusting entries.

7.   *Converting assets to expenses.* A cash expenditure (or cost) that will benefit more than one accounting period usually is recorded by debiting an asset account (for example, Supplies, Unexpired Insurance, and so on) and by crediting Cash. In each future period that benefits from the use of this asset, an adjusting entry is made to allocate a portion for the asset's cost from the balance sheet to the income statement as an expense. This adjusting entry is recorded by debiting the appropriate expense account (for example, Supplies, Expense or Insurance Expense) and crediting the related asset account.

8.   *Converting liabilities to revenue.* A business may collect cash in advance for services to be rendered in future accounting periods. Transactions of this nature are usually recorded by debiting Cash and by crediting a liability account (typically called, Unearned Revenue). In the period that services are actually rendered, an adjusting entry is made to allocate a portion of the liability from the balance sheet to the income statement to recognize the revenue earned for services provided during the period. The adjusting entry is recorded by debiting the liability (Unearned Revenue) and by crediting *Revenue Earned* (or a similar account) for the value of the services.

9.   *Accruing unpaid expenses.* An expense may be incurred in the current accounting period even though no cash payment will occur until a future period. These *accrued* expenses are recorded by an adjusting entry made at the end of each accounting period. The adjusting entry is recorded by debiting the appropriate expense account (for example, Interest Expense or Salary Expense) and by crediting the related liability (for example, Interest Payable or Salaries Payable).

10. *Accruing uncollected revenue.* Revenue may be earned (or accrued) during the current period, even though the collection of cash will not occur until a future period. Unrecorded earned revenue, for which no cash has been received, requires an adjusting entry at the end of the accounting period. The adjusting entry is recorded by debiting the appropriate asset (for example, Accounts Receivable or Interest Receivable) and by crediting the appropriate revenue account (for example, Service Revenue Earned or Interest Earned).

11. The concept of *materiality* allows accountants to use estimated amounts and even to ignore other accounting principles if these actions will not have a "material" effect upon the financial statements. Accountants must be sure that all material items are properly reported in financial statements, but may account for *immaterial items* and events in the *easiest and most convenient manner.* The concept of materiality allows the use of estimates in end-of-period adjustments, or even ignoring adjusting entries for immaterial items.

12. An item is *material* if knowledge of the item might reasonably influence the decisions of users of financial statements. Whether or not a specific item is "material" is a matter of *professional judgment,* in which accountants consider such factors as the absolute and relative dollar amount of the item, the cumulative effect of all such items, and the nature of the item under consideration.

13. Only after all adjusting entries have been made can a complete set of financial statements be prepared. The financial statements are prepared directly from the information reported by the *adjusted trial balance.*

14. The *income statement* is prepared first. It shows all of the revenue earned during the period, less all expenses incurred in generating revenue.

15. The *statement of retained earnings* is prepared second. It covers the same period of time as the income statement. This statement shows the net income or loss for the period, and any dividends the business made during the period by the owner.

16. The *balance sheet* is prepared next. It shows the financial position of a business at a particular point in time. Financial position refers to the relationship among assets, liabilities, and owners' equity.

17. The statement of cash flows is prepared last. This statement classifies various cash receipts and disbursements intro three categories: (a) operating, (b) investing, and (c) financing. It uses the cash flow figures from each of these categories to "tie" the cash balance reported in the balance sheet at the beginning of the period to the cash balance reported at the end of the period.

18. *Operating cash flows* arise primarily from day-to-day revenue and expense transactions. *Investing cash flows* arise primarily from buying and selling long-term assets, such as plant and equipment. *Financing cash flows* arise from transactions with owners and long-term creditors.

19. The income statement, the statement of retained earnings, and the statement of cash flows may be viewed as "links" between two successive balance sheets.

20. After the financial statements have been prepared, all revenue and expense accounts must be *closed*.

21. *Closing the accounts* means transferring the balances of revenues and expenses at the end of the period to an account used to measure net income, called *income summary*. After all revenue and expense balances have been transferred, the Income Summary account will show a *credit balance* if the business has earned *net income* for the period, or a *debit balance* if the business has suffered a *net loss* for the period. The balance of the Income Summary account is then transferred to the Retained Earning account.

22.   A Dividends account is used to record any distributions of assets to the stockholders during the period. It is closed by transferring its debit balance to the Retained Earnings account. *It does not get closed through the income summary because dividends are not an expense.*

23.   The principal purpose of closing revenue, expenses, and the drawing accounts is to reduce their balances to zero for the start of the next accounting period.

24.   After closing the accounts, an *after-closing trial balance* is often prepared to prove that the ledger is still in balance. The after-closing trial balance will contain only *balance sheet accounts*. All other accounts will have zero balances.

25.   A major step in preparing financial statements is drafting the *notes* which should accompany the statements. These notes should disclose any information that users of the statements may need to *interpret the statements properly*. Two items routinely disclosed are the useful lives used in depreciating major types of assets, and the due dates of major liabilities.

26.   When a business closes its accounts only at year-end, the revenue, expense, and dividend accounts throughout the period have balances reflecting year-to-date activity. To prepare an income statement for any period shorter than the year to date, *subtract* from the current balance in the revenue or expense account the balance in the account as of the beginning of the desired period. This process of subtracting prior balances from the current balance is repeated for each revenue and expense account. No such computations are required for the balance sheet accounts, as the balance sheet contains account balances at the balance sheet date.

27.*   A *worksheet* illustrates in one place the relationships between the unadjusted trial balance, and financial statements. A worksheet is simply a *spreadsheet,* which shows in columnar form the unadjusted trial balance, the effects of adjusting entries, adjusted trial balance, and the adjusted trial balance amounts arranged in the format of financial statements.

28.*   Preparation of a worksheet is *not* a step in the accounting cycle. Rather, a worksheet is simply a working paper (or software program) which enables accountants to "work out" the required adjusting entries.

---

*Supplemental Topic, "The Worksheet.:

TEST YOURSELF ON PREPARING AN ANNUAL REPORT

True or False

For each of the following statements, circle the T or the F to indicate whether the statement is true or false.

T　F　1.　If all transactions were originally recorded in conformity with generally accepted accounting principles, there would be no need for adjusting entries at the end of the period.

T　F　2.　Adjusting entries contribute to accurate financial reporting by allocating revenues to the period in which they were earned and expenses to the period in which they were incurred.

T　F　3.　Every adjusting entry must change both an income statement account and a balance sheet account.

T　F　4.　An account called Unearned Commissions Revenue is a revenue account.

T　F　5.　Accrued revenue is a term used to describe revenue which has been received but not yet earned.

T　F　6.　The adjusting entry to allocate part of the cost of a one-year fire insurance policy to expense will cause total assets to increase.

T　F　7.　The adjusting entry to recognize that commission revenue not previously recorded (or billed to a customer) has now been earned will cause total assets to increase.

T　F　8.　The adjusting entry to recognize an expense which has not yet been recorded and will not be paid until some future period will cause total assets to decrease.

T   F   9.   The adjusting entry to recognize that a fee received in advance from a customer has now been earned will cause total liabilities to increase.

T   F   10.   If employees have worked eight days in a period for which they will not be paid until the first payday next period, and if no adjusting entry is made at the end of this period, total liabilities will be understated and both net income and owners' equity will be overstated.

T   F   11.   The original cost of a building minus the accumulated depreciation is called the *book value*, or *carrying value*.

T   F   12.   The concept *of materiality* allows accountants to ignore transactions involving small dollar amounts.

T   F   13.   The dollar amounts appearing in financial statements can be taken directly from an adjusted trial balance prepared at year end.

T   F   14.   The dollar amounts appearing in financial statements cannot be determined until closing entries have been posted.

T   F   15.   Financial statements normally are accompanied by several pages of "notes" supplying additional information.

T   F   16.   A company that adjusts its books monthly and closes its books annually may prepare and close its books annually and may prepare quarterly financial statements directly from its adjusted trial balance at the end of each quarter.

T   F   17.   A company need not close its books in order to prepare financial statements.

T   F * 18.   A worksheet illustrates the relationship between an unadjusted trial balance, adjusting entries, and the amounts appearing in financial statements.

T   F * 19.   Preparing a worksheet is a basic step in the accounting cycle.

T   F * 20.   Worksheets are prepared only in manual accounting systems.

---

* *Supplemental Topic*, "The Worksheet."

Completion Statements

Fill in the necessary word to complete the following statements:

1. The four types of transactions requiring adjusting entries are _____ _____ , _____ _____ , _____ _____ , and _____ _____ transactions.

2. An adjusting entry at November 30 concerning the cost of an insurance policy serves two purposes: (a) it _____ the proper amount of _____ to November operations, and (b) it reduces the _____ account entitled _____ _____ so that the correct amount will appear in the November 30 balance sheet.

3. Adjusting entries always recognize either a _____ or an _____ .

4. The adjusting entry to record receiving some of the benefits in the current period from an expenditure made in an earlier period consists of a _____ to an _____ account and a _____ to an _____ account.

5. If a customer pays in advance for services to be rendered, the entry to record the receipt of the payment consists of a _____ to an _____ account and a _____ to a _____ account.

6. If an expense has been accumulating from day to day (such as wages) without being recorded, the proper adjusting entry would _____ an _____ account and _____ a account.

7. If an expenditure will yield benefits to a business only during the period in which it is made, the entry for the expenditure consists of a _____ to an _____ account and a _____ to an _____ account and/or a _____ account.

8. If an expenditure will yield benefits to the business over several periods, the entry for the expenditure consists of a _____ to an _____ account and a credit to an _____ account and/or a _____ account.

9. The South Bay Management Company agreed to manage an apartment building beginning May 15, 20__, for one year at a management fee of $400 per month. The first $400 payment is received June 15, 20__. The adjusting entry at May 31, 20__ should consist of a debit to _____ _____ _____ and a credit to _____ _____ _____ . When the first payment is received on June 15, the collection should be recorded by an entry debiting _____ for $400, and crediting _____ _____ _____ for $_____ and _____ _____ _____ for $_____ .

10. * In the worksheet prepared by a business operating at a loss, the Income Statement _____ column will exceed the _____ column and the excess of the _____ over the _____ will be entered in the _____ column in order to bring the two Income Statement columns into balance.

Multiple Choice

. Choose the best answer for each of the following questions and enter the identifying letter in the space provided.

__ 1. The *accounting period* of a business may best be described as:

    a. One month.

    b. One year.

    c. The time span covered by the balance sheet.

    d. The time span covered by the income statement.

__ 2. The purpose of *adjusting entries* is to:

    a. Correct errors made in the accounting records.

    b. Update the balance of the Retained Earnings account for changes in owners' equity temporarily recorded in revenue and expense accounts.

    c. Prepare the revenue and expense accounts for recording the transactions of the next accounting period.

    d. Allocate revenue and expenses among accounting periods when the related business transactions affect more than one period.

__ 3. The entry recording the liability to employees for work done during the period for which they have not yet been paid is an example of which type of adjusting entry?

    a. Converting an asset to expense.

    b. Converting a liability to revenue.

    c. Accruing unpaid expenses.

    d. Accruing uncollected revenue.

__ 4. A balance sheet account was debited in the amount of $1,240 for office supplies purchased during the first year of operations. At year-end, the office supplies on hand were counted and determined to represent a cost of $360. The appropriate adjusting entry would:

    a. Have no effect on net income.

    b. Consist of a debit to expense of $360 and a credit to the balance sheet account.

    c. Decrease assets by $1,240.

    d. Increase expenses $880.

---

* *Supplemental Topic*, "The Worksheet."

___ 5. Failure to make an adjusting entry to recognize accrued interest receivable would cause:

    a. An understatement of assets, net income, and owners' equity.

    b. An understatement of liabilities and an overstatement of net income and owners' equity.

    c. An overstatement of assets, net income, and owners' equity.

    d. No effect on assets, liabilities, net income, and owners' equity.

___ 6. Assets would be overstated if a necessary adjusting entry were omitted for:

    a. Expired insurance.

    b. Accrued salaries.

    c. Accrued interest earned.

    d. Revenue collected in advance during the period.

___ 7. Which of the following adjusting entries will result in a decrease in assets and owners' equity?

    a. The entry to record the earned portion of rent received in advance.

    b. The entry to record accrued wages payable.

    c. The entry to record revenue earned but not yet received.

    d. None of the above.

___ 8. Which of the following statements concerning materiality is *not* valid?

    a. Generally accepted accounting principles do not provide clear-cut guidelines as to what is considered "material" in each situation.

    b. The concept of materiality may result in financial statements that are not completely precise.

    c. Strict adherence to the matching principle or the realization principle is not required for items considered "immaterial."

    d. The concept of materiality results in financial statements that are less useful to decision makers because many important details have been omitted or estimated.

___ 9. A business that prepares quarterly financial statements:

    a. Must close its accounts quarterly.

    b. Must adjust its accounts at least quarterly.

    c. May not issue annual financial statements.

    d. Must obtain special permission from the IRS.

___ 10. The preparation of a *worksheet*:

    a. Constitutes creation of a formal financial statement.

    b. Eliminates the need for entering adjusting entries in the journal.

    c. Provides the information needed for journalizing adjusting and closing entries.

    d. Serves no purpose unless the books are to be closed.

___ 11. * When a worksheet is used, the normal sequence of accounting procedures would call for:

    a. Journalizing the adjusting entries before preparing the worksheet.

    b. Posting adjusting entries to the ledger after preparing an after-closing trial balance.

    c. Preparing a worksheet before journalizing adjusting and closing entries.

    d. Journalizing closing entries before preparing an adjusted trial balance.

___ 12. * Which of the following amounts appears in both the Income Statement credit column and the Balance Sheet debit column of a worksheet?

    a. Net income.

    b. Net loss.

    c. Accumulated depreciation.

    d. Dividends.

---

* *Supplemental Topic,* "The Worksheet."

Exercises

1. Listed below are eight technical accounting terms emphasized in this chapter.

Accrued revenue   *Adjusting entries*
Unearned revenue   *Closing entries*
Accrued expense   *Notes accompanying financial*
Interim statements   *statements*
*Worksheet

Each of the following statements may (or may not) describe one of these technical terms. In the space provided below each statement, indicate the accounting term described, or answer "None" if the statement does not correctly describe any of the terms.

a. An asset that becomes an expense as a good or service is used up.

_____

b. An expense that has been incurred, but not yet paid.

_____

c. A device for working out the end-of-period accounting procedures before adjusting and closing entries are entered into formal accounting records.

_____

d. Corrections of errors in financial statements discovered after the annual report has been printed, but before it has been issued.

_____

e. A liability that is usually settled by rendering services rather than by making cash payments.

_____

f. Revenue which has been earned during the accounting period, but has not been recorded or collected.

_____

g. Entries made to record revenue or expenses of the period that have not yet been recognized as a result of recording daily business transactions.

_____

2. Commuter Airlines prepares monthly financial statements. On August 31, the company's accountant made adjusting entries to record:

    a. Depreciation for the month of August.

    b. Earning ticket revenue which had been collected in advance. (When passengers buy tickets in advance, Commuter Airlines credits an account entitled Unearned Ticket Revenue.)

    c. The portion of the company's prepaid insurance policies which had expired in August.

    d. Salaries payable to employees which have accrued since the last payday in August.

    e. Interest revenue which had accrued on an investment in government bonds.

Indicate the effect of each of these adjusting entries upon the major elements of the company's financial statements—that is, upon revenue, expenses, net income, assets, liabilities, and owner's equity. Organize your answer in tabular form, using the column headings provided and the symbols + for increase, ! for decrease, and NE for no effect. The answer for adjusting entry **a** is provided as an example.

Adjusting entry	Income Statement			Balance Sheet			
	Revenue	! Expenses	= Net Income	Assets	=	Liabilities	+ Owners' Equity
a	NE	+	!	!		NE	!
b							
c							
d							
e							

*3. Use the following adjustments to complete the worksheet on the following page for the month ended June 30, 20___(ignore income taxes).

    a. Unexpired insurance at June 30 amounted to $300.

    b. Office supplies on hand were determined by count to amount to $250.

    c. The office equipment is being depreciated on the basis of a 10-year life with no salvage value. Record one month's depreciation.

    d. Accrued interest on notes payable at January 31 amounted to $50.

    e. Commissions still unearned at January 31, 20– amounted to $700.

    f. [1]Accrued salaries payable at January 31 were $2,100.

---

* *Supplemental Topic,* "The Worksheet."

54

SOLANA CORPORATION

Worksheet

For the Month Ended January 31, 20___

	Trial Balance		Adjustments		Adjusted Trial Balance		Income Statement		Balance Sheet	
	Debit	Credit	Debit	Credit	Debit	Credit	Debit	Credit	Debit	Credit
Balance sheet accounts:										
Cash	22,960									
Accounts receivable	17,300									
Unexpired insurance	360									
Office supplies	900									
Office equipment	25,200									
Accumulated depreciation:										
office equipment		3,150								
Notes payable		10,000								
Accounts payable		1,800								
Unearned commissions		1,500								
Capital Stock		20,000								
Retained Earnings		12,000								
Interest payable										
Salaries payable										
Income taxes payable		8,000								
Income statement accounts:										
Commissions earned		21,670								
Rent expense	2,400									
Salaries expense	11,000									
	70,120	70,120								
Insurance expense										
Office supplies expense										
Depreciation expense: office eqpt										
Interest expense										
Net income										

*4. On the journal page following, prepare adjusting and closing entries using the information
contained in the worksheet prepared in Exercise *3.

		General Journal		
20___		**Adjusting Entries**		
		a		
Jan.	31			
		b		
	31			
		c		
	31			
		d		
	31			
		e		
	31			
		f		
	31			
	31			
		Closing Entries		
	31			

---

* *Supplemental Topic*, "The Worksheet"

SOLUTIONS TO CHAPTER 4 SELF-TEST

True or False

1. **F** Adjusting entries are needed whenever transactions affect the revenue or expense of more than one accounting period.

2. **T** Adjusting entries are a result of applying the realization principle and the matching principle.

3. **T** Every adjusting entry changes owners' equity by recognizing revenue or expense. Any change in owners' equity must be offset by a corresponding change in either assets or liabilities.

4. **F** Unearned Commissions Revenue represents amounts that have been received but have not been earned yet; it is a *liability* account.

5. **F** Accrued revenue describes revenue which *has been earned* but has not been recorded before the end of the period.

6. **F** As the total cost of the policy is gradually allocated to expense, total assets decrease.

7. **T** The adjusting entry consists of a debit to an asset account (a receivable) and a credit to a revenue account.

8. **F** The adjusting entry debits an expense account and credits a liability account; liabilities are increased.

9. **F** Fees received in advance are recorded as a liability; this liability is *reduced* as the fees are earned.

10. **T** The appropriate adjusting entry should have been a debit to Salaries Expense and a credit to Salaries Payable.

11. **T** Both of these terms refer to the *net* amount at which an asset is shown on the balance sheet.

12. **F** The concept of materiality allows accountants to use estimates and to account for immaterial items in the easiest and most convenient manner, but does not justify simply not recording transactions involving small dollar amounts.

13. **T** Adjusted account balances form the basis for the preparation of formal financial statements.

14. **F** Closing entries are prepared *after* the preparation of financial statements. In fact, financial statements include the balances of many accounts which are closed in the closing process.

15. **T** The notes contain information necessary for users to properly interpret the statements. These notes are part of the generally accepted accounting principle of adequate *disclosure*.

16. **F** The adjusted trial balances contain year-to-date amounts for all revenue, expense, and dividend accounts. In order to prepare financial statements for, say, the third quarter, the company must *subtract* the balances at the end of the second quarter from the balances at the end of the third quarter for all revenue, expense, and dividend accounts.

17. **T** Many companies adjust their accounts monthly but close their books only at year-end. In this situation, temporary account balances reflect year-to-date amounts throughout the year. These businesses prepare interim financial statements by performing a series of revenue, expense and dividends for the desired interim period.

18* **T** A worksheet begins with an unadjusted trial balance, shows the proposed adjusting entries, the adjusted account balances, and how these adjusted balances will be used in the preparation of financial statements.

19.* **F** A worksheet is really just a "tool" for making adjusting entries.

20.* **F** Worksheets are often used in computer-based systems.

Completion Statements

1. defer expenses, defer revenue, accrue expenses, accrue revenue. 2(a). allocates, expense, (b) asset, Unexpired Insurance. 3. revenue, expense. 4. debit, expense, credit, asset. 5. debit, asset, credit, liability. 6. debit, expense, credit, liability. 7. debit, expense, credit, asset, liability. 8. debit, asset, asset, liability. 9. Management Fees Receivable, Management Fees Earned, Cash, Management Fees Receivable, $200, Management Fees Earned, $200. *10. debit, credit, debits, credits, credit.

Multiple Choice

1. Answer **d**—The period of time covered by the income statement. Answers **a** and **b** are incorrect because an accounting period is not limited to one specific time period. Some companies may use a month, while others use a quarter or a year. Answer **c** is incorrect because the balance sheet covers only a specific date, not an accounting period.

2. Answer **d**—when transactions affect the revenue or expenses of more than one period, adjusting entries are needed to allocate the effects of these transactions. Answer **a** is incorrect, because adjusting entries are needed even when no errors have been made in recording transactions. Answers **b** and **c** both describe the purpose of closing entries.

3. Answer **c**—accruing unpaid expenses. Prior to making an adjusting entry, work done by employees since the last payroll date is an expense that has not yet been recorded in the accounting records.

4. Answer **d**—the adjusting entry would transfer the cost of supplies used ($1,240 ! $360 = $880) from the asset account to an expense account.

5. Answer **a**—the entry to record accrued interest receivable increases total assets, revenue, and owner's equity. Therefore, failure to make this entry has the effects described in answer **a**.

6. Answer **a**—allocating expired insurance to expense reduces the asset account, Unexpired Insurance. Without this adjustment, the asset Unexpired Insurance would be overstated.

7. Answer **d**—the given answers all are incorrect. An adjustment that decreases owners' equity recognizes an expense; answers **a** and **c** relate to the recognition of revenue. Answer **b** recognizes expense, but increases a liability (wages payable) rather than decreasing an asset.

8. Answer **d**—by definition, a "material" item or event is one that might reasonably be expected to influence the decisions of financial statement users. All such material items must be reported properly; estimating or omitting immaterial details serves to make financial statements more useful in most cases, even if they are less precise. Materiality is a matter of professional judgment; GAAP do not provide definite materiality formulas to use in each situation.

9. Answer **b**—in order to ensure that proper amounts are reported, the company must adjust its accounts prior to preparing financial statements. Answer **a** is incorrect because quarterly financial statements may be prepared even if accounts are closed only at year end. There is no

---

prohibition against preparing quarterly or monthly financial statements as well as annual financial statements. The IRS has authority over matters of tax law, not the frequency with which a company issues financial statements.

*10.   Answer **c**—a worksheet is a "tool," from which accountants prepare formal adjusting and closing entries, as well as financial statements. It is not a formal financial statement, and does not eliminate the need to journalize and post the adjusting and closing entries. Answer **d** is incorrect, because a worksheet can be used to prepare interim financial statements even when the accounts are not being closed

*11.   Answer **c**—the steps in the accounting cycle following preparation of a worksheet, listed in sequence, are: (1) prepare financial statements, (2) adjust and close the accounts, and (3) prepare an after-closing trial balance. Answer **d** is incorrect because the adjusted trial balance is part of the worksheet and is prepared before closing entries are journalized.

*12.   Answer **b**—when a business incurs a net loss, the total of the debit column in the Income Statement columns of the work sheet exceeds the credit column. To bring these columns into balance, the amount of the loss is entered in the Income Statement credit column. Also, as a net loss reduces owners' equity, this amount is entered in the Balance Sheet debit column. Net income appears in the Income Statement debit column and Balance Sheet credit column. Accumulated depreciation and dividends do not enter into the determination of net income and do not appear in the Income Statement columns.

Solutions to Exercises

1.
a.   None (The statement describes either a pre-paid expense, depreciable asset, or recorded cost.)

b.   Accrued expense

c.   Worksheet

d.   None. (Notes accompanying financial statements contain additional information and are not used for correcting errors. If material errors were discovered, the annual report would be corrected and reprinted.)

e.   Unearned revenue

f.   Accrued revenue

g.   Adjusting entries

Supplemental Topic, "The Worksheet."

2.

Adjusting entry	Income Statement				Balance Sheet				
	Revenue	!	Expenses	=	Net Income	Assets	=	Liabilities	+	Owners' Equity
a	NE		+		!	!		NE		!
b	+		NE		+	NE		-		+
c	NE		+		!	!		NE		!
d	NE		+		!	NE		+		!
e	+		NE		+	+		NE		+

*3.

SOLANA CORPORATION
Worksheet
For the Month Ended January 31, 20__

	Trial Balance Debit	Trial Balance Credit	Adjustments Debit	Adjustments Credit	Adjusted Trial Balance Debit	Adjusted Trial Balance Credit	Income Statement Debit	Income Statement Credit	Balance Sheet Debit	Balance Sheet Credit
Balance sheet accounts:										
Cash	22,960				22,960				22,960	
Accounts receivable	17,300				17,300				17,300	
Unexpired insurance	360			a 60	300				300	
Office supplies	900			b 650	250				250	
Office equipment	25,200				25,200				25,200	
Accumulated depreciation:										
office equipment		3,150		c 210		3,360				3,360
Notes payable		10,000				10,000				10,000
Accounts payable		1,800				1,800				1,800
Unearned commissions		1,500	e 800			700				700
Capital Stock		20,000				20,000				20,000
Retained earnings		12,000				12,000				12,000
Interest payable				d 50		50				50
Salaries payable				f 2,100		2,100				2,100
Income statement accounts:										
Commissions earned		21,670		e 800		22,470		22,470		
Rent expense	2,400				2,400		2,400			
Salaries expense	11,000		f 2,100		13,100		13,100			
	70,120	70,120								
Insurance expense			a 60		60		60			
Office supplies expense			b 650		650		650			
Depreciation expense: office equipment			c 210		210		210			
Interest expense			d 50		50		50			
			3,870	3,870	72,480	72,480	16,470	22,470	56,010	50,010
Net income							6,000			6,000
							22,470	22,470	56,010	56,010

*Supplemental Topic, "The Worksheet."

*4.		General Journal		
20___		**Adjusting Entries**		
		a		
Jan	31	Insurance Expense	60	
		Unexpired Insurance		60
		To record insurance expired during January.		
		b		
	31	Office Supplies Expense	650	
		Office Supplies		650
		To record consumption of office supplies during January..		
		c		
	31	Depreciation Expense: Office Equipment	210	
		Accumulated Depreciation: Office Equipment		210
		To record depreciation expense for Jan ($25,200 ÷ 120 months).		
		d		
	31	Interest Expense	50	
		Interest Payable		50
		To record interest expense for January.		
		e		
	31	Unearned Commissions	800	
		Commissions Earned		800
		To record commissions earned during January.		
		f		
	31	Salaries Expense	2,100	
		Salaries Payable		2,100
		To record salary expense and related liability as of Jan. 31.		
		Closing Entries		
	31	Commissions Earned	22,470	
		Income Summary		22,470
		To close the revenue account.		
	31	Income Summary	18,870	
		Rent Expense		2,400
		Salaries Expense		13,100
		Insurance Expense		60
		Office Supplies Expense		650
		Depreciation Expense: Office Equipment		210
		Interest Expense		50
		Income Taxes Expense		2,400
		To close the expense accounts.		
	31	Income Summary	3,600	
		Retained Earnings		3,600
		To close the Income Summary account.		

Supplemental Topic, "The Worksheet."

5

ACCOUNTING FOR MERCHANDISING ACTIVITIES

HIGHLIGHTS OF THE CHAPTER

1. A *merchandising* company is one whose principal activity is buying and selling merchandise, or *inventory*. An inventory of merchandise consists of the stock of goods on hand and available for sale to customers. Inventory is a relatively liquid asset reported in the balance sheet immediately below accounts receivable. The same accounting concept and methods in use by the service-type business we studied in Chapters 1 to 4 are applicable to merchandising companies. A merchandising concern, however, requires some other accounts and techniques to control and record the purchase and sale of merchandise.

2. The *operating cycle* for a merchandising company is the period of time the business usually takes to perform its function of buying inventory, selling that inventory, and collecting the accounts receivable generated by those sales. This may be described as the period of time a business takes to convert cash into inventory, into accounts receivable, and then back into cash, as illustrated by the following diagram of the operating cycle:

(buy inventory)	(sell inventory)	(collect receivables)

Cash $\rightarrow$ Inventory $\rightarrow$ Accounts Receivable $\rightarrow$ Cash

3. Merchandising companies purchase their inventories from other business organizations in a *ready-to-sell* condition; companies that manufacture their inventories are called *manufacturers*. Merchandising companies include both *retailers*, who sell merchandise directly to the public, and *wholesalers*. Wholesalers buy large quantities of merchandise from several different manufacturers and then resell it to many retailers.

4. The principal source of revenue for a merchandising concern is from sale of goods. To succeed, it must sell its goods at prices higher than the prices paid in acquiring those goods from manufacturers or other suppliers. This cost is termed the *cost of goods sold*, and is an expense item of such importance that it is shown separately in the income statement of merchandising companies. The difference between revenue from sales and the cost of goods sold is called *gross profit*, which is not the same as net income. The company earns a net income only if the gross profit is large enough to cover the other expenses of the business.

5. A *subsidiary ledger* is an accounting record which shows separately the individual items which comprise the balance of a general ledger account. A general ledger account for which a subsidiary ledger is maintained is called a *controlling account*. Merchandising companies usually maintain the following subsidiary ledgers:

    a. Accounts Receivable subsidiary ledger, showing amount receivable from each customer;

    b. Accounts Payable subsidiary ledger, listing amount payable to each individual supplier;

    c. Inventory subsidiary ledger, listing separately a great many details about each product the company sells.

In addition to the three mentioned above, subsidiary ledgers are maintained for many other general ledger accounts.

6. Portions of a journal entry that affect a subsidiary ledger account must be *double-posted*—that is, posted both to the subsidiary ledger account and to the controlling account in the general ledger.

7. Subsidiary ledgers are not used in the preparation of financial statements and are not made available to persons outside of the business organization. Periodically, a subsidiary ledger must be *reconciled* with the controlling account. That is, the sum of the subsidiary ledger account balances is determined to be equal to that of the controlling account. In a computer-based accounting system, the computer automatically reconciles the subsidiary ledgers with controlling accounts.

8. There are two alternative approaches to accounting for merchandising transactions: (a) the *perpetual inventory method*, and (b) the *periodic inventory method*. Virtually all large merchandising companies use the perpetual approach, in which the accounting records are kept perpetually up-to-date as merchandise is purchased and sold to customers.

9. In a *perpetual inventory system*, purchases of merchandise are debited to an asset account entitled Inventory. As each unit is sold, *two* entries are necessary. One recognizes the *revenue earned* by debiting Cash or Accounts Receivable and crediting the *Sales* account with the selling price of merchandise sold. The second transfers the cost of the unit from the Inventory account to an account entitled *Cost of Goods Sold*. Thus we have a perpetual or running record of the cost of goods sold during the period, as well as the cost of goods on hand (the balance in the Inventory account).

10. A perpetual inventory system usually includes an *inventory subsidiary ledger*, which contains a separate account for each type of product in the company's inventory. The Inventory controlling account balance is the aggregate cost of merchandise on hand; the inventory subsidiary ledger provides quantity and unit cost data on a product by product basis.

11. Although the Inventory account is continuously updated for all purchases and sales of merchandise in a perpetual inventory system, a complete physical count of the merchandise on hand is made at least once a year. *Taking a physical inventory* discloses discrepancies between the quantities shown in the inventory records and the quantities of merchandise actually on hand. The Inventory controlling account is adjusted to the cost of merchandise actually on hand by crediting Inventory and debiting the Cost of Goods Sold account for the dollar amount of the discrepancy, called *inventory shrinkage*. The inventory subsidiary ledger is simultaneously adjusted also.

12. The closing entries for a merchandising business with a perpetual inventory system parallel those covered previously for a service-type business. The Sales account is closed into the Income Summary along with other revenue accounts. The Cost of Goods Sold account is closed into the Income Summary in the same manner as other expense accounts.

13. Under the *periodic inventory system*, the cost of merchandise acquired is debited to an account entitled *Purchases*, instead of being debited to Inventory. As units are sold, *no entry is made to record the cost of goods sold*. Thus, the accounting records do not show from day to day the cost of the goods on hand (inventory) or the cost of goods sold during the period. Instead, the value of the inventory is determined only *periodically* at the end of each accounting period by taking a physical count of merchandise in stock.

14. In a periodic inventory system, the *cost of goods sold* is computed by the following steps:

   a. Add the goods on hand at the beginning of the period (the ending inventory from last period) plus any additional goods acquired during the period (purchases) to get the *cost of goods available for sale*.

b. From the cost of goods available for sale, subtract the goods which were not sold (namely, the inventory on hand at the end of the current period) to get the *cost of goods sold* during the period.

15. The cost of goods sold section of the income statement of a merchandising company using the *periodic inventory method* would appear as follows for the month of May:

Inventory (Apr. 30)	$ 5,100
Purchases..	6,300
Cost of goods available for sale	$11,400
Less: Inventory (May 31)	5,400
Cost of goods sold	$ 6,000

16. Once computed, the ending inventory and cost of goods sold must be recorded. (Remember, in a periodic system, the inventory account has not been adjusted for merchandise purchased or sold during the period, and no cost of goods sold has yet been recorded.) One approach is to create a Cost of Goods Sold account and adjust the Inventory account to the proper balance as part of the closing process.

17. The following two special closing entries may be used to create a Cost of Goods Sold account:

a. Cost of Goods Sold	XXX	
Inventory (beginning balance)...........		XX
Purchases		XXX

To close temporary accounts contributing to
the cost of goods sold.

b. Inventory (year-end balance).......................	XXX	
Cost of Goods Sold		XXX

To reduce the balance of the Cost of Good
Sold account by the cost of merchandise still
on hand at year-end.

The first brings together the costs contributing to the cost of goods sold; the second adjusts the cost of goods sold to its proper balance and records ending inventory in the Inventory account. Once the Cost of Goods Sold account and the Inventory account have the proper balances, the closing process is the same as for a company using a perpetual inventory system.

18. Although perpetual and periodic inventory systems produce the same results in annual financial statements, a perpetual system provides much useful information throughout the year that is not available in a periodic system.

a. Ledger accounts for Inventory and for the Cost of Goods Sold are kept perpetually up-to-date in a perpetual system. Under the periodic system, the balance in the Inventory account does not change during the year as merchandise is purchased (remember a Purchases account is used) or sold. The cost of goods sold in a periodic system is determined by a computation made at the end of the year.

b. A perpetual inventory system includes an inventory subsidiary ledger showing for each type of product the cost and quantities of units purchased, sold, and currently on hand. A periodic system does not include an inventory subsidiary ledger.

19. In the preceding chapters we used the journal entry as a tool for analyzing the effects of various financial transactions and recorded each in the *general journal*. Although the general journal is flexible in that all types of transactions may be recorded, this approach is usually not cost-effective. Every general journal entry requires writing at least two account titles and an explanation of the transaction. In addition, the person maintaining a general journal must have

sufficient skill to analyze and record all types of transactions. Through the use of *special journals* a business can speed up and simplify the recording process.

20. A special journal is an accounting record or device designed to record a *particular type of transaction* quickly and efficiently. The person maintaining the special journal need not be an expert in accounting, since only one type of transaction is recorded in each special journal. Two points are basic to the design of an efficient special journal:

   a. The person recording the transaction should have to enter *as little data as possible*.

   b. The recording of transactions should be *combined with other essential business activities* to minimize time and effort involved in the accounting function.

21. Special journals may exist in several different forms, such as manual cash receipts or cash payments journals, and electronic point-of-sale terminals.

22. In addition to net income, two key measures used to evaluate performance of merchandising companies are trends in the company's *net sales* and *gross profit rate*. The trend in net sales from period to period is considered to be a key indicator of both past performance and future prospects. However, as some products are more profitable than others, increasing net sales alone is not enough to ensure increasing profitability. A company's *profit margin* (also called gross profit rate) is used to evaluate the profitability of sales transactions.

23. Profit margin is the dollar amount of gross profit expressed as a *percentage* of net sales revenue. Profit margins can be computed for the business as a whole, for specific departments, and for individual products. By concentrating sales efforts on the products and departments with the highest profit margins, management can increase the company's overall gross profit rate.

24. Manufacturers and wholesalers normally sell merchandise on account and may offer a *cash discount* to encourage customers to pay invoices early. Credit terms of *2/10, n/30* would mean that customers may take a deduction of 2% of their invoice amount if they pay within 10 days. Otherwise, they have 30 days to pay the full amount of the invoice. A cash discount is called a *purchase discount* by the buyer and a *sales discount* by the seller.

25. Most well-managed companies have a policy of taking advantage of all cash discounts available on purchases of merchandise, and therefore record purchases at the *net cost*— invoice price less any available cash discount. For example, if $1,000 of merchandise is purchased on terms of 2/10, n/30, Inventory is debited and Accounts Payable credited for $980, the net cost after discount. If the invoice is paid within 10 days, the purchaser simply records payment of a $980 account payable. If the invoice is not paid within 10 days, the purchaser must pay $1,000, rather than the recorded liability of $980, and a $20 *Purchase Discounts Lost* is debited and treated as a nonoperating expense in the income statement.

26. As an alternative to recording purchases at net cost, some companies record merchandise purchases at the gross invoice price. If payment is made within the discount period, these companies record the amount of the purchase discount *taken*. Purchase discounts taken is treated as a reduction in the cost of goods sold. Since the gross price method records only purchase discounts taken, it does not direct management's attention to discounts lost.

27. When merchandise purchased is found to be unsatisfactory and returned to the supplier, the return is recorded by debiting Accounts Payable and crediting Inventory for the net cost of the returned items.

28. The freight charges on goods acquired during the period are a legitimate part of the cost of the asset being acquired. Because it may be impractical to determine the portion of a shipping charge relating to specific product in inventory, many companies follow the convenient policy of debiting all transportation costs on *inbound* shipments to an account entitled *Transportation-in*.

This amount is generally included in the amount reported as cost of goods sold in the income statement. Do not confuse Transportation-in with the delivery expense on *outbound* shipments. Freight on outbound shipments is a *selling expense*, not part of the cost of goods being acquired.

TEST YOURSELF ON MERCHANDISING ACTIVITIES

True or False

T F 1. The operating cycle of a business is the period of time between payroll dates.

T F 2. Gross profit is the profit the business would have made if all the goods available for sale had been sold during the period.

T F 3. When a cash sale is made by a merchandising business, the revenue is recorded by a debit to Cash and a credit to sales, whether or not the sales price exceeded the cost of the goods sold.

T F 4. The gross profit rate is computed by dividing net sales by gross profit.

T F 5. A subsidiary ledger is used to account for items that are immaterial or of less significance than those recorded in the general ledger controlling account.

T F 6. Although general ledger accounts are used in the preparation of financial statements, the information contained in subsidiary ledgers must be disclosed in footnotes to the financial statements.

T F 7. The perpetual inventory method will reflect from day to day the cost of goods sold thus far during the period and the current balance of goods on hand.

T F 8. When a perpetual inventory system is in use, the accounting records contain an account, Cost of Goods Sold, which must be closed at the end of the accounting period.

T F 9. The perpetual inventory system is appropriate not only for businesses handling high unit cost goods, such as automobiles or fur coats, but also practical for stores with a computerized system handling a large quantity of low-priced items.

T F 10. When the periodic inventory method is used, the Inventory account is debited when merchandise is purchased and credited when goods are sold.

T F 11. In a periodic inventory system, the purchase of either merchandise or office equipment by a merchandising concern would be recorded as a debit to Purchases and a credit to either Cash or Accounts Payable.

T F 12. When a periodic inventory system is in use, the cost of goods sold section contains two amounts for Inventory: a beginning inventory which is added in arriving at the cost of goods available for sale, and an ending inventory which is subtracted to determine the cost of goods sold.

T F 13. When a periodic inventory system is used, the beginning inventory figure in this period's cost of goods sold computation was the ending inventory figure in last period's computation.

T F 14. When a periodic inventory system is in use, the income statement will report the "Cost of Goods Sold" even though the accounting records do not use a Cost of Goods Sold account on an ongoing basis.

T F 15. *Point-of-sale terminals* often make use of optical code recognition labels.

T F 16. The term "net sales" means gross sales less the cost of goods sold.

T F 17. A company with a trend of steadily increasing net sales has increasing profitability.

Completion Statements

Fill in the necessary word to complete the following statements:

1. The period of time a business usually takes to convert cash into inventory, then into receivables, and finally back into cash is called the _____ _____.

2. In a periodic inventory system, adding net purchases to the beginning inventory gives the _____ _____ _____ _____ _____ _____. Subtracting _____ _____ from this figure leaves the _____ _____ _____ _____.

3. The excess of sales revenue over the cost of goods sold is called _____ _____.

4. The Inventory account is debited when goods are acquired and credited when they are sold according to the _____ inventory method. Inventory is determined solely by a _____ _____ when the _____ inventory method is used.

5. _____ _____ is the dollar amount of gross profit expressed as a percentage of _____ _____.

6. When merchandising companies record all purchases at *net cost*, the accounting system is set up to keep track of _____ _____ _____. If purchases are recorded at *gross invoice price*, the accounting system keeps track of _____ _____ _____.

Multiple Choice

Choose the best answer for each of the following questions and enter the identifying letter in the space provided.

— 1. Carter Stores must determine how much it owes Hawkins Wholesale, one of Carter's merchandise suppliers, as of December 31, 2001. This information can be found *most directly* by examining:

a. Carter's accounts receivable subsidiary ledger.

b. Carter's accounts payable subsidiary ledger.

c. Carter's inventory subsidiary ledger.

d. The current liability section of Carter's balance sheet as of December 31, 2001.

___ 2.   Which of the following statements is *not* descriptive of the perpetual inventory system?

      a.   The amount of ending inventory is determined only by physical count and the cost of goods sold is determined by a computation made at year-end.

      b.   Two entries are made when merchandise is sold.

      c.   A ledger account keeps track of the cost of goods sold during the period.

      d.   The Inventory account balance is adjusted each time merchandise is purchased or sold during the period.

___ 3.   The inventory subsidiary ledger:

      a.   As well as the Inventory controlling account appears in the current asset section of the balance sheet.

      b.   As well as the Inventory controlling account must be adjusted each time merchandise is purchased or sold in a perpetual inventory system.

      c.   Is used to keep track of inventory items not accounted for in the Inventory controlling account.

      d.   Is an integral part of a periodic inventory system.

___ 4.   When a perpetual inventory system is used:

      a.   The dollar amount of inventory shrinkage is more difficult to determine than in a periodic inventory system.

      b.   Inventory shrinkage is more likely to occur than in a periodic inventory system.

      c.   Both the Inventory controlling account and the inventory subsidiary ledger accounts are adjusted to agree with the quantities determined by the physical inventory.

      d.   Taking a physical inventory is not necessary since up-to-date inventory and cost of goods sold information is provided by the accounting records.

Assume use of a *periodic* inventory system for 5 and 6.

___ 5.   By adding the purchases during the period to the beginning inventory and deducting the ending inventory, we obtain an amount called the:

      a.   Cost of goods available for sale.

      b.   Cost of goods sold.

      c.   Gross profit on sales.

      d.   Operating expenses.

___ 6. The ending inventory of Bar Marine was $42,000. If the beginning inventory had been $50,000 and the cost of goods available for sale during the period totaled $104,000, the cost of goods sold must have been:

    a. $196,000.

    b. $112,000.

    c. $ 62,000.

    d. None of the above.

___ 7. The net sales of Austin Saddlery were $200,000 for the current month. If the cost of goods available for sale was $180,000 and the gross profit rate was 35%, the cost of goods sold must have been:

    a. $ 70,000.

    b. $130,000.

    c. $ 50,000.

    d. $ 63,000.

___ 8. Special journals are advantageous:

    a. Only in noncomputerized (manual) accounting systems.

    b. Only in computerized accounting systems.

    c. Whenever a business must record an unusual or unique transaction.

    d. Whenever a business must record a large number of similar transactions.

___ 9. The net sales of Regent Musical Supply in October were $20,000. Regent Musical Supply uses a periodic inventory system. If the cost of goods available for sale during the month was $18,000, and the gross profit was $8,000, the ending inventory must have been:

    a. $ 4,800.

    b. $ 6,000.

    c. $10,000.

    d. Some other amount.

___ 10. Which of the following would be *least* useful in evaluating a company's profitability?

    a. Profit margin for the current year.

    b. Trend in profit margins for the most recent 5-year period.

    c. Trend in earnings for the most recent 5-year period

    d. Net sales for the current year.

Exercises

1.   Listed below are eight technical accounting terms emphasized in this chapter.

   Net sales   *Cost of goods sold*
   Periodic inventory system   *Inventory subsidiary ledger*
   Gross profit   *Gross profit rate*
   Perpetual inventory system   *Inventory shrinkage*

   Each of the following statements may (or may not) describe one of these technical terms. In the space provided below each statement, indicate the accounting term described, or answer "None" if the statement does not correctly describe any of the terms.

   a.   An item readily apparent upon taking a physical inventory in a perpetual inventory system, but difficult to determine in a periodic system.

   _____

   b.   Gross sales revenue less sales discounts and sales returns and allowances.

   _____

   c.   Beginning inventory, plus the delivered cost of goods purchased, minus ending inventory.

   _____

   d.   An accounting record generally not used in a periodic inventory system.

   _____

   e.   Net sales less the cost of merchandise sold.

   _____

   f.   Gross profit expressed as a percentage of net income.

   _____

   g.   System of accounting for merchandise in which a Purchases ledger account is not used.

   _____

2.   White Feather Corporation uses a *perpetual* inventory system. For each of the following merchandising transactions, give the title of the account(s) that are to be debited and credited in recording each transaction. (You may ignore sales taxes.)

	Transaction	Account(s) Debited	Account(s) Credited
a.	Purchased merchandise for cash.		
b.	Sold merchandise on account.		
c.	Collected cash from customer in b above.		
d.	Sold merchandise for cash.		
e.	A physical inventory at year-end disclosed a normal amount of inventory shrinkage.		

3. Alcala Corporation uses a *periodic* inventory system. Each of the following four horizontal lines represents data taken from a separate multiple-step income statement. Insert the missing amount in the space provided. Indicate a net loss by placing brackets around the amount, as for example, in line **a**, (20,000).

	Net Sales	Cost of Goods Available for Sale	Ending Inventory	Cost of Goods Sold	Gross Profit	Operating and Non-Operating Expenses	Net Income or (Loss)
a	$400,000	$325,000	$_____	$250,000	$_____	$_____	$ (20,000)
b	700,000	_____	90,000	_____	290,000	235,000	_____
c	250,000	210,000	_____	_____	72,000	105,000	_____
d	_____	_____	82,000	$330,000	_____	185,000	35,000

4. Kids' World sell children's furniture and clothing. The following information is available for sales during the month of May:

	Furniture	Clothing
Net sales	$6,400	$3,600
Cost of Goods Sold	4,160	1,440

Compute for May the profit margin (gross profit rate) for:

a. Furniture sales   _____%
b. Clothing sales   _____%
c. The company as a whole   _____%

SOLUTIONS TO CHAPTER 5 SELF-TEST

True or False

1. **F** The operating cycle of a business is the period of time between the purchase of merchandise and the conversion of this merchandise back into cash.

2. **F** Gross profit is the difference between revenue from sales and the cost of the goods sold.

3. **T** Sales revenue is the selling price of goods, not the cost of those goods to the seller.

4. **F** The gross profit rate is computed by dividing gross profit by net sales.

5. **F** A subsidiary ledger shows separately the *individual items* which comprise the balance of a general ledger controlling account.

6. **F** The information contained in subsidiary ledgers in not made available to persons outside the business organization and therefore would not appear in the financial statements or notes to the financial statements.

7. **T** The Cost of Goods Sold account keeps an up-to-date record of the cost of all merchandise sold; the Inventory account is continually adjusted each time merchandise is purchased from suppliers or sold to customers.

8. **T** The Cost of Goods Sold account keeps track of the cost of merchandise sold on an ongoing basis. It is a debit balance account which is closed into Income Summary at the end of the period along with other expense accounts.

9. **T** The perpetual inventory system requires recording the cost of each sale as it occurs. This approach is now feasible for stores handling large quantities of merchandise due to the use of computerized systems.

10. **F** The Inventory account is updated continually under the *perpetual* inventory system.

11. **F** The Purchases account is used only for merchandise acquired for resale.

12. **T** Beginning inventory plus net purchases equals cost of goods available for sale less ending inventory equals the cost of goods sold.

13. **T** The ending inventory of one period is the beginning inventory of the next period.

14. **T** In a periodic inventory system, the cost of goods sold reported in the income statement is determined by a computation, as illustrated in Highlight 15. The accounting records do not keep track of the cost of goods sold as merchandise is sold during the period. Some companies create a Cost of Goods Sold account and adjust the Inventory account to the proper balance during the closing process, but this account is then closed into Income Summary and is not used during the period to accumulate the cost of merchandise sold.

15. **T** From the code number, the computer is able to identify the item being sold, record the amount of the sale, and transfer the cost of the item from the Inventory account to the Cost of Goods Sold account.

16. **F** Net sales is equal to the balance of the Sales revenue account (gross sales), less some minor adjustments for transactions such as refunds to customers. Net sales less the cost of goods sold is equal to gross profit.

17. **F** Net sales is a dollar amount of sales volume. The dollar amount of sales may increase by simply selling merchandise at very low prices, even at prices that may not cover the cost of merchandise. In such cases, profitability may actually be decreasing while the dollar amount of net sales increases. The trend in profit margin on sales is a better indicator of a company's profitability than is the trend in net sales dollars.

Completion Statements

1. operating cycle. 2. cost of goods available for sale, ending inventory, cost of goods sold. 3. gross profit. 4. perpetual, physical count, periodic. 5. profit margin, net sales. 6. purchase discounts lost, purchase discounts taken.

Multiple Choice

1.   Answer **b**—the accounts payable subsidiary ledger contains an account for each creditor, showing the amount owed. The accounts receivable subsidiary ledger shows amounts due to Carter from each credit customer; the inventory subsidiary ledger shows for each product the quantities, per-unit costs, and total costs of all units purchased, sold, and currently on hand. Carter's balance sheet reports only aggregate accounts payable as of December 31, 2001. (Hawkins' accounts receivable subsidiary ledger would also show how much Carter owes Hawkins.)

2.   Answer **a** is descriptive of the periodic inventory system. In addition to recording the sale, an entry is made to record the cost of the merchandise sold under the perpetual inventory system. A ledger account entitled Cost of Goods sold is debited and Inventory is credited *each time* a sale is made when using a perpetual inventory system.

3.   Answer **b**—when merchandise is sold in a perpetual inventory system, the Inventory controlling account is credited for the cost of merchandise sold; the inventory subsidiary ledger is adjusted concurrently to reflect the specific items no longer in inventory. Since the inventory subsidiary ledger provides the detail comprising the balance in the Inventory controlling account, answer **c** is not accurate. Answer **a** would lead to a double counting of inventory in the balance sheet. Answer **d** is incorrect because periodic inventory systems do not generally use an inventory ledger.

4.   Answer **c**—the quantities of merchandise determined by the physical inventory differ from the perpetual inventory records, the accounting records are adjusted to reflect actual amounts. In a periodic inventory system, inventory shrinkage is included in the amount computed to be the cost of goods sold, and is difficult to isolate. Inventory shrinkage does not depend upon the type of inventory accounting method in use, hence answer **b** is inaccurate. (It might be the case, however, that shrinkage due to employee theft is more likely in a periodic system where the dollar amount of "shrinkage" is difficult to isolate because there are no perpetual records with which to compare the physical count.) Even in a perpetual system, a physical inventory is taken at least annually.

5.   Answer **b**—beginning inventory plus purchases (net of any discount and purchase returns and allowance) is the formula for cost of goods *available* (answer **a**). Answer **c** is computed by deducting cost of goods sold from net sales.

6.   Answer **c**—cost of goods sold is computed by deducting ending inventory ($42,000) from the cost of goods available for sale ($104,000). Since you are given the amount of cost of goods available for sale in the problem data, you do *not* have to use the beginning inventory amount provided in solving this problem.

7.   Answer **b**—since net sales were $200,000, gross profit was $70,000 (35% of $200,000) and the cost of goods sold must have been $130,000 ($200,000 net sales minus $70,000 gross profit).

8.   Answer **d**—a special journal is an accounting record or *device* designed to record a specific type of transaction quickly and efficiently. Although the *form* of special journals will vary according to the type of accounting system in use, use of special journals will speed up and simplify the recording process whenever routine transactions occur frequently, regardless of the type of accounting system in use.

9.   Answer **b**—net sales ($20,000) less gross profit ($8,000) equals cost of goods sold of $12,000. If the cost of goods available for sale is $18,000 and the cost of goods sold is $12,000, the cost of goods not sold (ending inventory) must be $6,000.

10. Answer **d**—trend analysis and profit margin (on current year net sales) are more meaningful statistics than simply the dollar amount of net sales for a particular year.

Solutions to Exercises

1.

a. Inventory shrinkage

b. Net sales

c. Cost of goods sold

d. Inventory subsidiary ledger

e. Gross profit

f. None (Gross profit rate [profit margin] is current year gross profit expressed as a percentage of current year net sales.)

g. Perpetual inventory system

2.

Transaction	Account(s) Debited	Account(s) Credited
a Purchased merchandise for cash.	Inventory	Cash
b Sold merchandise on account.	Accounts Receivable Cost of Goods Sold	Sales Inventory
c Collected cash from customer in b above.	Cash	Accounts Receivable
d Sold merchandise for cash.	Cash Cost of Goods Sold	Sales Inventory
e A physical inventory at year-end disclosed a normal amount of inventory shrinkage.	Cost of Goods Sold	Inventory

3.

	Net Sales	Cost of Goods Available for Sale	Ending Inventory	Cost of Goods Sold	Gross Profit	Operating and Non-Operating Expenses	Net Income or (Loss)
a	$400,000	$325,000	**$75,000**	$250,000	**$150,000**	**$170,000**	$(20,000)
b	700,000	**500,000**	90,000	**410,000**	290,000	235,000	**55,000**
c	250,000	210,000	**32,000**	**178,000**	72,000	105,000	**(33,000)**
d	**550,000**	**412,000**	82,000	330,000	**220,000**	185,000	35,000

4.

a. ($6,400 !$4,160) ÷ $6, 400 = 35%

b. ($3,600 !$1,400) ÷ $3,600 = 60%

c. ($6,400 + $3,600) ! ($4,160 + $1,440) = $4,400;
   $4,400 gross profit ÷ $10,000 total sales = 44%

FINANCIAL ASSETS

HIGHLIGHTS OF THE CHAPTER

1. The term *financial assets* includes cash and those assets easily and directly convertible into known amounts of cash. These assets include cash, short-term investments (also called marketable securities), and receivables. All of these assets represent forms of money; financial resources flow among these assets categories as businesses "store" money in these three basis forms.

2. In the balance sheet, financial assets shown at their *current values*, meaning the amounts of cash that these assets represent. The current value of cash is imply its *face amount*. The current value of short-term investments (marketable securities) fluctuates daily; therefore, short-term investments appear in the balance sheet at their current *market values*. Receivables appear in the balance sheet at *net realizable value* – the estimated collectible amount.

3. The term *cash* includes currency, coins, checks, money orders, money deposited in banks, and the charge slips signed by customers using bank credit cards. Cash is the most liquid of all assets and is listed first in the balance sheet. A company may have numerous bank accounts as well as cash on hand and several of the other items mentioned above, but these will be lumped together in the figure for Cash in the balance sheet. The balance of a bank account that is not available for use in paying current liabilities is *not* regarded as a current asset. Any such "restricted" cash is listed just below the current asset section of the balance sheet in the section entitled Long-Term Investments.

4. A *line of credit* is a prearranged borrowing agreement in which a bank has authorized a cash loan up to a specified credit limit. Once used, a line of credit becomes a liability. The *unused* portion of a line of credit represents the ability to borrow money quickly; it does not appear as either an asset or a liability in the balance sheet. Unused lines of credit are *disclosed* in notes accompanying the financial statements.

5. Some short-term investments are so liquid that they are termed *cash equivalents*. Examples include money market funds, U. S. Treasury bills, and commercial paper. These items are so similar to cash that they are usually combined with the amount of cash in the balance sheet. The first asset shown in the balance sheet for firms owning these types of short-term investments is *Cash and cash equivalents*.

6. Although the balance sheet reports the amount of cash and cash equivalents owned by a business at a particular date, a separate financial statement –the *statement of cash flows* – summarizes all of the cash receipts and cash disbursements during the accounting period. This required financial statement reports the cash activities that created the *change* in the cash and cash equivalents figure during an accounting period

7. The term *cash management* refers to planning, controlling, and accounting for cash transactions and cash balances. The basic objectives of cash management are:

    a. Provide accurate accounting for cash receipts, cash disbursements, and cash balances.

    b. Prevent loss from fraud or theft.

    c. Anticipate borrowing needs; assure adequate cash for business operations.

    d. Prevent excessive cash balances which produce no revenue.

    To meet these objectives, management needs a strong internal control structure.

8. Cash offers the greatest temptation to theft, and this makes the problem of internal control especially important. Basic rules to achieve strong internal control over cash include:

   a. Separating the handling of cash from the maintenance of accounting records.

   b. Preparing a *cash budget* for each department of planned cash receipts, cash payments, and cash balances for each month of the coming year.

   c. Preparing an immediate *control listing* of cash receipts at the time and place the money is received.

   d. Depositing all cash receipts in the bank daily.

   e. Making all significant cash disbursements by check.

   f. Requiring that every expenditure be verified and approved before payment is made.

   g. Promptly reconciling bank statements with the accounting record.

9. Cash receipts may be received over the counter from customers, or through the mail. All cash received over the counter should be promptly recorded on a cash register in plain view of the customer. The participation of two or more employees in each cash receipts transaction is desirable. The person who opens the mail should prepare a *control listing* of checks received, forwarding one copy of the list to the accounting department and another copy along with the checks to the cashier who will deposit them.

10. Employees who handle cash receipts should not also have the authority to issue credit memoranda for sales returns. Issuing a credit memoranda for a fictitious sales return could conceal the theft of money collected from the customer.

11. Good internal control over cash disbursement requires that all payments (except those from petty cash) be made by prenumbered checks. The officials authorized to sign checks should not have the authority to approve invoices for payment or to make entries in the accounting records. Before signing a check the official should review the documents supporting and approving the cash disbursement. These supporting documents should be stamped "Paid" and the checks should be mailed without going back to the person who prepared them.

12. One widely used means of controlling cash disbursements is the *voucher system*. A *voucher* (a serially numbered form) is prepared for each expenditure. Approval signatures are placed on the voucher to show that the expenditure was authorized, the goods or services received, the invoice prices verified, and the proper accounts debited and credited. A completed voucher must accompany every check submitted for signature. Before signing the check, the official authorized to make cash disbursements will review the voucher to determine that the expenditure has been approved.

13. Internal control is strong in a voucher system because each expenditure must be verified and approved before a check is issued and because the function of signing checks is separated from the functions of approving expenditures and recording cash transactions.

14. In a typical voucher system, the accounting department is responsible for approving cash payments and for recording the transaction. Once payment has been approved, the accounting department signs a voucher authorizing payment and records the transaction in the accounting records. The voucher and supporting document are then sent to the finance department, where an official reviews the voucher and supporting documents, issues and signs the check. After the check is signed, the voucher and supporting documents are perforated to prevent reuse and filed in a paid voucher file in the accounting department.

15. Each month the bank will provide the depositor with a *statement* of his or her account, showing the beginning balance, dates and amounts of deposits, deductions for checks paid, other charges, and the ending balance. All paid checks are returned to the depositor with the bank statement. When numerous checks are being deposited daily, it is inevitable that occasionally one will

78

bounce; that is, the drawer of the check will have insufficient funds on deposit to cover it. The check will be marked *NSF* (not sufficient funds), charged back against the depositor's account, and returned to the depositor. An NSF check should be regarded as a receivable rather than cash until it is collected directly from the drawer, redeposited, or determined to be worthless.

16. The amount of *cash* included in the cash and cash equivalents figure reported in the balance sheet of a business should be the correct amount of cash owned at the close of business on that date. To determine this amount, it is necessary to **reconcile** the monthly bank statement with the balance of cash as shown by the depositor's accounting records. The balance shown on the bank statement will usually not agree with that shown on the depositor's books because certain transactions will have been recorded by one party but not by the other. Examples are outstanding checks, deposits in transit, service charges, NSF checks, and errors by the bank or by the depositor.

17. The *bank reconciliation* will identify the items which cause the balance of cash per books to differ from the balance of cash shown on the bank statement, and it will show the adjusted or correct amount of cash. Those reconciling items which have not yet been recorded by the depositor (or which reflect errors on the depositor's part) must be entered on the books to make the accounting records correct and up-to-date at the end of the period.

18. As previously stressed, it is desirable that all cash payments be made by check; however, in every business some small expenditures are necessary for which it is not practicable to issue checks. Postage, taxi fares, and small purchases of office supplies are common examples. To control these small payments almost every business established a *petty cash fund*. A check is written for perhaps $100 or $200 and is cashed, and the cash is kept on hand for making small expenditures. A receipt or *petty cash voucher* should be obtained and placed in the fund to replace each cash payment. Therefore the fund always contains constant amount of cash and vouchers. The expenses are recorded in the accounts when the fund is replenished, perhaps every two or three weeks. The entry for the replenishment check will consist of debits to the proper expense accounts and a credit to Cash.

19. *Cash budgets* which forecast monthly cash expenditures for each department contribute to control over cash disbursements. Management or the internal auditors will investigate any expenditures in excess of budgeted amounts. Comparison of actual with budgeted levels of performance on a departmental basis requires the use of a responsibility accounting system.

20. Companies with large amounts of liquid resources often invest in *marketable securities*. Marketable securities consist of investments in bonds and in the capital stocks of publicly traded corporations. A basic characteristic of all marketable securities is that they are *readily marketable* – purchased or sold easily at *quoted market prices*. These investments are almost as liquid as cash itself and are listed second among the current assets, immediately after cash.

21. Short-term investments in marketable securities are reported in the balance sheet at their *current market value as of the balance sheet date*. The valuation principles of *mark-to market* requires adjusting the balance sheet valuation of these investments to market value at each balance sheet date. An offsetting entry must also be made in a special stockholders' equity account, *Unrealized Holding Gain (or Loss) on Investments*. Since the mark-to-market adjustment affects only the balance sheet (an asset account and a stockholders' equity account), it has no effect on the net income of the period.

22. Whether higher or lower than cost, the current market value is the amount reported in the balance sheet for short-term investments in marketable securities. When market value differs from cost, the cost figure is usually disclosed in the footnotes to the financial statements. For investments classified as available for sale securities, the difference between cost and market also appears as an element of stockholders' equity, labeled Unrealized Holding Gain (or Loss) on Investments. The account increases total stockholders' equity in the case of a *gain*, and decreases total stockholders' equity in the case of a *loss*.

23. An important factor in the growth of the American economy has been the increasing tendency to sell goods on credit. In most large businesses, the major portion of total sales is actually sales on credit. Since every credit sale creates some sort of receivable from the customer, it follows that accounts receivable and/or notes receivable will be large and important assets in the balance sheets of most businesses.

24. Accounts receivable are very liquid assets, usually being converted into cash within a period of 30 to 60 days. Some companies sell merchandise on longer-term installment plans, allowing customers to take as long as 48 months to pay. As long as the accounts receivable arise from "normal" sales transactions accounts receivable are classified as current assets.

25. A business can increase sales by giving its customers easy credit terms. But no business wants to sell on credit to customers who will be unable to pay their accounts. Consequently, many businesses have a credit department which investigates the credit records of new customers to see if they are acceptable credit risks.

26. Accounts receivable are shown in the balance sheet at the estimated collectible amount – the net realizable value. Even in companies with sound credit policies, a few accounts receivable will prove to be uncollectible. As long as the portion of uncollectible accounts is relatively small, it is to the advantage of the business to go ahead and incur these losses because the extension of credit to customers is also bringing in a lot of profitable business. The losses from accounts that do prove uncollectible are an *expense* resulting from the use of credit to increase sales.

27. A most fundamental accounting principle is that **revenue must be matched with the expenses incurred in securing that revenue**. Uncollectible Accounts Expense is caused by selling goods or services to customers who fail to pay their bills. The expense is therefore incurred in the **period the sale is made** even though receivable is not determined to be uncollectible until some following period. At the end of each accounting period, we must therefore **estimate** the amount of uncollectible accounts expense. This estimate is brought on the books by an adjusting entry debiting **Uncollectible Accounts Expense** and crediting **Allowance for Doubtful Accounts**. The Allowance for Doubtful Accounts is **a contra- asset account.** It appears in the balance sheet as a deduction from Accounts Receivable and thus leads to an **estimated net realizable** value for receivables.

28. Allowance for Doubtful Accounts is sometimes called **Allowance for Bad Debts**. Uncollectible Accounts Expense is sometimes referred to as **Bad Debts Expense**.

29. Since the allowance for doubtful accounts is necessarily an estimate rather than a precise calculation, there is a fairly wide range within which the amount may be set. Accountants' **professional judgment** and the **concept of conservatism** in the valuation of assets both play considerable parts in determining the size of the allowance. Conservatism suggests that the allowance for doubtful accounts should be at least adequate. Establishing a relatively large allowance for doubtful also means recording a relatively large amount of uncollectible accounts expense, thus tending to reduce net income for the current period.

30. When a customer's account is determined to be uncollectible, it should immediately be written off. The write-off consists of a debit to the Allowance for Doubtful Accounts and a credit to Accounts Receivable. The credit will be posted to the customer's account in the subsidiary ledger as well as to the controlling account in the general ledger. Since the write-off reduces both the asset Accounts Receivable and the contra-asset Allowance for Doubtful Accounts, **there is no change in the net carrying value of receivables**. Nor is there any recognition of expense at the time of the write-off. The write-off merely confirms the validity of our earlier estimate in recording uncollectible accounts expense in the period the sale was made.

31. Two methods of estimating uncollectible accounts expense are in wide use. The first method, which we call the **balance sheet approach**, relies on aging the **accounts receivable** and thereby arriving at the total amount estimated to be uncollectible. The allowance for uncollectible

accounts is then adjusted (usually increased) to this estimated uncollectible amount, after *giving consideration to the existing balance* in the allowance account.

32. An *aging schedule* for accounts receivable is a list of the balances due from all customers, with each amount placed in a column indicating its age. Thus, we might use columns with headings such as Not Yet Due, Past Due 1 to 30 Days, Past Due 31 to 60 Days, etc. Based upon past experience, the credit manager estimates the uncollectible portion for each column. The *required balance* in the Allowance for Doubtful Accounts is simply the sum of the estimated uncollectible portions for all age groups.

33. The alternative method of estimating uncollectible accounts expense stresses that the *expense* is usually a fairly constant *percentage of sales* (or of sales on credit). Therefore the amount of the adjustment is computed as a percentage of the period's sales *without regard to any existing balance* in the allowance account. This method is often called the *income statement approach* to estimating uncollectible accounts expense.

34. Some companies do not use valuation allowance for accounts receivable. Under the *direct write-off* method of recognizing uncollectible accounts a business does not recognize any expense until a particular account receivable is determined to be uncollectible. At this point the receivable is written off with an offsetting debit to Uncollectible Accounts Expense. A shortcoming in the direct write-off method is that uncollectible account expense is not properly matched against the related revenue. However, the method is acceptable in financial statements if the distortion in net income is not material in dollar amount. Current income tax regulations *require* the use of the direct write-off method in computing taxable income.

35. For purposes of internal control, employees who maintain the accounts receivable subsidiary ledger must not have access to cash receipts. Also, they must not have authority to issue credit memoranda or to write off receivables as uncollectible

36. Although offering credit terms is an effective means of generating sales revenue, accounts receivable are a "*nonproductive*" asset which produces no revenue prior to collection. In order to minimize the amount "tied up" in the form of accounts receivable, management may offer customers cash discounts for early payment, accept national credit cards, or factor their accounts receivable.

37. Instead of waiting until receivables are collected, management can obtain cash immediately by factoring account receivable. The term *factoring* means either (a) selling accounts receivable to a financial institution (factor), or borrowing money by pledging accounts receivable as collateral for the loan.

38. Making credit sales to customers who use major credit cards avoids the risk of uncollectible accounts because the account receivable is paid promptly by the credit card company. Making sales through credit card companies also has the advantages of eliminating the work of credit investigations, billing, and maintaining an accounts receivable subsidiary ledger. However, credit card companies charge a fee equal to a percentage (usually 3% to 7%) of each credit sale.

39. The manner in which a credit card is recorded depends upon the type of credit card used by the customer. When the credit card company is a *bank* (as for Visa or MasterCard), the retailing business deposits signed credit card drafts directly into its *bank* account. Sales to customers using bank credit cards are recorded as *cash sales*. When customers use *nonbank* credit cards (such as American Express or Diners Club), the merchant records and *account receivable* from the credit card company for the full sales price.

40. In analyzing financial statements it is common practice to consider the relationship between average receivables and annual credit sales. To evaluate whether the company is successful in its policies of granting credit and collecting receivables, the ratio of net sales to average receivable is computed. For example, if annual credit sales were $2,400,000 and average receivables were $600,000, the accounts receivable turnover is 4 times per year. This *accounts receivable turnover*

ratio indicates how many times the receivables were converted into cash during the year. The higher the turnover rate, the greater the profit opportunity.

41. Another statistic useful in analyzing the liquidity of a company's receivable is the average number of days required to collect these accounts. The *average number of days to collect accounts receivable* is computed by dividing the number of days in a year (365) by the accounts receivable turnover rate.

42. Companies should disclose in notes to the financial statements significant *concentrations of credit risk*. Concentrations of credit risk occur if substantial portions of a company's total accounts receivable are due from a single customer, or from a group of customers in the same industry or geographic region.

43.* There are four basic "accountable events" relating to investments in marketable securities: (1) purchase of the investment, (2) receipt of dividend revenue and interest revenue, (3) sales of securities owned, and (4) the end-of-period "mark-to-market" adjustment.

44.* Investments in marketable securities are recorded at *cost*, which includes any brokerage commissions. In additions to the Marketable Securities ledger account (controlling), most investors also maintain a *marketable securities subsidiary ledger*, with a separate account for each type of security owned.

45.* Investments in marketable securities generate revenue in the form of interest or dividends. Most investors recognize interest and dividend revenue as it is received. Unlike dividend revenue, interest revenue accrues from day to day. An adjusting entry to accrue revenue receivable could be made at the end of each accounting period, but recognition upon receipt is justified by the concept of materiality.

46* When an investment in marketable securities is sold, a gain or loss results whenever the sales price is different from cost. A sales price in excess of cost produces a gain, whereas a sale price below cost results in a loss.

47.* At the end of each accounting period, the balance in the Marketable Securities controlling account is adjusted to its current market value. This adjustment is termed "mark-to-market," and represents a *departure from the cost principle*. For those investments classified as available for sale securities, the mark-to-market adjustment involves two balance sheet accounts: (1) the Marketable Securities account, and (2) a special stockholders' equity account- Unrealized Holding Gain (or Loss) on Investments.

48.* The adjustment to the asset account may be a debit or a credit, whichever is needed to adjust the Marketable Securities controlling account to current market value. For those investments classified as available for sale securities, there is a corresponding change recorded in the stockholders' equity account - Unrealized Holding Gain (or Loss) on Investments. This special account may have either a credit or debit balance. When the current market value of the securities exceeds cost, the holding gain is represented by a credit balance. When the market value of the securities is below cost, the holding results is represented by a debit balance.

49.* For investments classified as available for sale securities, the gains and losses recorded in the mark-to-market adjustment process are *unrealized*, and are *not* included in the investor's income statement. At any balance sheet date, the Unrealized Holding Gain (or Loss) account represents the difference between the aggregate cost of the marketable securities owned and the aggregate current market value.

50.* Investment transactions are reflected in the financial statements in a variety of ways. Interest revenue, dividend revenue, and gains and losses from sales of investments appear in the multiple-step income statement as *nonoperating* items, after the determination of income from operations. In the statement of cash flows, receipts of dividends and interest are classified as *operating*

---

* *Supplemental Topic A*, "Accounting for Marketable Securities."

activities; purchases and sales of marketable securities are classified as *investing activities*. Unrealized holding gains (or losses) recorded by the "mark-to-market," adjustment process are reported in the stockholders' equity section of the balance sheet.

51.** A promissory note is an unconditional promise in writing to pay on demand or at a future date a definite sum of money. Most notes are for periods of a year or less and are therefore classified as current assets by the payee and as current liabilities by the maker of the note. Most notes bear interest (a change made for the use of money). Interest rates are stated on an annual basis, and a 360-day year is sometimes assumed to simplify computations. The formula for computing interest is *Interest = principal x rate of interest x time*.

52.** The face amount of each note receivable is debited to the Notes Receivable account in the general ledger. The notes themselves when properly filed are the equivalent of a subsidiary ledger. An adjusting entry for interest accrued on notes receivable is necessary at the end of the period. The entry will debit Interest Receivable and will credit Interest Revenue. When the note is collected in the following period, the entry will be a debit to Cash offset by a credit to Notes Receivable for the face amount of the note, credit to Interest Receivable for the amount of the accrual, and a credit to Interest Revenue for the remainder of the interest collected.

53.** If the maker of the note defaults (fails to pay as agreed), an entry should be made to transfer the note and any interested earned to an account receivable. If both parties agree that a note should be renewed rather than paid at maturity, an entry should be made debiting and crediting the Notes Receivable account and explaining the terms of the new note.

54.** In the past, some businesses *discounted* their notes receivable to a bank – that is, sold the notes to a bank at a discount from the maturity value of the note. Discounting notes receivable actually is a form of factoring.

TEST YOURSELF ON FINANCIAL ASSETS

True or False

For each of the following statements, circle the T or the F to indicate whether the statement is true or false.

T   F   1.   The term "financial asset" has the same meaning as the term "cash equivalents."

T   F   2.   The balance sheet item of Cash and Cash Equivalents includes amounts on deposit with banks and also currency, money orders, and customers' checks on hand.

T   F   3.   For strong internal control, the employee who opens incoming mail should not also be responsible for preparing a control listing of checks received in the mail.

T   F   4.   Internal control over cash should include measures to prevent fraud or loss, to provide accurate records of cash transactions, and to ensure the maintenance of adequate but not excessive cash balances.

T   F   5.   For strong internal control, an employee who handles cash receipts should not be responsible for issuing credit memoranda for sales returns.

T   F   6.   Internal control over cash receipts is most effective when one person is made solely responsible for receiving and depositing cash and making related entries in the accounting records.

** *Supplemental Topic B,* "Notes Receivable and Interest Revenue."

T F 7. All cash receipts should be deposited intact in the bank daily, and all material cash payments should be made by check.

T F 8. The principal advantage of a *voucher system* is that it provides strong internal control over the making of expenditures and the payment of liabilities.

T F 9. A voucher is a document which shows that the necessary steps to verify the propriety of an expenditure have been performed and that a cash disbursement is justified.

T F 10. No entry is made in the accounting records at the time a small payment is made from the petty cash.

T F 11. The Petty Cash account should be debited at the time it is replenished.

T F 12. Reconciling a bank account means determining that all deductions shown on the bank statement represent checks issued by the depositor in the current period.

T F 13. The purpose of preparing a bank reconciliation is to identify those items which cause the balance of cash per the bank statement to differ from the balance of cash per the ledger, and thereby to determine the correct cash balance.

T F 14. In preparing a bank reconciliation, outstanding checks should be deducted from the balance shown on the bank statement, and deposits in transit (or undeposited receipts) should be added to the bank balance.

T F 15. After preparing a bank reconciliation, journal entries should be made to record each of the items shown as adjustments to the balance per depositor's records.

T F 16. James Company deposited a check from a customer, Ray Prince, but the bank returned the check with the notation NSF and deducted it on James Company's bank statement. A telephone call to Prince's office indicated that he would be out of town for some weeks. James Company decided to hold the check until Prince returned. The check should be included in the figure for Cash on the balance sheet of James Company.

T F 17. Short-term investments in marketable securities are reported in the balance sheet at *cost*, but their *current market value* must be disclosed in footnotes to the financial statements.

T F 18. The practice of estimating uncollectible accounts expense at the end of each accounting period is designed to match revenue and expenses so that all expenses associated with the revenue earned in the period are recognized as expense in that same period.

T F 19. During the first year of its existence. Cross Company made most of its sales on credit but made no provision for uncollectible accounts. The result would be an overstatement of assets and owners' equity, an understatement of expense, and an overstatement of net income.

T F 20. Conservatism in the valuation of accounts receivable would call for holding the amount entered in Allowance for Doubtful Accounts to a bare minimum.

T F 21. The *balance sheet* approach to estimating uncollectible accounts expense emphasizes the aging of accounts receivable and the adjustment of the allowance account to the level of the estimated uncollectible amount.

T F 22. The *income statement* approach to estimating uncollectible accounts expense does not require the use of an allowance account.

T F 23. When the year-end provision for uncollectible accounts expense is estimated as a percentage of sales, the estimate is recorded without regard for the existing balance in the allowance account.

T F 24. The *direct write-off* method does not cause receivables to be stated in the balance sheet at their estimated realizable value.

T F 25. When a given account receivable is determined to be worthless, it should be written off the books by an entry debiting Uncollectible Accounts Expense and crediting the Allowance for Doubtful Accounts.

T F 26. When a company collects an account receivable previously written off as worthless, an entry should be made debiting Accounts Receivable and crediting Allowance for Doubtful Accounts. A separate entry is then made to record collection of the account.

T F 27. The write-off of an account receivable determined to be worthless by debiting the Allowance for Doubtful Accounts will not affect the net carrying value of the receivables in the balance sheet.

T F 28. *Factoring accounts receivable* refers to the process of categorizing accounts receivable according to age.

T F 29. A retailer who sells to a customer using a national credit card will have an uncollectible account if the customer never pays the credit card company.

T F 30. When a retail store sells merchandise to a customer who uses a bank card (such as Visa or MasterCard), the account to be debited is Cash rather than Accounts Receivable.

T F 31. Effective management of accounts receivable include efforts to maximize this asset and to reduce accounts receivable turnover rate.

T F 32. A company with an accounts receivable turnover rate of 12 requires, on average, less than two weeks to collect its accounts receivable.

T F* 33. When an investment in marketable securities is *sold*, gain or loss is computed by comparing sales price with the current market value of the investment reported in the most recent balance sheet.

T F* 34. The balance of the Unrealized Holding Gain (or Loss) account represents the difference between the cost of securities owned and their current market values as of the balance sheet date.

T F* 35. The mark-to-market adjustment for the current period is the same dollar amount as the balance of the Unrealized Holding Gain (or Loss) on Investments in Marketable Securities account.

T F** 36. When a company accepts an interest-bearing note from a customer, the interest charges should be recognized as revenue at the time the note is received.

Completion Statements

Fill in the necessary word to complete the following statements:

1. The term *financial assets* includes _____, short-term investments (such as _____ _____ and _____ _____), and _____.

2. The term *cash* includes not only currency, coin, and money orders, but also _____ and the balances of _____ _____.

3. An adequate system of internal control over cash should include separating the function of handling cash from the _____ _____ _____ _____.

4. Cash frauds often begin with temporary unauthorized "borrowing" by employees of cash received from customers. One effective step in preventing such irregularities is to insist that each day's cash receipts be _____ _____ in the bank.

5. Among the most common reconciling items in a bank reconciliation are _____ _____, which should be deducted from the balance shown by the banks, and _____ _____ _____, which should be added to the balance shown by the bank statement.

6. The abbreviation *NSF* applied to a check return by a bank means _____ _____ _____, and calls for an entry on the depositor's book debiting _____ _____.

* Supplemental Topic A, "Accounting for Marketable Securities."
** Supplemental Topic B, "Notes Receivable and Interest Revenue."

7. In the preparation of a bank reconciliation, various reconciling items are added to or deducted from the balance per the bank statement or the balance per the depositor's records. Outstanding checks should be _____ _____ the balance per the _____ _____. Deposits in transit to the bank should be _____ _____the balance per the _____ _____. Collections made by the bank on behalf of the depositor should be _____ _____ the balance per the _____ _____.

8. In a voucher system, every cash disbursement must be authorized by personnel of the _____ department, but the related check must be signed by an officer of the _____ department. After a check is signed, it should be mailed directly to the _____; the related voucher should be _____ and returned to the _____ department.

9. Short-term investments in marketable securities are reported in the balance sheet at _____ _____ _____; the valuation principle applicable to marketable securities is termed _____-_____-_____.

10. The accounting principle which underlies the practice of estimating uncollectible accounts expense each period is known as the _____ _____. This process is essential to the periodic determination of _____ _____.

11. If the Allowance for Doubtful Accounts is understated, the net realizable value of accounts receivable will be _____, equity will be _____, and net income will be _____.

12. The income statement approach to uncollectible accounts emphasizes estimating the _____ _____ _____ for the period, while the balance sheet approach emphasizes estimating the proper level for the _____ _____ _____ _____.

13. The Inn Place made credit sales of $4,200 to customers using Global Express credit cards. Global Express charges retailers a fee of 4%. The entry to record collecting the cash from these credit sales would be a debit to Cash for $_____-, a _____ to _____ _____ _____ for $ _____, and a _____ to _____ _____ for $_____.

14. * When an investment in marketable securities is sold, the gain or loss recognized in the income statement is determined by comparing _____ _____ with _____ _____ _____. The required balance in the Unrealized Holding Gain (or Loss) is determined by comparing _____ _____ _____ with _____ _____ of securities owned at the balance sheet date.

15. ** If the interest on a 60-day note with a face value of $10,000 amounts to $250, the rate of interest is _____% (express as an annual rate.)

* Supplemental Topic A, "Accounting for Marketable Securities."
** Supplemental Topic B, "Notes Receivable and Interest Revenue."

16. ** The entry to record interest accrued on notes receivable at year-end consists of a debit to _____ _____ and a credit to _____ _____. Of these accounts, the one to be closed into the Income Summary is _____ _____.

Multiple Choice

Choose the best answer for each of the following questions and enter the identifying letter in the space provided.

___ 1.   Which of the following is *not* accurate with respect to financial assets?

    a.   Financial assets include accounts receivable and notes receivable, as well as short-term investments in the stock of publicly traded corporations.

    b.   Financial assets are reported in the financial statements at values determined in accordance with the cost principle.

    c.   Financial assets are reported in the balance at the amounts of cash these assets represent.

    d.   All financial assets are current assets, but not all current assets are financial assets.

___ 2.   Which of the following practices is undesirable from the standpoint of maintaining adequate internal control over cash?

    a.   Appointing as custodian of a petty cash fund an employee who has no responsibility with respect to maintenance of accounting records.

    b.   Recording overages and shortages from errors in handling over-the-counter cash receipts in a ledger account, Cash Over and Short.

    c.   Authorizing the cashier to make bank deposits.

    d.   Authorizing the official who approves invoices for payment to sign checks.

___ 3.   Checks received through the mail should be:

    a.   Transmitted to the accounts receivable department without delay.

    b.   Deposited by the mail-room employee.

    c.   Listed by the mail-room employee and forwarded to the cashier; a copy of the list should be sent to the accounting department.

    d.   Handled first by the accounting department, which, after making appropriate entries in the accounts, should turn over the checks to the cashier to be made a part of the daily bank deposit.

** *Supplemental Topic B*, "Notes Receivable and Interest Revenue."

___ 4. Which of the following is *not* a significant element of internal control over cash disbursements?

    a. Perforating or stamping "Paid" on supporting invoices and vouchers.

    b. Using serially numbered checks and accounting for all numbers in the series.

    c. Use of a Cash Over and Short account.

    d. Establishment of a petty cash fund.

___ 5. Which of the following is *not* a significant element of internal control over cash receipts?

    a. Preparing a control listing of checks received in the mail.

    b. Establishing a petty cash fund.

    c. Depositing each day's cash receipts intact in the bank.

    d. Prenumbering sales tickets.

___ 6. Which of the following statements describes an advantage of use of a voucher system?

    a. Assures that every expenditure is reviewed and verified before payment is made.

    b. Provides automatically a comprehensive record of business done with particular suppliers.

    c. Provides a highly flexible system for handling unusual transactions.

    d. Reduces the number of checks that will be written during any given period.

___ 7. In establishing and maintaining a petty cash fund:

    a. The Petty Cash account is debited only when the fund is first established or subsequently changed in size.

    b. The Petty Cash account is debited whenever the fund is replenished.

    c. The contents of the fund should at all times be limited to currency, coin, and checks.

    d. The contents of the fund should at all times be limited to currency, coins, checks, money orders, undeposited cash receipts, petty cash vouchers, and notes receivables from employees.

___ 8. An NSF check held by the payee should be carried on its records as:

    a. An element of cash on hand.

    b. Notes receivable.

    c. Accounts receivable.

    d. Cash over and short.

9. When a bank reconciliation has been satisfactorily completed, the only related entries to be made on the depositor's books are:

   a. To record items which explain the difference between the balance per the books and the adjusted cash balance.

   b. To record items which explain the difference between the balance per the books and the balance per the bank statement.

   c. To correct errors existing in the bank statement.

   d. To record outstanding checks and deposit in transit.

10. Before a bank reconciliation was prepared, the accounting records of Adams Company showed a cash balance of $26,440 and the bank statement showed a balance of $32,500. The bank statement showed a balance of $32,500. The reconciling items are a deposit in transit of $2,620; outstanding checks of $8,700; and bank service charges of $20. Based upon these facts, the amount of cash that should be shown on Adam's balance sheet is:

    a. $35,120.

    b. $26,420.

    c. $20,360.

    d. Some other amount.

11. The *mark-to-market* concept:

    a. Is the valuation applied to all financial assets.

    b. Involves recognition of a current period gain or loss, as well as the adjustment of an asset account.

    c. Requires footnote disclosure of the current market values of marketable securities.

    d. Has no effect upon the net income of the period.

12. When an allowance for estimating uncollectible accounts is in use, the writing off of an individual account receivable as worthless will:

    a. Be recorded by a debit to Uncollectible accounts Expense.

    b. Increase the balance in the allowance account.

    c. Decrease the debit balance in the allowance account.

    d. Have no effect on the working capital of the company.

___ 13.   Bryan Company, after aging its accounts receivable, estimated that $3,500 of the $125,000 of receivables on hand would probably prove uncollectible. The Allowance for Doubtful Accounts contained a credit balance of $2,300 prior to adjustments. The appropriate accounting entry is:

    a.   A debit to Uncollectible Accounts Expense and a credit to Allowance for Doubtful Accounts for $1,200.

    b.   A debit to Uncollectible Accounts Expense and a credit to Allowance for Doubtful Accounts for $3,500.

    c.   A debit to Uncollectible Accounts expense and a credit to Allowance for Doubtful Accounts for $5,800.

    d.   A debit to Allowance for Doubtful Accounts and a credit to Accounts Receivable for $3,500.

___ 14.   Pine Company uses the income statement approach in estimating uncollectible accounts expense and has found that such expense has consistently approximated 1% of net sales. At December 31 of the current year receivables total $150,000 and the Allowance for Doubtful Accounts has a credit balance of $400 prior to adjustment. Net sales for the current year were $600,000. The adjusting entry should be:

    a.   A debit to Uncollectible Accounts Expense and a credit to Allowance for Doubtful Accounts for $5,600.

    b.   A debit to Uncollectible Accounts Expense and a credit to Allowance for Doubtful Accounts for $6,400.

    c.   A debit to Allowance for Doubtful Accounts and a credit to Accounts Receivable for $6,000.

    d.   A debit to Uncollectible Accounts Expense and a credit to Allowance for Doubtful Accounts for $6,000.

___ 15.   Crawford Company uses the direct write-off method in accounting for uncollectible accounts. Crawford recognizes uncollectible accounts expense:

    a.   As indicated by aging the accounts receivable at the end of the period.

    b.   As a percentage of net sales during the period.

    c.   As accounts receivable from specific customers are determined to be worthless.

    d.   As a percentage of net credit sales during the period.

___ 16.   The entry to record a sale to a customer who uses a bank credit card (such as Visa or MasterCard) includes a debit to:

    a.   An account receivable from the customer.

    b.   An account receivable from the bank.

    c.   Cash.

    d.   Notes receivable.

_____ 17.   Hayden Manufacturing's net credit sales for the current year are $5,400,000 and average accounts receivable amount to $675,000. Using 365 days to a year, which of the following is accurate?

     a.   Hayden's accounts receivable turnover ratio is 1 to 8.

     b.   Hayden's accounts receivable were converted into cash 46 times during the current year.

     c.   Hayden's average days' sales uncollected is 8 days.

     d.   Hayden's average days' sales uncollected is 46 days.

_____ 18. *   Scott Corporation sold marketable securities costing $500,000 for $516,000 cash. This transaction is reported in Scott's income statement and statement of cash flows, respectively, as:

     a.   A $516,000 gain and a $516,000 cash receipt.

     b.   A $16,000 gain and a $516,000 cash receipt.

     c.   A $16,000 gain and a $16,000 cash receipt.

     d.   No effect on the income statement; a $516,000 cash receipt in the statement of cash flows.

_____ 19 *   Fisher Corporation invested $400,000 cash in marketable securities early in December. The entire investment was classified as available for sale securities. On December 31, the quoted market price for these securities is $419,000. Which of the following is an accurate statement?

     a.   If Fisher sells these investments on January 2 for $410,000, it will report a loss of $9,000 in the January income statement.

     b.   Fisher's December 31 balance sheet reports and marketable securities at $400,000 and an Unrealized Holding Gain on Investments of $19,000.

     c.   Fisher's December 31 balance sheet reports and marketable securities at $419,000 and an Unrealized Holding Gain on Investments of $19,000.

     d.   Fisher's December income statement includes a $19,000 gain on investments.

_____ 20. **   Which of the following statements regarding notes receivable is *false*?

     a.   The person who signs the note and promises to pay is called the maker of the note.

     b.   When a company lends money, the company's financial statements should report a note receivable and accrued interest revenue.

     c.   The maker of a note receivable records an asset by debiting Note Receivable in his or her accounting records.

     d.   In determining the number of days used in computing interest, the note's date of origin is not included, but the note's maturity date is included.

---

*Supplemental Topic A, "Accounting for Marketable Securities."
**Supplemental Topic B, "Notes Receivable and Interest Revenue."

_____ 21.[**] Mann Company accepts numerous notes receivable from its customers. When the maker of a note defaults, Mann Company should:

      a. Transfer the principal of the note to Accounts Receivable and write off the accrued interest as a loss.

      b. Make no accounting entry if the maker of the defaulted note will sign a renewal note on equally favorable terms.

      c. Debit Accounts Receivable for the principal of the note plus interest earned, offset by credit to Notes Receivable and Interest Revenue.

      d. Record a liability for the maturity value of the note.

Exercises

1. Listed below are eight technical accounting terms emphasized in this chapter.

Accounts receivable turnover	*Bank reconciliation*
Direct write-off method	*Allowance method*
Concentration of credit risk	*Cash equivalent*
Financial asset	*Mark-to-Market*

Each of the following statements may (or may not) describe one of these technical terms. In the space provided below each statement, indicate the accounting term described, or answer "None" if the statement does not correctly describe any of the terms.

a. A large portion of receivables due from customers vulnerable to the same economic environment.

_____

b. A determination of the items making up the difference between the bank balance and the balance according to the depositor's records.

_____

c. Method of accounting for uncollectible receivables which fails to match revenue and related expenses.

_____

d. Balance sheet valuation standard applicable to investments in marketable securities.

_____

e. A ratio, computed by dividing average receivables by net sales, that indicates the liquidity of the receivables.

_____

f. Contra-asset account representing the portion of receivables estimated to be uncollectible.

_____

[**] *Supplemental Topic B*, "Notes Receivable and Interest Revenue."

g.   Cash and assets convertible directly into known amounts of cash, such as marketable securities and receivables.

_____

2.   Indicate the proper sequence of the following events in the operation of a voucher system by numbering the steps in order of their normal occurrence.

____ Voucher reviewed by treasurer and check signed and mailed.
____ Preparation of voucher, including verification of process, quantities, terms, and other data on vendor's invoice.
____ Receipts of goods and preparation of receiving report.
____ Issuance of purchase order.
____ Purchase and related liability recorded.
____ Voucher filed in paid voucher file.
____ Voucher filed in unpaid voucher file by payment date.
____ Voucher and supporting documents perforated to prevent reuse.
____ Accounting department forwards voucher and supporting documents to finance.

3.   Your are to fill in the missing portions of the bank reconciliation shown below for Hunter Construction at July 31, 20__, using the following additional information:

a.   Outstanding checks: no. 301, $2,500; no. 303 $600; no. 304 $1,800; no. 306, $1,282.

b.   Service charge by bank, $6.

c.   Deposit made after banking hours on July 31, $1,950.

d.   A $264 NSF check drawn by our customer Jay Kline was deducted from our account by the bank and returned to us.

e.   An $1,800 note receivable left by us with the bank for collection was collected and credited to our account. No interest is involved.

f.   Our check no. 295, issued in payment of $688 for office supplies, was written as $688 but was erroneously recorded in our accounts as $580.

HUNTER CONSTRUCTION
Bank Reconciliation
July 31, 20__

Balance per bank statement, July 31, 20__ $17,018
Add:

Deduct:

Adjusted balance .... $_____
Balance per depositor's records, July 31, 20__ $11,364

Deduct:

Adjusted balance (as above)................................. $_____

4.   A list of account titles, each preceded by a number, appears below. In the space provided, indicate the accounts to be debited and credited in properly recording the five transactions described. In some cases more than one account may be debited or credited.

(Note that X designates any account not specified in the list.)

  1.   Cash
  2.   Notes Receivable
  3.   Interest Receivable
  4.   Accounts Receivable
  5.   Allowance for Doubtful Accounts
20.   Interest Revenue
30.   Uncollectible Accounts Expense
31.   Credit Card Discount Expense
  X   Any account not listed

Transaction	Account(s) Debited	Accounts(s) Credited
a. **Example** Rendered services, receiving part cash and the balance on account.	1,4	X
b. Wrote off the account of J. Smith as uncollectible.		
c. Collected cash from a national credit card company (not a bank) for credit card sales made this week.		
d. Reinstated the account of J. Smith, written off in 1 above, when Smith promised to make payment.		
e. Collected the J. Smith account in full.		
f.** Collected a note receivable, plus interest at maturity date. A portion of the interest collected had been accrued as of the end of the preceding month.		

** *Supplemental Topic B,* "Notes Receivable and Interest Revenue.

5.	The balance sheet of Carsoni, Inc., included the following items at November 30:

Marketable securities	$510,000
Note receivable..	10,000
Interest receivable	200
Accounts receivable	100,000
Less: Allowance for doubtful accounts............	2,400
Unrealized holding gain on investments in
marketable securities.......................................	15,000

In the space provided, on the following page, prepare general journal entries to record the following events occurring in December (explanations not required):

Dec 4	An account receivable for $230 previously written off is unexpectedly collected. (Make two separate entries.)

Dec. 8	A $2,275 account receivable is written off as uncollectible.

Dec. 16[**]	A 20%, 60-day note receivable is received from a customer in settlement of a $6,000 account receivable due today.

Dec. 30[**]	Collected in full a 12% 90-day $10,000 note receivable and interest due today. As of November 30, $200 interest receivable had been accrued on this note. (Remember to record interest revenue earned in December.)

Dec. 31	An aging of accounts receivable indicates the need for a balance of $3,500 in the allowance for doubtful accounts. (Consider the effects of the transactions on December 4 and December 8 before making the month-end adjusting entry.

Dec. 31[**]	Prepared an adjusting entry to record accrued interest on the note received on December 16. (Assume a 360-day year in your interest computation.)

Dec. 31.[*]	On December 31, the current market value of Carsoni's marketable securities is $518,000. This investment had originally cost Carsoni $495,000 several months ago, and had been classified as available for sale securities.

[**] *Supplemental Topic B*, "Notes Receivable and Interest Revenue."
[*] *Supplemental Topic A*, "Accounting for Marketable Securities."

		General Journal		
20__				
Dec. 4				

6.**   Compute the interest on the following amounts using the assumption of a 360-day year.

a. $12,000 at 14% for 60 days: $_____

b. $ 8,400 at 18% for 75 days: $_____

c. $ 4,000 at 12% for 90 days: $_____

d. $ 9,000 at 12 ½% for 120 days: $_____

e. $13,000 at 15% for 180 days: $_____

SOLUTIONS TO CHAPTER 6 SELF-TEST

True or False

1.   **F** The term "Financial asset" describes cash and those assets convertible into known amounts of cash (cash equivalents, marketable securities, and receivables). Cash equivalents are only one type of financial asset–very liquid short-term investments in money market funds, U. S. Treasury bills and high-grade commercial paper.

2.   **T** All items that a bank will accept for immediate deposit, as well as certain short-term investments, are classified as Cash and Cash Equivalents.

3.   **F** A copy of the control listing is sent to the cashier who makes deposits and to the accounting department. Daily comparison of the control listing with actual deposits and amounts recorded by the accounting department should reveal any errors.

4.   **T** These are some of the measures essential to a good system of internal control.

5.   **T** This combination of duties would enable the employee to conceal cash shortages by issuing fictitous credit memoranda.

6.   **F** Subdivision of duties requires that employees who handle cash receipts should not have access to the accounting records.

7.   **T** These are two of the major steps in achieving internal control over cash.

8.   **T** Each transaction requiring a cash payment is verified, approved, and recorded by the accounting department before a check is issued by the finance department.

9.   **T** Approval signatures are placed on the voucher as evidence that the expenditure was authorized, the goods or services received, the invoice prices verified, and the proper accounts debited and credited.

10.   **T** Expenses are recorded in the accounting records only when the fund is replenished.

11.   **F** The entry to replenish the fund consists of debits to various expense accounts and a credit to Cash.

12.   **F** A bank reconciliation is a schedule explaining any difference between the bank statement and the balance shown in the depositor's records.

13.   **T** The balance shown in the bank statement and that shown in the accounting records are each adjusted for any unrecorded transactions.

14.   **T** These two items are the most common examples of transactions recorded by the depositor that have not been recorded by the bank.

15.   **T** All reconciling items which adjust the depositor's records are entered on the books so that the accounting records reflect the correct amount of cash.

** *Supplemental Topic B, "Notes Receivable and Interest Revenue."*

16. **F** An NSF check should be viewed as an account receivable from the maker of the check, not as cash. An entry should be made consisting of a debit to the account receivable from the customer and a credit to Cash.

17. **F** Under the mark-to market approach, marketable securities are adjusted to market value at the balance sheet date. This current market value is used in the money columns of the balance sheet, while the cost of the investment is disclosed in notes to the financial statements.

18. **T** A fundamental principle of accounting is that revenue should be offset by the expenses incurred in generating that revenue.

19. **T** As a result of making no provision for uncollectible accounts expense is understated and accounts receivable are overstated. Net income is therefore too big and so is owners' equity.

20. **F** Conservatism implies reporting assets at their minimum value. The Allowance for Doubtful Accounts is subtracted from Accounts Receivable to arrive at a net figure; the larger the allowance, the smaller the net amount.

21. **T** The expense is the amount of adjustment required to bring the existing balance in the allowance account to the amount determined by aging the accounts receivable.

22. **F** Uncollectible accounts expense is determined by a percentage of sales; the allowance account is credited for this amount without regard for any balance already existing.

23. **T** This approach is called the income statement approach to estimating uncollectible accounts.

24. **T** Accounts receivable are stated at face amount unless they are determined to be worthless, at which time they are written off (expensed).

25. **F** When the allowance method of estimating bad debts is being used, the write-off of a specific account receivable consists of a debit to the Allowance for Doubtful Accounts and a credit to Accounts Receivable.

26. **T** Note that the entry to reinstate the account receivable is exactly the opposite of the entry that was made to write off the account as worthless.

27. **T** The write-off reduces both the asset and the contra-asset account by the same amount; the net realizable value of accounts receivable shown in the balance sheet does not change.

28. **F** The term *factoring accounts receivable* refers to the practice of obtaining cash immediately either by selling the accounts receivable, or using them as collateral for a loan. Accounts Receivable are classified according to age in the preparation of an *aging schedule* (used in the balance sheet approach to estimating uncollectible accounts.)

29. **F** The credit card company sustains the loss.

30. **T** Bank credit card drafts are deposited at the bank for immediate credit and are the equivalent of cash.

31. **F** Management should strive to *minimize* amounts "tied up" in the nonproductive asset by offering cash discounts, accepting national credit cards, and factoring receivables. *Increasing* accounts receivable turnover is desirable, since this indicates that accounts receivable are being converted to cash more quickly.

32. **F** The average period to collect accounts receivable is approximately 30 days (365 days/12).

33.* **F** Gain or loss on a sale of an investment in marketable securities is determined by comparing sales price with *original cost* of the security.

34.* **T** This account may have either a debit or credit balance, and is reported as a component of total stockholders' equity in the balance sheet.

---

* *Supplemental Topic A,* "Accounting for Marketable Securities."

35.* **F** The *balance* of the Unrealized Holding Gain (or Loss) account is the difference between current market value and original cost of marketable securities owned at the balance sheet date. The current period *adjustment* is the difference between the current market value of the marketable securities and the existing balance in the marketable securities account (which may be different from cost due to previous year's mark-to-market adjustments).

36.** **F** Interest revenue is earned throughout the life of the note.

Completion Statements

1. cash, cash equivalents, marketable securities, receivables. 2. checks, bank accounts. 3. maintenance of accounting records. 4. deposited intact. 5. outstanding checks, deposits in transit. 6. not sufficient funds, Accounts Receivable. 7. deducted from bank statement, added to bank statement, added to depositor's records; added to, depositor's records. 8. accounting finance, payee, perforated (or stamped paid) accounting. 9. current market value, mark-to-market. 10. matching principle, net income. 11. overstated, overstated, overstated. 12. uncollectible accounts expense, allowance for doubtful accounts. 13. $4,032; debit; credit card discount expense, $168; credit; Accounts Receivable; $4,200. *14. sales price, original cost, current market value, original cost. **15. 15%. **16. Interest Receivable, Interest Revenue, Interest Revenue.

Multiple Choice

1. Answer **b** – all financial assets are reported at current values, although current value is determined differently for each category of financial asset. The valuation of marketable securities at current market value represents an exception to the cost principle.

2. Answer **d** – a major step in achieving internal control over cash disbursements is separation of the function of approving expenditures from the function of signing checks. Answer **a** is an example of proper segregation of duties; answer **b** provides a means of identifying weakness in internal control over cash receipts. Because control listings exist for both over-the-counter sales and for cash received in the mail, there is no breakdown of internal control in having the cashier make the bank deposits.

3. Answer **c** – the control listing prepared by the mailroom employee (who then ceases to have access to the receipts) is compared to the daily bank deposits made by the cashier.

4. Answer **c** – use of a Cash Over and Short accounts is a means of achieving control over the receipts. Cash on hand in the drawer at the end of the day is compared to the cash sales as shown on the register tape (control listing); any difference is debited or credited to the Cash Over and Short account.

5. Answer **b** – establishment of a petty cash fund is a mean of achieving control over small cash *disbursements* that are not normally made by check. The other answers listed are examples of internal control measures over cash receipts.

6. Answer **a** – the *accounting* department examines supporting documents for cash disbursements and signs a voucher indicating that payment is authorized. The *finance* department issues the check and marks the supporting documents in some manner to prevent them from being used again.

7. Answer **a** – when the petty cash fund is replenished, individual expense accounts are debited and Cash is credited. The petty cash box should contain cash and/or vouchers totaling the exact amount of the fund. Undeposited cash receipts should *not* be held in the petty cash fund.

8. Answer **c** – an NSF check does not constitute cash or a note receivable from the customer (A note receivable is a *written promise to pay* at a specified time a definite sum of money.)

---

* *Supplemental Topic A,* "Accounting for Marketable Securities."
** *Supplemental Topic B,* "Notes Receivable and Interest Revenue."

9.   Answer **a** – the depositor wants to adjust his or her accounting records to the adjusted balance shown on the bank reconciliation–this is the amount that is be shown on the balance sheet as "cash." Answers **c** and **d** are items that have already been recorded properly in the depositor's accounting records, so no adjusting entry is necessary.

10.   Answer **b** – of the three reconciling items shown, only the bank service charges need to be subtracted from the cash balance in Adams' accounting records. We can also arrive at the adjusted cash balance an alternate way: balance on the bank statement plus the deposit in transit minus outstanding checks.

11.   Answer **d** – the mark-to-market concept requires adjustment of the balance of the Marketable Securities account to the current market value at the balance sheet date. This adjustment affects an asset account and a stockholders' equity account, but has no effect upon net income. Marketable securities are reported in the balance sheet at current market value, with the *cost* of the securities disclosed in notes to the financial statements.

12.   Answer **d** – working capital consists of current assets minus current liabilities. The writing off of an account receivable entails a debit to Allowance for Doubtful Accounts and a credit to Accounts Receivable. This entry to decreases Accounts Receivable and also decreases the balance in the contra-asset account – Allowance for Doubtful Accounts. The *net realizable value* of accounts receivable is the same before and after the write-off; thus, there is no effect on working capital.

13.   Answer **a** – the balance sheet approach of aging the accounts receivable determines the desired credit balance that should be in the Allowance for Doubtful Accounts. Since the Allowance for Doubtful Accounts already contains a credit balance of $2,300, Bryan Company must increase (credit) this account $1,200 – the debit part of the entry is to Uncollectible Accounts Expense.

14.   Answer **d** – under the income statement approach, the uncollectible accounts expense is estimated at some percentages of net sales (or net credit sales). The adjusting entry is made in the full amount of this estimated expense, without regard for the current balance in the Allowance for Doubtful Accounts.

15.   Answer **c** – companies using the direct write-off method do not estimate uncollectible accounts expense. Instead, this expense is only recognized when specific accounts are identified as uncollectible.

16.   Answer **c** – banks accept for immediate deposit the drafts signed by customers using bank credit cards. Therefore, these sales are viewed as cash sales rather than as sales on account.

17.   Answer **d** – Hayden's accounts receivable turnover ratio is 8 ($5,400,000 divided by $675,000). This means that Hayden's accounts receivable turned over (were converted into cash) 8 times during the current year. The average days' sales uncollected is computed by dividing 365 days by the turnover rate – 365 ÷ 8 = approximately 46 days.

18.*   Answer **b** – the gain recognized the income statement is computed by comparing the sales price of $516,000 with the cost of $500,000. In the statement of cash flows, the cash proceeds from the sale constitute a cash receipt from investing activities.

19.*   Answer **c** – the mark-to-market adjustment has no effect upon the December income statement. If the marketable securities are sold in January for $410,000. Fisher recognizes a $10,000 gain in January on the sale ($410,000 sales price)- ($400,000 cost).

20.**   Answer **c** – the maker of the note is the borrower of the money and records a *liability* – Note Payable.

---

* *Supplemental Topic A*, "Accounting for Marketable Securities."
** *Supplemental Topic B*, "Notes Receivable and Interest Revenue."

21.[**] Answer **c** – interest earned on the note is recorded through the maturity date and is included in the account receivable from the maker. The interest receivable on a defaulted note is just as valid a claim against the maker as the principal amount.

Solutions to Exercises

1.

a.   Concentration of credit risk

b.   Bank reconciliation

c.   Direct write-off method

d.   Mark-to-market

e.   None (The accounts receivable turnover is net sales divided by average receivables.)

f.   None (The statement describes the Allowance for Doubtful Accounts.)

g.   Financial assets

2.

7	Voucher reviewed by treasurer and check signed and mailed.
3	Preparation of voucher, including verification of process, quantities, terms, and other data on vendor's invoice.
2	Receipts of goods and preparation of receiving report.
1	Issuance of purchase order.
4	Purchase and related liability recorded.
9	Voucher filed in paid voucher file.
5	Voucher filed in unpaid voucher file by payment date.
8	Voucher and supporting documents perforated to prevent reuse.
6	Accounting department forwards voucher and supporting documents to finance.

[**] *Supplemental Topic B*, "Notes Receivable and Interest Revenue."

HUNTER CONSTRUCTION
Bank Reconciliation
July 31, 20__

Balance per bank statement, July 31, 20__			$17,018
Add: Deposit on July 31			1,950
			$18,968
Deduct:	Outstanding check:		
	No. 301	$2,500	
	No. 303	600	
	No. 304	1,800	
	No. 306	1,282	6,182
Adjusted balance			$12,786
Balance per depositor's records, July 31, 20__			$11,364
Add: Note receivable collected for us by bank			1,800
			$13,164
Deduct:	Service Charge	$ 6	
	NSF check on Jay Kline	264	
	Error on check no. 295	108	378
Adjusted balance (as above).................................			$12,786

4.

Accounts

	Debited	Credited
a	30	5
b	5	4
c	1,31	4
d	4	5
e	1	4
f**	1	3,20,2

** *Supplemental Topic B*, "Notes Receivable and Interest Revenue."

General Journal		
20__		
Dec. 4 Accounts Receivable	230	
Allowance for Doubtful Accounts		230
To reinstate as an asset an account receivable		
previously written off as uncollectible		
4 Cash	230	
Accounts Receivable		230
To record collection of account reinstated in preceding entry.		
8 Allowance for Doubtful Accounts	2,275	
Accounts Receivable		2,275
To write off an account receivable determined to be uncollectible		
**16 Notes Receivable	6,000	
Accounts receivable		6,000
Received a 10%, 6-day note in settlement of an account receivable		
**30 Cash	10,300	
Notes Receivable		10,000
Interest Receivable		200
Interest Revenue		100
To record collection of note receivable and interest due today.		
31 Uncollectible Accounts Expense	3,145	
Allowance for Doubtful Accounts		3,145
To increase balance in allowance account to $3,500:		
Required balance.. $3,500		
Current balance ($2,400 + $230 - $2,275)...... 355		
Required adjustment $3,145		
**31 Interest Receivable	25	
Interest Revenue		25
To accrue interest on note receivable for 15 days in December		
($6,000 x 10% x 15/360 = $25)		
*31 Marketable Securities	8,000	
Unrealized Holding Gain on Investments in Marketable Securities.		8,000
To adjust Marketable Securities account to current market value		
of $518,000 and to adjust Unrealized Holding Gain to $23,000		
($518,000 less $495,000 cost).		

** *Supplemental Topic B*, "Notes Receivable and Interest Revenue."
* *Supplemental Topic A*, "Accounting for Marketable Securities."

6.**

a. $280 ($12,000 x .14 x 60/360)

b. $315 ($8,400 x .18 x 75/360)

c. $120 ($4,000 x .12 90/360).

d. $375 ($9,000 x .125 x 120/360)

e. $975 ($13,000 x .15 180/360)

** *Supplemental Topic B*, "Notes Receivable and Interest Revenue."

INVENTORIES AND THE COST OF GOODS SOLD

HIGHLIGHTS OF THE CHAPTER

1. In a retail or wholesale business, inventory consists of all goods owned and held for sale in the regular course of business. In manufacturing businesses there are three major types of inventories: finished goods, work in process, and materials. In the current asset section of the balance sheet, inventory is listed immediately after accounts receivable.

2. The primary basis of accounting for inventory is cost, which includes all expenditures necessary to place the merchandise in the proper location and condition for sale, such as transportation-in, storage, insurance while in transit, etc.

3. A *perpetual* inventory system maintains a continuously updated inventory account. As merchandise in acquired, its cost is added to the Inventory account; as goods are sold, their cost is transferred from inventory into the cost of goods sold. A sale of merchandise requires two entries: (a) a debit to Cash (or Accounts Receivable) and credit to Sales for the sales price, and (b) a debit to Cost of Goods Sold and a credit to Inventory for the cost of merchandise.

4. When several lots of identical merchandise are purchased at different prices during the year, which of these costs should be used as the *cost of goods sold* in recording sales transactions? In determining the cost of merchandise sold in a particular sales transaction, accountants may use *specific identification*, or they may adopt one of the following three cost flow assumptions: (a) *average cost*, (b) *first-in, first-out (FIFO)*, or (c) *last-in, first-out (LIFO)*.

5. The *specific identification* method may be used only when the actual costs of individual units can be determined from the accounting records. The actual cost of units sold is transferred from inventory into cost of goods sold.

6. If the items in inventory are similar in function, cost, and sales price, a seller may follow the convenient and practice using *cost flow assumption*, such as average cost, FIFO, LIFO. The cost flow assumption *need not correspond to the physical movement of the company's merchandise*. Use of a flow assumption eliminates the need for separately identifying each unit sold and looking up its actual cost.

7. The *average cost* method values all merchandise–units sold and units remaining in inventory–at the *average* per-unit cost. Average cost (computed after every purchase) is computed by dividing the total cost of goods available by the number of units in inventory. Since the average cost may change following each purchase, this method also is called *moving average*. When units are sold, the average per-unit cost is transferred into cost of goods sold.

8. The *first-in, first-out* (*FIFO*) method is based upon the assumption that the first units purchases are the first units sold. When units are sold, the cost of the oldest units on hand is transferred into cost of goods sold. Remaining inventory, therefore, is comprises of the most recent purchases.

9. The *last-in, first-out* (*LIFO*) method assumes that the most recently acquired units are sold first. When units are sold, the *most recent* purchase costs are transferred from inventory into cost of goods sold. Remaining inventory, therefore, consists of the "old" merchandise acquired in the earliest purchases.

10. During a period of changing prices, each of the four alternative inventory valuation methods will lead to different figures for cost of goods sold, gross profit on sales, net income, inventory, and owners' equity. All are acceptable, however, because they are merely alternative methods of determining *cost*.

11. During a period of rising prices, the *LIFO* method will lead to the highest figure for cost of goods sold, the smallest inventory value, the lowest net income, and the lowest income tax. This is because the most recent (and higher) costs are considered to be the cost of the units sold and the earlier (and lower) purchase prices are considered to be the cost of the unsold units comprising the ending inventory. Supporters of LIFO argue that income is most accurately measured by matching the *current* cost of merchandise against *current* sales prices, regardless of which physical units of merchandise are actually delivered to the customers.

12. The *FIFO* method produces a realistic balance sheet amount for inventory close to current replacement cost, whereas the *LIFO* method produces a balance sheet value for inventory reflecting prices in the distant past.

13. Continuing inflation and high income tax rates have led to increased interest by business managers in LIFO. The LIFO method causes reported net income to reflect the increasing cost of replacing the goods sold during the year, and tends to avoid basing income tax payments on an exaggerated measurement of taxable income. Income tax regulations allow a corporation to use LIFO in its tax return only if the company also uses LIFO in its financial statements.

14. A company may use different inventory valuation methods to account for different types of inventory, or for inventories in different geographic locations. The principle of *consistency* stresses that the chosen inventory method be followed consistently from period to period. A company is permitted to change its method provided the reasons for the change are explained and the effects of the change on net income are fully disclosed.

15. When a manufacturer uses a *just-in-time (JIT)* inventory system, purchases of raw materials and component parts arrive just in time for use in the manufacturing process; in addition, the manufacturing process is completed just in time to ship finished goods to customers. A just-in-time system greatly reduces the size of raw material and finished goods inventories, but does not eliminate them entirely.

16. Taking a physical inventory, is necessary at the end of each year in order to adjust the perpetual inventory records to the physical count of items actually on hand. In most cases, the year-end physical count reveals some shortages or damaged merchandise. The costs of missing or damaged units are removed from the inventory records using the same flow assumption as is used in recording the cost of goods sold. If shrinkage losses are small, the costs removed from inventory are debited directly to the Cost of Goods Sold account. If these losses are material in amount, the offsetting debit should be to a special loss account, such as Inventory Shrinkage Loss.

17. Although inventory is recorded in the accounting records at cost when purchased, the *lower-of-cost-or-market-rule (LCM)* requires that inventory be reported in the balance sheet at the lower of its (a) cost or (b) market value. In the LCM rule, "market rule" means *current replacement cost*. Inventory, therefore is valued at the lower of its cost (as determined under specific identification, average cost, FIFO, or LIFO methods) or its current replacement cost. If the current replacement cost of the ending inventory is substantially *below* the cost determined under any of the above four methods, the inventory is written down to the replacement cost; the offsetting debit is to the Cost of Goods Sold (or if material, to a special loss account.)

18. Inventory includes all goods owned regardless of location. A *proper cutoff* means that purchase and sale transactions occurring near year-end are *recorded in the right accounting period.* A sale should be recorded when title to the merchandise passes to the buyer. For goods in transit at year-end, we must consider the terms of shipment. If the terms of shipment are *F.O. B. shipping point*, the goods in transit are the property of the buyer. If the terms are *F.O. B. destination*, the goods remain the property of the seller while in transit.

19. Although most businesses use a perpetual inventory system, some small businesses use the *periodic* system. In a periodic system, the Inventory account remains unchanged until the end of the accounting period. The cost of merchandise purchases during the year is debited to a

Purchases account, rather than to the Inventory account. When merchandise is sold to a customer, an entry is made recognizing the sales revenue, but no entry is made to reduce the Inventory account or to recognize the cost of goods sold. At the end of the year, the physical inventory is taken. The cost assigned to this ending inventory is used in computing the cost of goods sold according to the following formula:

Beginning inventory XXXX
Add: Purchases during the year........................... XXXX
Cost of goods available for sale........................... XXXX
Less: Ending Inventory .... (XXX)
Cost of goods sold XXXX

20. The same inventory flow assumptions used in perpetual inventory systems to determine the cost of goods sold may be used with a periodic system. In the periodic system, however, we use the flow assumption to determine the costs which are to be assigned to the *inventory* remaining at the end of the period. The cost assigned to the ending inventory (using specific identification, average cost, FIFO, or LIFO) is then subtracted from the costs of goods available for sale to arrive at the cost of goods sold.

21. Both LIFO and average cost methods result in different valuations of ending inventory (and consequently cost of goods sold) under perpetual and periodic costing procedures. Many companies that use the LIFO in a perpetual inventory system *restate* their year-end inventory at the lower cost determined by the *periodic* LIFO costing procedures in order to receive the maximum tax benefit from the LIFO method. When specific identification or the FIFO method is in use, the perpetual and periodic costing procedures result in exactly the same valuation of inventory.

22. The importance of properly accounting for ending inventory derives from the *matching principle* –the accounting standard matching appropriate costs against revenue to determine net income. When we assign a value to the ending inventory, we are thereby also determining the *cost of goods sold* and the *gross profit on sales*.

23. The ending inventory of one year is the beginning inventory of the next year. Therefore an error in the valuation of ending inventory will cause the income statements of two successive years to be in error by the full amount of the error in inventory valuation.

24. a. When *ending* inventory is understated, net income will be understated.

    b. When *ending* inventory is overstated, net income will be overstated.

    c. When *beginning* inventory is understated, net income will be overstated.

    d. When *beginning* inventory is overstated, net income will be understated.

25. In other words, an inventory error is *counterbalancing* over a two-year period. If ending inventory is overstated, the income for the current year will be overstated, but income for the following year will be understated by the same amount. The reverse is also true if ending inventory is understated, the income for the current year will be understated, but income for the following year will be overstated.

26. An error in inventory valuation will cause several parts of the financial statements to be in error. In the income statement, the cost of goods sold, the gross profit on sales, and the net income will all be wrong by the full amount of the inventory error (ignoring income taxes). In the balance sheet of the year in which the inventory error occurs, the owners' equity, the total current assets, and the balance sheet totals will also be in error.

27. Since an error in inventory has a counterbalancing effect on income over a two-year period, the owner's equity and the balance sheet totals will be correct at the end of the second year.

28. The *gross profit method* of estimating inventories is useful when inventory is lost by fire or theft, or when it is desired to prepare monthly financial statements without incurring the expense of taking a physical inventory.

29. An assumption underlying the gross profit method is that the gross profit rate does not change from period to period. Thus, we may determine the current cost percentage from the income statement of the last period. The cost percentage (or cost ratio) is found by dividing the cost of goods sold by net sales. (The cost percentage also is equal to 100% minus the gross profit rate).

30. Once the ratio is known, the gross profit method is applied as follows:

    a. Determine the cost of goods available for sale from the general ledger records of beginning inventory and net purchases.

    b. Estimate the cost of goods sold by multiplying net sales for the period by the cost ratio.

    c. Deduct the estimated cost of goods sold from the cost of goods available for sale to find the estimated ending inventory.

31. The *retail method* may be used to estimate the cost of the ending inventory, as follows:

    a. Determine the retail price of goods available for sale by adding the retail value of the beginning inventory to the retail price of goods purchased during the period.

    b. Compute the *cost percentage* by dividing the cost of goods available for sale by the retail price of these goods.

    c. Estimate the *retail value* of the ending inventory by subtracting net sales from the retail value of the goods available for sale.

    d. Convert the ending inventory valuation to *cost* by multiplying the ending inventory at retail prices by the cost percentage determined in *b* above.

32. The retail method also may be used to simplify the pricing of the annual physical inventory taken at a retail store. The inventory would be counted and priced as follows:

    a. Take a physical inventory, pricing the goods at *retail prices*. This is easier than pricing the goods at cost, because the goods have price tags showing their retail price.

    b. Determine the cost percentage.

    c. Use the cost percentage to reduce the valuation of the ending inventory from retail to cost.

33. The *inventory turnover rate* (a measure of the *liquidity* of inventory) is equal to the cost of goods sold divided by the average amount of inventory. Short-term creditors are interested in this ratio because it indicates how many *times* in the course of a year the company is able to sell its average inventory. The higher this rate, the more quickly the company sells its inventory. The number of *days* required to sell inventory is computed by dividing 365 days by the inventory turnover rate.

34. The length of the *operating cycle* is the average time period between the purchase of merchandise and the conversion of this merchandise back into cash. To determine how quickly inventory converts into cash, we must combine the number of days required to *sell the inventory* (365 days divided by the inventory turnover rate) with the number of days required to *collect the accounts receivable* (365 days divided by the accounts receivable turnover rate.)

35. Users of financial statements should understand that accounting methods in use by a company have an effect on financial statement ratios. A company using LIFO in a period of rising prices generally reports lower net income than if FIFO were used, which affects such ratios as return on assets and return on equity. Inventory turnover rate, current ratio, current assets, and working capital are additional statistics directly affected by the choice of inventory method.

36.* The difference between the LIFO cost of an inventory and its current replacement cost is called a *LIFO reserve*. Existence of a LIFO reserve indicates that the company's inventory is **understated**

---

* *Supplemental Topic*, "LIFO Reserves."

in terms of its current replacement cost, and in terms of the valuation that would have resulted from the use of the FIFO method. Companies using LIFO disclose in notes to their financial statements the current replacement cost (or the FIFO cost) of inventories.

37.* *Liquidation of the LIFO reserve* occurs if inventory falls to an abnormally low level at year-end. In this case, the costs transferred to the cost of goods sold will come from older and lower-cost layers. The inclusion of these low costs in the cost of goods sold may cause a company's profits to rise dramatically. The abnormal profits which result from the liquidation of a LIFO are a onetime occurrence and do not represent an improvement in financial performance. Whenever a company using LIFO ends its fiscal year with substantially less inventory than at the beginning of the year, liquidation of part of the LIFO reserve has occurred.

38.* The dollar amount of the LIFO reserve can be determined by comparing the LIFO inventory valuation shown in the balance sheet with the current replacement cost of inventories disclosed in the notes to the financial statements. A LIFO reserve represents the amount by which a company has reduced its taxable income *over a period of years* through use of the LIFO method. The aggregate tax benefit since LIFO was adopted can be computed by multiplying the LIFO reserve by the income tax rate for the company.

TEST YOURSELF ON INVENTORIES AND THE COST OF GOODS SOLD

True or False

T F 1. A major objective of accounting for inventories is proper measurement of net income.

T F 2. In a perpetual inventory system, ledger accounts for inventory and the cost of goods sold are continuously updated for purchases and sales of merchandise.

T F 3. The specific identification method of inventory valuation is particularly appropriate for low-priced, high-volume articles.

T F 4. Inventories are usually valued at cost, but the cost figure for inventory can differ significantly depending upon which inventory method is used.

T F 5. The average-cost method places more weight on the prices at which large purchases were made than on the price at which small purchases were made.

T F 6. Using the first-in, first-out (FIFO) method during a period of rising prices implies that the cheaper goods have been sold and the more costly goods are still on hand.

T F 7. If we consider the "true" cost of sales to be the replacement cost of goods sold, income statements using historical costs tend to understate net income during periods of inflation.

T F 8. During a period of rapid inflation, using LIFO will maximize reported net income.

T F 9. Using the LIFO method implies that the ending inventory consists of the most recently acquired goods.

T F 10. Consistency in the valuation of inventory requires that a method once adopted cannot be changed unless the company is sold.

---

* *Supplemental Topic*, "LIFO Reserves."

T F   11.   It is acceptable practice to understate inventories at year-end as long as it is done consistently from year to year.

T F   12.   Taking physical inventory refers to the physical count to determine the quantity of inventory on hand; pricing the inventory means determining the cost of the inventory on hand.

T F   13.   The use of the lower-of-cost-or-market produces a conservative inventory valuation because unrealized losses are treated as actually incurred.

T F   14.   If the terms of shipment are F.O.B. shipping point, the goods in transit should normally belong to the seller.

T F   15.   The recording of a sale in the wrong period will have no effect on the net income for each period if the goods are excluded from inventory in the period in which the sale is recorded.

T F   16.   An error in the valuation of inventory at the end of the period will cause errors in net income for two periods.

T F   17.   Errors in the valuation of inventory are counterbalancing; an error which causes an overstatement of net income this period will cause an understatement next period.

T F   18.   An overstatement of ending inventory will cause an understatement of net income.

T F   19.   In tax audits, the IRS often investigates the taxpayer's inventory because overstated inventory will cause the taxpayer's net income to be understated.

T F   20.   The gross profit method permits a business to estimate inventory without actually taking a physical count of the goods on hand.

T F   21.   The retail method of inventory valuation permits a business to take the physical inventory and price it at current retail prices rather than look up invoices to determine the cost of goods on hand.

T F   22.   The operating cycle for a merchandising business is equal to 365 days divided by the inventory turnover rate.

T F   23.*   A LIFO reserve is the reduction in taxable income over the years due to the use of the LIFO inventory method.

Completion Statements

Fill in the necessary word to complete the following statements:

Supplemental Topic, "LIFO Reserves."

112

1. In a perpetual inventory system, purchases are recorded by a debit to _____ and a credit to Accounts Payable. Sales are recorded by two entries: (a) a debit to Accounts Receivable and a credit to _____ for the _____ price of the merchandise and (b) a debit to _____ _____ _____ _____ and a credit to _____ for the _____ of the goods.

2. The four most commonly used inventory valuation methods are: _____ _____, _____ _____, _____, and _____.

3. During a period of rising prices, using the _____ method implies that the cheaper goods are still on hand while the more expensive ones were sold.

4. A _____ inventory system is designed to minimize a company's investment in inventory.

5. The lower-of-cost-or-market rule results in the recognition of a _____ in the _____ cost of inventory. However, an _____ in the _____ cost would not be recognized.

6. If goods are shipped F.O. B. destination, the _____ to the goods while in transit belongs to the _____ and the goods should be excluded from the inventory of the _____.

7. In a periodic inventory system, purchases are recorded by a debit to _____ and a credit to Accounts Payable or Cash. Sales are recorded by a single entry which debits _____ _____ and credits _____ for the _____ price of the merchandise.

8. Ending inventories are overstated as follows: Year 1 by $20,000; Year 2 by $8,000; and Year 3 by $15,000. Net income for each of the three years was computed at $25,000. The corrected net income figure (ignoring the effect of income taxes)for each of the three years is: Year 1, $_____; Year 2, $_____; Year 3 $_____.

9. The method of inventory valuation frequently used by retail stores is first to value the inventory at _____ and then to convert this amount to a _____ figure by applying the _____ of cost to selling prices during the current period.

10. The inventory turnover rate is computed by dividing _____ _____ _____ _____ by _____ _____. The accounts receivable turnover rate is computed by dividing _____ by _____ _____ _____; the number of days required to collect receivables is computed by dividing _____ by the _____ _____ _____ _____.

Multiple Choice

Choose the best answer for each of the following questions and enter the identifying letter in the space provided.

____ 1. Which of the following four items would *not* be included in inventories on the balance sheet?

      a. Raw materials used in manufacture of chemicals.

      b. Building materials used in construction.

      c. Cars left by customers at an auto repair shop.

      d. Goods purchased but not yet delivered to premises (title passed).

____ 2. A *perpetual* inventory system:

      a. Requires the use of the first-in, first-out (FIFO) basis of pricing inventory sold.

      b. Provides such strong internal control that custody of assets need not be separate from the accounting records for inventory.

      c. Eliminates the need for taking an annual physical inventory.

      d. Maintains a continuously updated Inventory account as well as a continuously updated Cost of Goods Sold account.

____ 3. Which of the following is *not* an acceptable inventory method?

      a. Lower of cost or market.

      b. Sales value.

      c. Specific identification.

      d. First-in, first-out.

____ 4. During a period of rising prices, which inventory pricing method might be expected to give the *lowest* valuation for inventory on the balance sheet and the *lowest* net income figure?

      a. Cost on a LIFO basis.

      b. Cost on a FIFO basis.

      c. Average cost.

      d. FIFO, lower of cost or market.

____ 5. A physical inventory should be carefully planned in order to ensure each of the following *except*:

      a. Goods located in the receiving department are included.

      b. The correct inventory valuation method is used.

      c. Damaged goods are excluded.

      d. Merchandise for which an order has been received, but which has not been shipped, is included.

___ 6. Goods costing $750 are sold for $1,000 at the end of Year 1, but the sale is recorded in Year 2. The goods *were* included in the ending inventory at the end of Year 1. The most likely effect of this error is:

    a. Net income for Year 1 was understated by $1,000.

    b. Net income for Year 2 was overstated by $250.

    c. Beginning inventory for Year 2 was understated by $750.

    d. Net income for Year 1 was overstated by $250.

___ 7. Which of the following statements regarding inventory costing methods is *true*?

    a. Cost flow assumptions are not used in a periodic inventory system; the cost of ending inventory is determined by specific identification based upon units counted in the physical inventory.

    b. Perpetual and periodic inventory systems will always result in different figures for ending inventory, even if the same inventory costing method is used in each.

    c. Perpetual and periodic inventory systems will always result in the same figure for ending inventory, as long as the same inventory costing method is used in each.

    d. Applying LIFO costing procedures in a periodic system may result in a lower "cost" for ending inventory than if LIFO were applied on a perpetual basis.

___ 8. An overstatement of $1,000 in the inventory at the end of Year 4 would:

    a. Understate the beginning inventory of Year 5.

    b. Have no effect on net income of Year 3.

    c. Overstate purchases for Year 5.

    d. Have no effect on net income of Year 4.

___ 9. The *gross profit* method of estimating inventories:

    a. Is a useful means of determining the rate of gross profit without taking a physical inventory.

    b. Is a useful means of verifying the reasonableness of a physical inventory count.

    c. Provides information about the number of units in the ending inventory.

    d. Provides information about changes in the rate of gross profit.

___ 10. The *retail method* of estimating inventory:

    a. Converts ending inventory at retail selling price to cost by multiplying the gross profit percentage.

    b. Computes the cost of goods sold by multiplying net sales by the cost percentage; and then deducts this amount from cost of goods available to find ending inventory.

    c. Requires a business to maintain records showing beginning inventory and purchases at both cost and retail prices.

    d. Assumes that the gross profit rate remains the same as it was in preceding years.

_____ 11.   Assume Franco Company and Limerick Corporation are *identical in all respects* except that Franco uses FIFO and Limerick uses LIFO in accounting for inventory. In a period of rising prices, each of the following statements is accurate *except*:

        a.   Limerick reports lower net income and lower income tax expense than does Franco.

        b.   Limerick will appear to have a higher inventory turnover rate and longer operating cycle than will Franco.

        c.   Limerick's current ratio is lower than Franco's.

        d.   Limerick's cost of goods sold figure more closely approximates current cost of merchandise sold than does Franco's.

_____ 12. *   A *LIFO reserve*:

        a.   Is reported as a current asset.

        b.   Represents the amount of money a company no using LIFO could have saved if it had been using LIFO since the business was organized.

        c.   Causes an abnormal decline in net income when it is liquidated.

        d.   Is the amount by which the LIFO cost of inventory understates the current replacement cost of the inventory.

Exercises

1.   Listed below are eight technical accounting terms emphasized in this chapter.

LCM rule	*Gross profit method*
Cost ratio	*Retail inventory method*
FIFO method	*Inventory shrinkage*
LIFO method	*Consistency*

Each of the following statements may (or may not) describe one of these technical terms. In the space provided below each statement, indicate the accounting term described, or answer "None" if the statement does not correctly describe any of the terms.

a.   Loss due to missing or damaged units which is recorded in a separate adjusting entry in a perpetual inventory system.

_____

b.   A method of inventory valuation in which inventory is reported at retail prices.

_____

c.   A method of estimating the cost of the ending inventory based on the assumption of a constant gross profit rate.

_____

_____
* *Supplemental Topic*, "LIFO Reserves."

d.   A method of inventory valuation that assumes the ending inventory consists of goods acquired in the earliest purchases.

_____

e.   The ratio of cost to selling price.

_____

f.   A method of pricing in which inventory is valued at the lower of original cost or replacement cost.

_____

g.   Accounting standard that requires use of the same method of inventory pricing from year to year, with full disclosure of the effects of any change in method.

_____

2.   Hom Corporation uses the FIFO method in a perpetual system and adjusts the accounting records to the physical inventory taken at year-end. In each of the situations described below, indicating the effects of the error on the various elements of financial statements prepared at the end of the *current* year, using the following code: *O* = overstated, *U* = understated, *NE* = no effect.

Situation	Revenue	Cost and/or Expenses	Net Income	Assets	Liabilities	Owners' Equity
a. No record made of goods purchased and received on Dec. 31; goods omitted from physical count of inventory.						
b. Made sale in late December; goods were delivered on Dec. 31 but were also included in physical inventory Dec. 31						
c. In taking the physical inventory, some goods in a warehouse were overlooked.						
d. A purchase made late in year was recorded properly on the books, but the goods were not included in the physical count of inventory.						

Use the following information for Exercises 3,4,and 5.

Widmer Corporation's accounting records disclose the following information regarding purchases of inventory item no. 329 during May:

	Units	Unit Cost	Total Cost
Beginning inventory, May 1...............	50	$10.10	$505
Purchase, May 3	40	11.00	440
Purchase, May	90	12.00	1,080
Purchase, May	20	13.75	275

On May 15, Widmer sold 150 units at a price of $16.10 each.

3. Assume Widmer uses a *perpetual inventory system*. Compute the cost of goods sold and the cost of the ending inventory of 50 units under each of the following inventory methods.

		Cost of Goods Sold	Inventory
a.	FIFO cost..............................	$_____	$_____
b.	LIFO cost	$_____	$_____
c.	Average cost.........................	$_____	$_____

4. Assume Widmer uses a *periodic inventory system*. Compute the cost of goods sold and the cost of the ending inventory of 50 units under each of the following inventory methods.

		Inventory	Cost of Goods Sold
a.	FIFO cost..............................	$_____	$_____
b.	LIFO cost	$_____	$_____
c.	Average cost.........................	$_____	$_____

5. Assume the replacement cost of each unit of item no. 329 on May 31 is $12.50, and that Widmer uses the FIFO cost flow assumption. Compute the cost of ending inventory and the cost of goods sold applying the *lower-of-cost-or-market rule* (with "cost" being defined as the FIFO cost computed in exercises 3 and 4 above).
    a.   Cost of ending inventory using LCM rule .... $_____
    b.   Cost of goods sold using LCM rule .... $_____

6. On July 20, 20__, the accountant for **b** company is in the process of preparing financial statements for the year ending June 30, 20__. The physical inventory, however, was not taken until July 10, 20__, and the accountant finds it necessary to establish the approximate inventory cost at June 30, 20__ from the following data:

Physical inventory, July 20__ $30,000
Transactions for period July 1 – July 10:
    Sales 14,800
    Purchases... 16,950

The gross profit on sales of the past couple of years has averaged 22.5% of net sales. In the space below, compute the approximate inventory cost at June 30, 20__.

7.   Toy Mart uses the retail method to estimate its inventory at the end of each month. The following information is available at July 31:

	Cost	Retail
Inventory, June 30..	$292,500	$450,000
Purchases during July.......................................	187,500	300,000
Goods available for sale during July................	$480,000	$750,000

a.   The cost percentage that would be used in applying the retail method for the month of July .... _____%

b.   The estimated inventory at July 31, stated in retail prices .... $_____

c.   The estimated inventory at July 31, stated at cost .... $_____

SOLUTIONS TO CHAPTER 7 SELF-TEST

True or False

1.   **T** Determining the proper valuation of inventory establishes the cost of goods sold for the period, which is used in computing net income.

2.   **T** The key feature of a perpetual inventory system is that the records show continuously the amount of inventory on hand and the cost of goods sold.

3.   **F** This method is best suited to inventories of high-priced, low-volume items.

4.   **T** There are four inventory valuation methods discussed in the text; these methods represent alternative definition of *cost.*

5.   **T** Average cost is computed by dividing the *total* cost of goods available for sale by the total number of units available for sale.

6.   **T** FIFO is based on the assumption that the first merchandise acquired (cheaper prices) is sold first.

7.   **F** The use of historical costs tends to *overstate* net income because the replacement cost of the merchandise sold is really higher than the cost of goods sold deducted on the income statement.

8.   **F** LIFO causes the more current (higher) costs to be included in the cost of goods sold, thus *minimizing* net income.

9.   **F** Under LIFO, the ending inventory is assumed to consists of merchandise acquired in the *earliest* purchases.

10. **F** Charges are permitted, however, when a change is made, the effects of the change upon reported net income should be disclosed fully in the footnotes accompanying the financial statements.

11. **F** The validity of both the balance sheet and the income statement depend on the accuracy in the valuation of inventory.

12. **T** Establishing a dollar value for inventory of multiplying the quantity of each inventory item by the unit cost per item.

13. **T** LCM is a method of inventory valuation in which merchandise is valued at original cost or replacement cost (market), whichever is lower.

14. **F** Title to the goods passes at point of shipment; the goods are the property of the buyer while in transit.

15. **F** The difference between sales price and cost of the inventory (the profit) will be included in net income in the wrong period.

16. **T** The ending inventory of one year is the beginning inventory of the next year.

17. **T** The ending inventory of one year is also the beginning inventory of the following year; total net income for the two-year period is correct.

18. **F** If ending inventory is overstated, the cost of goods sold figure will be understated and net income will be overstated.

19. **F** A business which wants to **understate** taxable income would understate ending inventory.

20. **T** Knowing the gross profit rate enables us to separate the net sales into the gross profit and the cost of goods sold. This cost of goods sold figure is deducted from cost of goods available for sale to estimate ending inventory.

21. **T** These retail price figures are then converted to *cost* by application of cost-to-retail percentage.

22. **F** Dividing 365 by the inventory turnover rate equals the average number of days required to sell inventory. The operating cycle consists of the average number of days required to sell inventory PLUS the average number of days required to collect accounts receivable.

23.* **F** The term "LIFO reserve" refers to the difference between current replacement cost (or FIFO cost) of a company's inventory and the LIFO cost shown in the accounting records. The cumulative tax benefit of using LIFO may be computed by multiplying the LIFO reserve by the income tax rate.

Completion Statements

1. inventory; a. sales, sales; b. cost of goods sold, inventory, cost. 2. specific identification; average cost; first-in, first-out (FIFO); last-in, first-out (LIFO). 3. LIFO. 4. just-in-time (JIT). 5. decrease, replacement, increase, replacement. 6. title, seller, buyer. 7. purchases, accounts receivable (or cash), sales, sales. 8. $5,000; $37,000; $18,000. 9. retail, cost, percentage (or ratio). 10. cost of goods sold, average inventory, sales (or credit sales), average accounts receivable, 365, inventory turnover rate, 365, accounts receivable turnover rate.

Multiple Choice

1. Answer **c** – is not included in the definition of inventory for either a merchandising firm or a manufacturing business. For a merchandising company, inventory consists of all goods owned and held for sale in the regular course of business (answer **d**). In a manufacturing business, there are three types of inventories: raw materials (answers **a** and **b**), goods in process of manufacture, and finished goods.

---

* *Supplemental Topic*, "LIFO Reserves."

2. Answer **d** – a perpetual inventory system can be used with any acceptable inventory costing method. Although an updated inventory account is maintained, basic internal control measures such as subdivision of duties, control of documents by serial numbers, and separation of the accounting function from custody of inventory are necessary. Even though perpetual inventory records show an up-to-date balance for inventory, an annual physical inventory still is taken to determine any "shrinkage" losses and correct any errors in the perpetual inventory records.

3. Answer **b** – is not one of the acceptable inventory methods. The acceptable methods are (1) specific identification; (2) average cost; (3) first-in, first-out (FIFO); and (4) last-in, first-out (LIFO). Lower of cost of market is a method of inventory pricing in which goods are values at original cost or replacement cost (market), whichever is lower.

4. Answer **a** – (LIFO) yields the lowest value for ending inventory because the ending inventory is presumed to consists of units acquired in the *earliest* purchases which were the lowest costs. This smaller ending inventory figure results in a higher cost of goods sold amount than the other methods and hence a *smaller* net income.

5. Answer **b** – the selection of an inventory method is a decision made by management. The physical inventory is undertaken to establish a true count of all merchandise owned by the company and will be carried out in the same manner regardless of the inventory method selected.

6. Answer **b** – net income for Year 2 was overstated by $250, the *profit* on the sale that should have been recorded in Year 1. If the goods were sold in Year 1, the goods should not have been included in Year 1's ending inventory. Year 1's ending inventory, therefore was *overstated* by the *cost* of these goods ($750); the beginning inventory of Year 2 was also *overstated* by $750.

7. Answer **d** – under a periodic system, the cost of items purchases at year-end and not yet sold are considered part of the cost of goods sold during the year; periodic LIFO *assumes* that the latest purchases are sold and that the ending inventory comes from the earliest purchases. Under a perpetual system, the cost of unsold year-end purchases is included in inventory, since the determination of the cost of goods sold is made as each sale occurs and these items were not available before year-end. Answer **a** is incorrect–all four inventory costing methods may be used in either perpetual or periodic systems. In the LIFO and average cost methods, ending inventory and cost of goods amounts would differ under perpetual and periodic systems. Under FIFO and specific identification methods, ending inventory and cost of goods amounts are the same for the perpetual and periodic systems.

8. Answer **b** – Year 3 will be unaffected by an inventory error at the end of Year 3. Beginning inventory of Year 5 will be overstated because Year 4's ending inventory is Year 5's beginning inventory, but purchases for Year 5 will be unaffected. Year 4's net income will be overstated.

9. Answer **b** – the gross profit method uses the gross profit percentage to compute an estimate of the *cost* of ending inventory (not the number of *units* as in answer **c**).In using the gross profit method, it is assumed that the rate of gross profit earned in the preceding year will remain the same for the current year.

10. Answer **c** – in order to compute the cost percentage for use in the retail inventory method, a business must have amounts for the goods available at both cost and retail prices, "Goods available for sale" is the total of beginning inventory plus purchases during the current period. Answer **a** is incorrect because it mentions multiplying by the *gross profit percentage* instead of the *cost percentage*. Answer **b** is descriptive of the *gross profit method* of estimating inventory. The retail method is based upon the cost ratio of the *current year,* rather than that of the prior year.

11. Answer **b** – due solely to the use of LIFO, Limerick's inventory turnover rate will appear to be higher than Franco's, and therefore Limerick will appear to require fewer days to sell its average inventory. The operating cycle consists of the number of days required to sell inventory PLUS the number of days to collect accounts receivable. Assuming the accounts receivable turnover rate

and sales are identical for both companies, Limerick would appear to have a *shorter* operating cycle than Franco. Answers **a, c**, and **d** are all accurate.

12.[*] Answer **d** – the amount of a LIFO reserve is computed as the difference between LIFO cost and the current replacement of ending inventory. This amount is *not* specifically reported in the financial statements, although it can be determined by comparing LIFO cost to the current replacement cost of inventory disclosed in notes to the financial statements. When inventory levels decline substantially, liquidation of part or all of the LIFO reserve occurs and results in a one-time *increase* in net income

Solutions to Exercises

1.

a.   Inventory shrinkage

b.   none (Only in specialized industries would inventories be valued at market prices.)

c.   Gross profit method

d.   LIFO method

e.   Cost ratio

f.   LCM rule

g.   Consistency

2.

	Revenue	Cost and/or Expenses	Net Income	Assets	Liabilities	Owners' Equity
a.	NE	NE	NE	U	U	NE
b.	NE	U	O	O	NE	O
c.	NE	O	U	U	NE	U
d.	NE	O	U	U	NE	U

3.

		Cost of Goods Sold	**Inventory**
a.	FIFO cost	$1,665($505+$440+$270)	$635($2,300-$1,665)
b.	LIFO cost	$1,722($1,080+$440+$202)	$578($2,300-$1,722)
c.	Average cost	$1687.50(11.25 x 150)	$612.60($2,300 -$1,687.50)

4.

		Inventory	**Cost of Goods Sold**
a.	FIFO cost	$635 ($275 + $360)	$1,665($2,300 - $635)
b.	LIFO cost	$505	$1,795 ($2,300 - $505)
c.	Average cost	$575($11.50 x 50)	$1,725 ($2,300 - $575)

5.

a.   Ending inventory (LCM rule) $625(50 x $12.50 is lower than FIFO)

b.   Cost of goods sold: $1,675 ($2,300-$625 ending inventory)

---

[*] *Supplemental Topic*, "LIFO Reserves."

6.

Physical inventory, July 10, 20__		$30,000
Less: Net purchases for period July 1-July 10..............		16,950
		$13,050
Add: Cost of goods sold for period July –July10:		
$14,800 x 77.5% (cost percentage..............................		11,470
Approximate inventory, June 30, 20__		$24,520

7.

a.   64%   ($480,000/$750,000)

b. $400,000   ($750,000- $350,000)

c. $256,000   ($400,000 x 64%)

8

PLANT ASSETS AND DEPRECIATION

HIGHLIGHTS OF THE CHAPTER

1.   The term *plant and equipment* is used to describe long-lived assets used in the operation of the business. A plant asset is a *stream of services* to be received by the owner over a long period of time. As the services are received, a portion of the asset is consumed and should be recognized as an expense (depreciation).

2.   The major categories of plant and equipment include:

   a.   Tangible plant assets, such as land, buildings, and machinery. Most of these assets are *subject to depreciation*, whereas land is generally *not subject to depreciation*.

   b.   Intangible assets, such as patents, copyrights, trademarks, franchises, organization costs, leaseholds, and goodwill. The term *intangible assets* is used to describe non-current assets which have *no physical form*. The cost of intangible assets is subject to *amortization.*

   c.   Natural resources, such as mining properties, oil and gas reserves, and tracts of standing timber. These assets are physically consumed and converted into inventory.

3.   The major "accountable events" and the accounting issues relating to plant and equipment are:

   a.   Acquisition – determining the cost of the plant asset.

   b.   Allocation of the acquisition cost to expense over the asset's useful life (depreciation).

   c.   Sale or disposal – determining any gain or loss to be recognized.

4.   All *reasonable* and *necessary* expenditures incurred in acquiring a plant asset and placing it in use should be recorded in an asset account. The cost may include the list price, sales or use taxes paid, freight and handling costs, installation costs, and insurance prior to the time that the asset is placed in service.

5.   Cash discounts reduce the net cost of the asset. Interest paid when an asset is purchased on the installment plan should be recorded as an expense rather than as part of the cost of acquiring the asset.

6.   The cost of land may include real estate commissions, escrow fees, title insurance fees, delinquent taxes (including penalties and interest), etc. Separate ledger accounts are always maintained for land and buildings. Certain land-improvement costs, such as fences, driveways, parking lots, sprinkler systems, and landscaping, have a limited life and should be recorded in a separate account and depreciated.

7.   When a building is purchased, the total cost includes the price paid plus all incidental costs, such as termite inspection fees, legal fees, and major repairs necessary before the building is occupied. When a building is constructed by the owner, the total cost of the building includes all direct expenditures (labor, materials, building permit, etc.) plus interest charges during the construction period.

8.   A *capital expenditure* is one that will benefit many accounting periods; a *revenue expenditure* is one that will benefit only the current accounting period. Capital expenditures are recorded in asset accounts and are deducted from revenue through the process of depreciation; revenue expenditures are recorded in expense accounts as incurred.

9.   *Depreciation* is the process of *allocating the cost of plant assets* to the periods in which services are received from the assets. A separate depreciation expense account should be maintained for

each major group of depreciable assets, and the total amount of depreciation expense for the fiscal period should be disclosed in the income statement.

10. Depreciation is *not* a process of assigning a market value (or realizable value) to plant assets, nor is it a process of accumulating a fund for the replacement of assets when they become worn out or obsolete. Depreciation is an *allocation process*: The cost of an asset, less residual value, is allocated to the years that are benefited from the use of the asset.

11. The balance in the Accumulated Depreciation account represents the portion of the historical cost of plant assets which has expired to date; this account does *not* represent a fund of cash accumulated to replace plant assets.

12. The two major causes of depreciation are:
    a. Physical deterioration from use.
    b. Obsolescence due to technological changes or changing needs of the company.

13. The two most commonly used methods of computing periodic depreciation for financial statement purposes are:
    a. *Straight-line:*

    $$\text{Depreciation Expense} = \frac{\text{Cost - Residual Value}}{\text{Estimate Years of Useful Life}}$$

    b. Fixed-percentage-of-declining-balance:

    An accelerated method in which the book value of the asset is multiplied by a rate which is a specified percentage of the straight-line rate.

    $$\frac{\text{Depreciation}}{\text{Expense}} = \frac{\text{Remaining}}{\text{Book Value}} \times \frac{\text{Accelerated}}{\text{Depreciation Rate}}$$

    (The above two methods are illustrated and explained in the chapter. Two other depreciation methods are discussed briefly in the Supplemental Topic at the end of the chapter.)

14. The *straight-line method* is the simplest and the most widely used method of computing depreciation. Under this method an *equal portion* of the cost of the asset (less residual value) is allocated to each period of use.

15. Under *accelerated depreciation* methods, larger amounts of depreciation are recorded in the early years of use and reduced amounts in later years. In some cases the use of an accelerated depreciation method tends to equalize the total expense of using an asset because decreasing periodic depreciation charges are offset by increasing repair outlays as the asset gets older.

16. The most widely used accelerated depreciation method is the *fixed-percentage-of-declining-balance*, often referred to as the declining-balance method. Annual depreciation expense is computed by multiplying a depreciation rate by the current book value (undepreciated cost) of the asset. The accelerated depreciation *rate* remains *constant*; the book value of the asset declines each period. Under the *double-declining-balance* method, the depreciation rate is 200% of the straight-line rate. Another variation is *150% declining-balance*, in which the depreciation rate is 150% of the straight-line rate.

17. When an asset is acquired in the middle of an accounting period, depreciation can be computed by rounding the calculation to the *nearest whole month*. Another approach, called the *half-year convention*, is to record six months' depreciation on all assets acquired or sold during the year.

18. A business need not use the same method of depreciation for all its assets. Also, different methods may be used for tax purposes than are being used in the accounting records and financial statements.

19. The Modified Accelerated Cost Recovery System (MACRS) is the only accelerated depreciation method allowed for federal income tax purposes for assets acquired after 1986. MACRS is used for income tax purposes only. The use of MACRS for financial reporting is **not** permitted because this system departs from generally accepted accounting principles.

20. Depreciation rates are based on estimates of useful life. If the estimate of useful service life is found to be in error, the estimate should be revised, and the **undepreciated cost of the asset should be allocated over the years of remaining useful life**. A change in annual depreciation expense may also result from a change in the **estimate of residual value** or from a change in the **method** of computing depreciation.

21. When units of plant and equipment wear out or become obsolete they must be discarded, sold, or traded in. To record the disposal of a depreciable asset, the cost of the asset must be removed from the asset account, **and the accumulated depreciation** (on that asset) **must be removed** from the contra-asset account.

22. When plant assets are disposed of at a date other than the end of the year, depreciation is recorded for the fractional period preceding disposal.

23. The **book value**, or carrying value, of a depreciable asset is its cost minus accumulated depreciation. If the asset is sold for a price above book value, there is a **gain** on the sale. If the asset is sold for less than book value, there is a **loss**.

24. When a depreciable asset is sold, the amount of the gain or loss is determined by comparing the book value of the asset sold with the amount received from the sale. The amount of a gain would be **credited** to a **Gain on Disposal of Plant Assets** account, and a loss would be **debited** to **Loss on Disposal of Plant Assets**.

25. As a result of using different depreciation methods, an asset's basis for income tax purposes may differ from its book value. In this event, the gain or loss on disposal of the asset computed for tax purposes will differ from that reported in the financial statements.

26. A gain or loss on the trade-in of a plant asset for a similar kind of asset is recognized for financial reporting purposes whenever 25% or more of the transaction value involves cash or the creation of debt.

27. **Intangible assets** are those noncurrent assets which do not have physical substance but which contribute to the process of earning revenue. Intangibles are recorded at cost and should be **amortized** over their useful lives. It is often difficult to estimate the useful life of an intangible asset, but the maximum amortization period **may not exceed 40 years**. Intangible assets generally are amortized by the straight-line method.

28. Despite the fact that expenditures for research and development often lead to discoveries or knowledge that contribute to the earning process for many periods, the Financial Accounting Standards Board has ruled that all research and development expenditures are to be **expensed when incurred**. Hence, these types of expenditures are not reported in the balance sheet as intangible assets.

29. **Goodwill** is the amount paid for a business **in excess of** the fair market value of the net identifiable assets of the business. It represents the **present value** of expected future earnings in excess of the normal return on the net identifiable assets of the business. The term **net identifiable assets** refers to all assets except goodwill minus liabilities.

30. Goodwill may exist in many businesses, but it should be recorded in the accounts **only when it is purchased**.

31. The following two methods are often used in **estimating** the value of goodwill owned by a business unit:

   a. Negotiated agreement between buyer and seller. If a business with net assets (at market value) of $80,000 is sold for $100,000, this suggests that goodwill of $20,000 is possessed by this business.

   b. The capitalized value of excess earning power. For example, if excess earnings amount to $5,000, and the capitalization rate agreed upon is 20%, the goodwill can be estimated at $25,000 ($5,000 ÷ .20 = $25,000).

32. Natural resources, such as mines or timber stands, are physically extracted and converted into inventory. These assets are recorded at cost and reported separately in the balance sheet.

33. **Depletion** is the process **allocating the cost** of the natural resource to the units removed. The depletion rate is computed by dividing the cost of the natural resource by the estimated number of units available to be removed. The rate is then multiplied by the number of units removed during a period to determine the total depletion charge for the period.

34. **Impairment** of an asset occurs when its economic usefulness declines, usually due to a change in economic conditions. If the book value of an asset cannot be recovered through future sale or use, the asset should be written down to its net realizable value and a loss recognized. When and if permanent impairment has occurred, as well as the dollar amount of "net realizable value," is largely a matter of professional judgment on a case by case basis.

35. The **cash effects** of plant and equipment transactions do **not** parallel the effects reported in the income statement. Depreciation expense, amortization expense, and write downs due to impairment of assets all reduce net income, but have no immediate effects upon cash flows. These are examples of **"noncash" charges** against earnings. Cash flows occur upon purchase (cash payments) and sale (cash receipts) of plant assets. Cash flows relating to acquisitions and disposals of plant assets are reported in the **statement of cash flows**, classified as **investing activities**. (Although the income statement may report a gain or loss upon disposal, the entire cash proceeds is considered a cash flow from investing activities in the statement of cash flows.)

36.* Under the **units-of-output** method, depreciation is based upon some measure of output, other than the passage of time. When the usage of an asset fluctuates and the output can be estimated in terms of some unit (such as* tons produced or miles driven), a more equitable allocation of the cost of a plant asset can be obtained by computing depreciation on the basis of output. Cost (less residual value) is divided by estimated output to obtain a depreciation rate per unit. Depreciation for a period is computed by multiplying the rate per unit by the number of units of output for the period.

$$\frac{\text{Depreciation}}{\text{Expense}} = \frac{\text{Cost - Residual Value}}{\text{Total Estimated Units of Output}} \times \frac{\text{Units of}}{\text{Output}}$$

_____

* *Supplemental Topic*, "Other Depreciation Methods."

128

37.* A form of accelerated depreciation termed the sum-of-the-years'-digits, or SYD, results in depreciation expense between the double-declining-balance and the 150%-declining-balance methods. Coverage of this method, as well as of decelerated depreciation methods (in which less depreciation expense is recognized in the early years), is deferred to later accounting courses.

TEST YOURSELF ON PLANT ASSETS AND DEPRECIATION

True or False

For each of the following statements, circle the T or the F to indicate whether the statement is true or false.

T   F   1.   In a broad sense, the cost of a machine or a building may be viewed as a long-term prepaid expense.

T   F   2.   An auto owned by a glass manufacturer would be reported under Plant and Equipment, while glass owned by an auto manufacturer would be classified as Inventory.

T   F   3.   The cost of land should not include any transaction costs, such as real estate commissions paid.

T   F   4.   *Capital expenditures* are those disbursements which are allocated to several accounting periods; *revenue expenditures* are charged off as current expenses.

T   F   5.   The cost of a plant asset should include all costs necessary to get the asset ready for use, including the cost of the units spoiled in production while the asset was being adjusted and tested.

T   F   6.   A small expenditure, such as $10 for a set of spark plugs, may reasonably be charged to expense even though the expenditure may benefit several periods.

T   F   7.   Obsolescence may be a more significant factor than wear and tear through use in putting an end to the usefulness of many depreciable assets.

T   F   8.   Depreciation expense for a period should be a reasonably good estimate of the change in the fair market value of an asset during the period.

T   F   9.   In practice, the residual value of an asset is often ignored in estimating annual depreciation expense.

T   F   10.   The Accumulated Depreciation account is a fund established for the replacement of assets, but it will not be large enough to cover the cost of replacement during a period of inflation.

T   F   11.   The fixed-percentage-of-declining-balance method of depreciation has a "built-in" residual value and can never allocate 100% of the original cost of an asset to expense.

T F   12.   Generally accepted accounting principles require a business to use the same depreciation methods in its financial statements that it uses for income tax purposes.

T F   13.   When it becomes evident that a plant asset will have a useful life longer than had been originally estimated, the depreciation rate will be revised according to the new estimate of useful life.

T F   14.   Whenever a depreciable asset is sold, both the cost of the asset and the accumulated depreciation must be removed from the accounts.

T F   15.   For both tax purposes and preparing financial statements, no gain is recognized when used plant assets are traded in on new plant assets of "like kind."

T F   16.   Depletion refers to the allocation of the cost of an intangible asset over the periods that benefits are received.

T F   17.   Intangible assets are assets that cannot be sold.

T F   18.   The systematic write-off of intangible assets to expense is known as amortization.

T F   19.   Goodwill is the present value of future earnings in excess of the normal return on net identifiable assets.

T F   20.   When a business has superior earnings for many years, goodwill probably exists and should be recorded on the books.

T F   21.   If a buyer of a business pays a price for the business in excess of the fair market value of the net identifiable assets, the buyer may record goodwill as one of the assets being acquired.

T F*   22.   The units-of-output method of depreciation yields results similar to accelerated methods of depreciation when the rate of output increases steadily over a period of years.

Completion Statements

Fill in the necessary words to complete the following statements:

1.   The two causes of depreciation are: (a) _____ _____ and (b) _____.

2.   If a _____ expenditure is erroneously recorded as a expenditure, net income will be _____ in the current period, and overstated in every future period in which depreciation should have been recognized.

Supplemental Topic, "Other Depreciation Methods."

3.   Net income for three consecutive years was reported as follows:

Year 1........ $30,000
Year 2........ $39,000
Year 3........ $40,000

At the beginning of Year 1, a capital expenditure of $15,000 for a new machine, which should have been depreciated over a five-year life using the 150%-declining-balance method, was erroneously charged to repair expense. The correct net income for the three years should have been as follows.

Year 1, $_____; Year 2, $_____; Year 3, $_____.

4.   The entry to record the disposal of a depreciable asset will always include a credit to the asset account for the _____ _____ of the asset, and a debit to the _____ _____ account.

5.   The cost of intangible assets should be _____ by the _____ method over a period not to exceed _____ years.

Multiple Choice

Choose the best answer for each of the following questions and enter the identifying letter in the space provided.

___ 1.   Big Company purchased land for $80,000 subject to delinquent property taxes of $4,000. These taxes were paid immediately by Big Company along with interest of $320 on the delinquent taxes. The cost of this land should be recorded by Big Company at:

a. $80,000.

b. $84,000.

c. $84,320.

d.   Some other amount.

___ 2.   If a revenue expenditure is debited to a plant asset account in error:

a.   Revenue for the current period is understated.

b.   Net income of the current period is overstated.

c.   Net income in future periods will be unaffected by this error.

d.   Expenses for the current period are overstated.

_ 3.   Depreciation, as the term is used in accounting, means:

    a.   The systematic write-off of the cost of a natural resource over its productive life.

    b.   The allocation of the cost of a plant asset to expense to reflect the use of asset services.

    c.   The physical deterioration of an asset.

    d.   The decrease in the market value of an asset.

_ 4.   The book value or carrying value of a depreciable asset is best defined as:

    a.   The undepreciated cost of the asset.

    b.   The price that the asset would bring if offered for sale.

    c.   Accumulated depreciation on the asset since acquisition.

    d.   Original cost of the asset.

_ 5.   The straight-line method of depreciation:

    a.   Generally gives best results because it is easy to apply.

    b.   Ignores fluctuations in the rate of asset usage.

    c.   Should be used in a period of inflation because it accumulates, at a uniform rate, the fund for the replacement of the asset.

    d.   Is the best method to use for income tax purposes.

_ 6.   Accumulated depreciation, as used in accounting, may be defined as:

    a.   Earnings retained in the business that will be used to purchase another asset when the present asset is depreciated.

    b.   Funds (or cash) set aside to replace the asset being depreciated.

    c.   The portion of the cost of a plant asset recognized as expense since the asset was acquired.

    d.   An expense of doing business.

_ 7.   A and B Companies purchase identical equipment having an estimated service of 10 years. A Company uses the straight-line method of depreciation, and B Company uses the double-declining-balance method. Assuming that the companies are identical in all other respects:

    a.   B Company will record more depreciation on this asset over the entire 10 years than will A Company.

    b.   At the end of the third year, the book value of the asset will be lower on A Company's books than on B Company's.

    c.   A Company's depreciation expense will be greater in the first year than B Company's.

    d.   A Company's net income will be lower in the ninth year than B Company's.

8. Which of the following is not an intangible asset?

    a.   A patent.

    b.   A trademark.

    c.   An investment in marketable securities.

    d.   Goodwill.

9. The best evidence of goodwill existing in a business is:

    a.   The appearance of goodwill on the balance sheet.

    b.   Numerous contributions to charitable organizations.

    c.   A long-standing reputation for manufacturing a high-quality product.

    d.   A long record of earnings greater than those of like-size firms in the same industry.

10. Lucky Strike Mines recognizes $2 of depletion for each ton of ore mined. This year 750,000 tons of ore were mined, but only 700,000 tons were sold. The amount of depletion that should be deducted from revenue this year is:

    a. $2,900,000

    b. $1,500,000

    c. $1,400,000

    d. $100,000

11. Which of the following statements regarding *impairment of long-lived assets* is not accurate?

    a.   Impairment of an asset may involve recognition of a loss and writing the asset down to net realizable value.

    b.   Regardless of whether or not potentially impaired assets are written down, the circumstances should be fully disclosed in footnotes accompanying the financial statements.

    c.   The FASB has issued strict guidelines to be followed in determination of whether or not permanent impairment has occurred, as well as in computation of the dollar amount of any loss.

    d.   At the present time, professional judgment on a case-by-case basis determines the accounting treatment to be used in cases of potentially impaired assets.

Exercises

1. Listed below are eight technical accounting terms emphasized in this chapter.

   Half-year convention   *Goodwill*
   Revenue expenditure   *Book value*
   Straight-line depreciation   *Net identifiable assets*
   Accelerated depreciation   *Declining-balance method*

   Each of the following statements may (or may not) describe one of these technical terms. In the space provided below each statement, indicate the accounting term described, or answer "None" if the statement does not correctly describe any of the terms.

   a. Depreciation methods which take less depreciation in the early years of the asset's life and more in the later years of the asset's life

   _____

   b. The total of all assets except goodwill, less liabilities.

   _____

   c. The present value of future earnings in excess of the normal return on net identifiable assets.

   _____

   d. A method of allocating the cost of an asset equally to each year of its life.

   _____

   e. An expenditure that will benefit only the current accounting period.

   _____

   f. The cost of an asset minus the related accumulated depreciation.

   _____

   g. An approach to computing depreciation which records six months' depreciation on all assets acquired during a year, regardless of actual dates of purchase.

   _____

2. A truck with an estimated life of four years was acquired on March 31, Year 1, for $11,000. The estimated residual value of the truck is $1,000, and the service life is estimated at 100,000 miles. Compute depreciation for Year 1 and Year 2 using the following methods (where appropriate, round depreciation to the nearest month).

	Year 1	**Year 2**
a. Straight-line	$_____	$_____
b. Fixed-percentage-of-declining-balance (twice the straight-line rate)	$_____	$_____
*c. Output (miles driven: Year 1, 20,000; Year 2, 40,000)	$_____	$_____

3.   Equipment which cost $6,000 had an estimated useful life of six years and an estimated salvage value of $600. Straight-line depreciation was used. In the space provided at the top of the next page, prepare the journal entry (omitting explanation) to record the disposal of the equipment under each of the following assumptions:

   a.   The equipment was sold for $4,000 cash after two years' use.

   b.   After three years' use, the equipment was sold for $3,500 cash.

   c.   After four years' use, the equipment was traded in on a similar equipment with a fair market value of $8,000. The trade-in allowance was $3,100.

---

* *Supplemental Topic*, "Other Depreciation Methods."

General Journal

a			
b			
c			

4. The Golden Calf, a Las Vegas gambling casino, had net identifiable assets with a fair market value of $8,000,000, and earned an average net income of $2,080,000 per year. Other Las Vegas casinos averaged a net income equal to 20% of their net identifiable assets. An investment group negotiating to buy the Golden Calf offers to pay $8,000,000 for the casino's net identifiable assets, plus an amount for goodwill.

The investment group determined the amount to be paid for goodwill by capitalizing the Golden Calf's annual earnings in excess of the industry average earnings at a rate of 25%. Compute the total price the investment group is offering to pay for the Golden Calf.

Computations:

Answer: $_____

SOLUTIONS TO CHAPTER 8 SELF-TEST

True or False

1. **T** As the stream of services from the machine is utilized, the cost of the asset is transferred to depreciation expense.

2. **T** Plant and Equipment describes long-lived assets acquired for use in the operations of the business and not intended for resale to customers.

3. **F** When land is purchased, various incidental costs (real estate commissions, escrow fees, legal fees, delinquent taxes) are added to capitalized cost in the accounting records.

4. **T** A material expenditure benefiting several accounting periods is a *capital* expenditure. An expenditure benefiting only the current period, or one that is not material in amount, is a *revenue* expenditure.

5.   **T** An asset's cost equals the purchase price plus any costs necessary to make the asset ready for its intended use.

6.   **T** Expenditures which are not material in dollar amount are expensed in the current period.

7.   **T** Long-lived assets may become obsolete as a result of technological changes or changing needs of the company before they physically deteriorate.

8.   **F** Depreciation is a process of cost allocation over an asset's useful life; it is not a process of valuation.

9.   **T** Residual value is often difficult to estimate accurately; it is frequently not material in amount.

10.   **F** The Accumulated Depreciation account represents the expired cost of an asset—it is *not* a fund of cash.

11.   **T** Since each year's depreciation expense is computed as a percentage of the undepreciated cost of the asset, the total cost will never be written off entirely.

12.   **F** Different methods may be used for tax purposes than are being used in the accounting records and financial statements.

13.   **T** The remaining undepreciated cost of the asset is simply spread over the remaining useful life.

14.   **T** The desired result is that the book value, or carrying value, of the asset is removed from the books.

15.   **F** For tax purposes, no gain is recognized on a "like-kind" exchange. If more than 25% of the transaction value is comprised of cash or debt, however, gains *are* recognized in a company's financial statements.

16.   **F** Depletion is the allocation of the cost of a *natural resource* over the periods benefited.

17.   **F** Intangible assets are assets used in the operation of the business which have no physical substance and are noncurrent; they may be bought and sold.

18.   **T** The usual accounting entry for amortization consists of a debit to Amortization Expense and a credit to the intangible asset account.

19.   **T** Goodwill is evident when investors will pay a higher price because the business earns more than the normal rate of return on its resources.

20.   **F** Although goodwill probably exists, it is recorded in the accounting records only when it is purchased.

21.   **T** The fair market value of all identifiable assets is first recorded on the books of the buyer; any *excess* purchase price is then allocated to an asset account entitled Goodwill.

22[*] **F** Accelerated depreciation means larger amounts of depreciation in the early years of an asset's life; units-of-output yields similar results when the rate of output *decreases* steadily.

Completion Statements

1 a. physical deterioration, b. obsolescence. 2. capital, revenue, understated. 3. $40,500; $35,850; $37,795. 4. original cost, accumulated depreciation. 5. amortized, straight-line, 40.

---

[*] *Supplemental Topic*, "Other Depreciation Methods."

Multiple Choice

1.   Answer **c**—the of land includes incidental costs such as delinquent property taxes and interest on the delinquent taxes. The taxes and interest are obligations of the former owner that were paid by Big Company as part of the acquisition cost—they are not current period expenses of Big Company, but are capitalized. Answer **a** ignores both the delinquent taxes and interest; answer **b** does not capitalize the interest.

2.   Answer **b**—a revenue expenditure benefits only the current period and should be recorded by a debit to an expense account. Even though the plant asset debited in error is subject to depreciation, the depreciation expense will be smaller than the expense that should have been recorded. Since expense is understated, net income of the current period is overstated. Revenue for the current period is unaffected. Net income of future periods will be understated if the error is not corrected due to depreciation on the plant asset debited in error.

3.   Answer **b**—depreciation is the allocation of the cost of a plant asset to expense in the periods in which services are received from the asset. Physical deterioration, as well as obsolescence, are justifications for this cost allocation procedure. Answer **d** is incorrect because accounting records do not purport to reflect fluctuating market values of plant assets. Answer **a** is a definition of depletion.

4.   Answer **a**—book value is cost minus accumulated depreciation; that is, the undepreciated cost. Answer **b** is incorrect because accounting records contain historical cost data, not liquidation values or market values.

5.   Answer **b**—straight line depreciation allocates equal portions of an asset's cost to expense each period, regardless of actual usage. From a matching principle point of view, the straight-line method gives "best" results when usage of the asset is uniform year to year. Answer **c** is incorrect because no depreciation method accumulates a fund for the replacement of an asset. Most companies use accelerated depreciation methods in preparing income tax returns because these methods provide larger deductions for depreciation in the early years of an asset's life.

6.   Answer **c**—each year the amount debited to depreciation expense is also credited to a balance sheet account called Accumulated Depreciation. The credit balance in accumulated depreciation represents the expired cost (i.e., amount expensed) since acquisition, not cash or earnings that could be used to purchase another asset. Answer **d** could be a description of the current period's depreciation expense, but not the balance in accumulated depreciation.

7.   Answer **d**—by the ninth year of the asset's life, A Company's straight-line depreciation will be greater than B Company's double-declining-balance amount; therefore A Company's net income will be lower. Company and B Company will record an equal amount of depreciation over the entire 10-year life of the asset. A Company's straight-line depreciation expense will be lower than double-declining-balance method in the early years of the asset's life, and A Company's book value for the asset will be higher during the early years.

8.   Answer **c**—intangible assets are used in operation of the business, but have no physical substance and are noncurrent. Answers **a, b,** and **d** meet this definition. An investment in marketable securities is not used in the operation of a business.

9.   Answer **d**—although answers **b** and **c** are often associated with the existence of goodwill in a *general* sense, goodwill in an *accounting* sense is the present value of future earnings in excess of a normal return on net identifiable assets. Answer **d** indicates higher than normal earnings which is evidence of the existence of goodwill, assuming the earnings continue. The appearance of goodwill on a balance sheet occurs only when one company purchases another business in its entirety; internally generated goodwill may exist, but is not recorded in the accounting records.

10. Answer **c**—total depletion is $1,500,000 (750,000 tons mined at $2 per ton). The depletion deducted from revenue is $1,400,000 (700,000 tons sold at $2 per ton). $100,000 (50,000 tons not sold at $2 per ton) should be assigned to inventory.

11. Answer **c**—the FASB currently is studying the issue of impairment of long-lived assets, but it has **not** yet taken an official position. Answers **a, b,** and **d** are all accurate statements.

Solutions to Exercises

1.

a. None (Accelerated depreciation takes **more** depreciation in the early years of the asset's life and **less** in the later years.)

b. Net identifiable assets

c. Goodwill

d. Straight-line depreciation

e. Revenue expenditure

f. Book value

g. Half-year convention

2.

		Year 1	Year 2
a.	($11,000- $1,000) x 1/4 x 9/12	$1,875	
	$10,000 x 1/4		$2,500
b.	$11,000 x 50% x 9/12	$4,125	
	($11,000- $4,125) x 50%		$3,438
*c.	20,000 x 10 cents	$2,000	
	40,000 x 10 cents		$4,000

---

* *Supplemental Topic*, "Other Deprecation Methods."

3.

	General Journal		
A	Cash	4,000	
	Accumulated Deprecation	1,800	
	Loss of Disposal of Equipment	200	
	Equipment		6,000
B	Cash	3,500	
	Accumulated Depreciation	2,700	
	Gain on Disposal of Equipment		200
	Equipment		6,000
C	Equipment	8,000	
	Accumulated Depreciation	3,600	
	Equipment		6,000
	Cash		4,900
	Gain on Disposal of Plant Assets		700

4.

Normal earnings ($8,000,000 x .20)	$1,600,000
Excess earnings ($2,080,000- $1,600,000)	$ 480,000
Goodwill ($480,000 / .25)	$1,920,000
Price offered ($8,000,000 + $1,920,000)	$9,920,000

HIGHLIGHTS OF THE CHAPTER

1.   Liabilities are *obligations* arising from past transactions. The liability is recorded by a credit; the offsetting debit generally is either to an asset or an expense account. The dollar amount of the liability is usually clearly stated in a written or oral agreement between the debtor and the creditor. Most liabilities eventually are paid in cash. A few liabilities, such as unearned revenue, are discharged by rendering future services rather than by making a cash payment.

2.   Although both creditors and owners supply financing to a business, liabilities differ from owners' equity in several respects. All liabilities eventually mature; owners' equity does not mature. The claims of creditors have *legal priority* over the claims of owners; creditors are paid in full before any distributions to owners when a business ceases operations. Creditors do not have the right to manage the business but may set restrictions on certain aspects of business operations in *indenture contracts*.

3.   Many liabilities create a contractual obligation for the borrower to pay interest, as well as repaying the principal amount of the debt. Obligations to pay interest stem only from liabilities; a business does not pay interest upon its owners' equity.

4.   Most liabilities are of definite dollar amounts clearly stated on an invoice or in a contract. These liabilities can be recorded promptly as the transactions occur. Sometimes, however, the amount of a liability can only be estimated at the time that it comes into existence. An example is the liability of a manufacturer to make future warranty repairs on the products it sells. *Estimated liabilities* usually are recorded by means of adjusting entries at the end of each accounting period.

5.   *Current liabilities* are amounts payable to creditors within one year or the operating cycle, whichever is longer. A second requirement for classification as a current liability is the expectation that the debt will be paid from current assets (or by rendering services). A company's debt paying ability is judged, in part, by the relationship of its current assets to its current liabilities.

6.   Examples of current liabilities include accounts payable, short-term notes payable, the "current portion" of long-term debt, accrued liabilities, and unearned revenue.

7.   A note payable may be issued as evidence of indebtedness to banks or to other creditors.

8.   A note usually is drawn for the *principal amount borrowed*, Cash is debited, and Notes Payable is credited at the time the note is issued. No liability is recorded for the interest charges upon issuance; the liability for interest accrues daily over the life of the loan.

9.   The entry to record the payment of principal and interest at maturity requires a debit to Notes Payable for the amount of principal, a debit to Interest Expense for the interest related to the current period, a debit to Interest Payable for any interest accrued (and recorded) in prior periods, and a credit to Cash for the total paid.

10. If a note is not repaid in the same period it was issued, it will be necessary to recognize the interest which has accrued (become owed) on the note during each period. The interest which has accrued during the period is recognized by a debit to Interest Expense and a credit to the liability account Interest Payable.

11. Many long-term liabilities, such as mortgages, call for monthly installment payments equal to the accrued interest charges plus a portion of the principal amount. The portion of unpaid principal

which will be repaid within one year is called the ***current portion of long-term debt,*** and is classified as a current liability.

12. As the maturity date of a long-term liability approaches, the obligation eventually becomes due within the current period. At this time, the obligation generally is reclassified as a current liability. An exception to this rule exists if the maturing obligation is expected to be ***refinanced*** (see Highlight 17).

13. ***Accrued liabilities*** arise from the recognition of an expense for which payment will be made in a future period. Expenses often paid *after* recognition of the expense in the accounting records includes payrolls, interest, and—for corporations—income taxes.

14. Every business incurs a number of accrued liabilities relating to payrolls. The largest of these liabilities is the amount owed to employees—that is, their ***net pay***. However, employers also accrue liabilities for various payroll tax expenses and for amounts withheld from employees' gross pay.

15. A liability for ***unearned revenue*** arises when a customer pays in advance. Often this liability is discharged by rendering services or delivering merchandise to the customer in a future period.

16. ***Long-term liabilities*** are those liabilities which do not mature within one year, or the operating cycle of the business, whichever is longer. In addition, some obligations maturing in the current period are classified as long-term liabilities if certain conditions are met regarding the refinancing of the liability.

17. If a liability is maturing in the current period, but management has both the ***intent*** and the ***ability*** to refinance the debt on a ***long-term basis***, the liability is classified as long-term. Although "refinancing on a long term basis" may be accomplished in several ways, the simplest examples involve extending the maturity date beyond the next year, or paying off one obligation by taking out another loan with a maturity date beyond the current point.

18. Purchases of real estate or equipment frequently are financed by ***installment notes***, which call for a series of payments. Although installment notes may involve a variety of payment schemes, two commonly used approaches are the following:

    a. Installment payments are ***equal*** to the periodic interest charges with the principal amount due at a specified maturity date.

    b. Installment payments are ***greater*** than the amount of interest accruing each period. A portion of each payment represents interest expense, and the remainder reduces the principal amount of the liability.

19. If the installment payments are greater than the interest accruing each period and continue until the debt is completely repaid, the loan is said to be fully amortizing. A common example of a ***fully amortizing*** loan is a mortgage incurred upon purchase of real estate, payable in equal monthly installments over a period of 30 years. Over the life of a fully amortizing loan, the monthly payments include interest charges as well as repayment of the entire principal; there is no "balloon payment" at the due date for any remaining principal amount.

20. An ***amortization table*** is a schedule that indicates how installment payments are allocated between interest expense and repayment of principal. An amortization table begins with the original amount of the liability. If we assume equal ***monthly payments, interest*** expense is computed by applying the monthly interest rate to the unpaid balance at the beginning of that month. The portion of each payment that reduces the amount of the liability is simply the remainder of the payment. Although the amount of the monthly payment remains the same, the amount of interest expense ***decreases*** every month.

21. Up to this point, we have discussed liabilities common to most business organizations. We will now focus upon special types of liabilities found primarily in the financial statements of publicly owned corporations.

22. The issuance of bonds payable is a popular form of long-term financing in which a large loan is split into a great many units, called bonds, usually in the face amount of $1,000 each. A corporation issuing bonds to the general public must first obtain approval from the SEC, and usually utilizes the services of an **underwriter**. The underwriter guarantees the issuing corporation a specific price for the entire bond issue and makes a profit by selling the bonds to the public at a higher price. (The corporation records the issuance of bonds at the net amount received from the underwriter.)

23. Bonds of large, well-established companies are readily transferable because they are generally traded on one or more securities exchanges. The quotations for bonds are usually given in terms of a percentage of the par value. Thus, a $1,000 bond sold at 101 7/8 would bring $1,018.75, before deducting commissions or taking accrued interest into account.

24. A major advantage of raising capital by issuing bonds rather than stock is that bond interest payments are **deductible** in determining taxable income, whereas dividend payments are not. Also, if a company can earn a return higher than the fixed cost of bonds, net income and earnings per share will increase. If stock were issued, the additional shares would tend to offset the increase in earnings on a per share basis.

25. Bonds generally pay interest every six months. If bonds are issued or sold between interest dates, the buyer pays the seller for any accrued interest.

26. There usually are three accountable events in the life of a bond issue; (1) issuance, (2) interest payments, and (3) retirement of the bonds.

27. In the chapter, we assume that bonds are issued "at par"—that is, at their face amount or **maturity value**. The basic entry is a debit to Cash and a credit to Bonds Payable. If the bonds are issued **between interest dates**, the buyer is charged for the interest which has accrued since the last interest payment date. The amount of this accrued interest is included in the debit to Cash and also is credited to an account entitled Accrued Interest Payable. (The issuance of bonds at a discount or premium is discussed in the *Supplemental Topic section of this chapter, beginning with Highlight 56.)

28. Interest payments are recorded by debiting Interest Expense (and Accrued Interest Payable, if any), and crediting Cash. At the end of the accounting period, an adjusting entry is made to accrue a liability for any bond interest payable relating to the current period.

29. When bonds mature, the last interest payment is made and recorded, and the bonds are retired. If the bonds are retired at their maturity value, the entry consists of a debit to Bonds Payable and a credit to Cash.

30. While they are outstanding, bonds trade at market prices. These prices represent the **present value** to investors of the future interest payments and the maturity value of the bonds.

31. The **present value** of a future cash payment is the amount that a knowledgeable investor would pay today for the right to receive that future payment. The present value will always be less than the future amount because money on hand today can be invested to become equivalent to a larger amount in the future. This principle is sometimes called the **time value of money**.

32. The rate of interest that will cause a given present value to increase to a given future amount is called the **discount rate**, or effective rate. At any given time, the effective interest rate required by investors is the **going market rate** of interest.

33. The price at which bonds sell is the present value to investors of the future principal and interest payments. The **higher** the going market rate of interest, the **less** investors will pay for bonds with a given contract rate of interest.

34. Thus, bond prices **vary inversely** with market interest rates. As interest rates rise, bond prices (the present value of the future cash flows) fall. As interest rates fall, bond prices rise.

35. If the market rate of interest is higher than the contractual rate stated on the bond, the bond will sell at *discount*—that is, at a price below its maturity value. If the market rate is below the contract rate, the bond will sell at a *premium*—a price *above* maturity value.

36. Corporate bonds are traded on organized securities exchanges at quoted market prices. After bonds are issued, their market prices vary inversely with changes in market interest rates. These fluctuations in interest rates have a far greater effect upon the market prices of long-term bonds than upon the prices of short-term bonds. In addition to the impact of current interest rates, the market prices of bonds are influenced by the length of time remaining until maturity. As a bond nears its maturity date, its market price normally moves closer to maturity value.

37. If bonds are retired before maturity at a price above their carrying value, a loss results; if bonds are retired at a price below their carrying value, a gain is realized. Gains and losses on the early retirement of bonds should be shown in the income statement as *extraordinary items*.

38. A *lease* is a contract in which the *lessor* gives the *lessee* the right to use an asset in return for periodic rental payments. Lease contracts may be *operating leases*, in which the lessor retains the risks and returns of ownership, or *capital leases*, in which the objectives are to provide financing to the lessee for the eventual purchase of the property. Lessees should make full disclosure of the terms of all noncancelable leases in their financial statements.

39. In an operating lease, the periodic rentals are recorded as revenue by the lessor and as rental expense by the lessee. No liability is recognized by the lessee other than for any accrued monthly rentals.

40. A capital lease, which is essentially equivalent to a sale and purchase, should be recorded as a sale by the lessor and as a purchase by the lessee. The asset and related liability should be recorded by the lessee at the *present value* of the future lease payments. The lessee should depreciate the asset over its estimated useful life rather than over the life of the lease.

41. A lease which meets *any one* of the following criteria must be accounted for as a *capital* lease:

    a. Lease *transfers ownership* of the property to the lessee at the end of the lease.

    b. Lease contains a *bargain purchase option*.

    c. *Lease term* is *at least 75%* of the estimated useful life of the leased property.

    d. *Present value of the minimum lease payments is at least 90%* of the fair value of the leased property.

42. A pension plan is a contract between a company and its employees under which the company agrees to pay retirement benefits to eligible employees. In a *funded* pension plan, the employer makes regular payments into a pension fund managed by an independent trustee, such as an insurance company (debit Pension Expense and credit Cash). A pension plan is considered *fully funded* when the company pays to the trustee the entire amount calculated by the actuary as the current year's expense. In a fully funded pension plan, the trustee assumes all responsibility for paying retirement benefits to employees and *no pension liability* appears in the company's balance sheet.

43. *Nonpension retirement benefits*, such as health insurance, are accounted for in the same manner as are pension benefits, with one major difference: most companies have not fully funded their obligations for nonpension retirement benefits. That is, the amount of current year expense computed by the actuary is only partially paid in cash each year. Recognition of annual expense in this situation involves a debit to Nonpension Retirement Benefit Expense and credits to Cash (amount funded) and to Unfunded Liability for Nonpension Retirement Benefits (amount not funded).

44. Unfunded postretirement costs, like depreciation, are *noncash* expenses, meaning that no cash outlay is required in the near term. As these costs can be very large, they represent a major difference *between net income and net cash flow*.

45. Income taxes expense reported in a company's *income statement* is based upon the items of revenue and expense recognized during the current year according to *generally accepted accounting principles*. *Income tax regulations* govern items to be reported in the *income tax return* and often allow corporations to postpone payment of taxes to a future period. The portion of a company's income taxes expense that must be paid when the current tax return is filed is credited to Income Taxes Payable, a current liability. That portion which is deferred to future tax returns is credited to *Deferred Income Taxes*.

46. A company should *disclose* in notes to its financial statements the interest rates and maturity dates of all long term notes, and the total amounts maturing in each of the next five years. The FASB also requires businesses to disclose the *fair value* of long-term liabilities if this value differs significantly from the amount shown in the balance sheet.

47. In evaluating debt-paying ability of a company, short-term creditors and long-term creditors have different perspectives. *Short-term creditors* (interested primarily in immediate solvency) use indicators of fluidity such as working capital, current ratio, and turnover rates for receivables and inventory. *Long-term creditors* are interested in the company's ability to pay ongoing interest obligations and to retire maturing debts.

48. Another measure of short-term liquidity is the *quick ratio*, consisting of "quick" assets divided by current liabilities. Quick assets include only cash, short-term investments, and short-term receivables. Thus, the quick ratio is a more rigid test of short-term solvency than is the current ratio.

49. The *debt ratio* and the *interest coverage ratio* are statistics examined by long-term creditors. The *debt ratio* is computed by dividing total liabilities by total assets, and indicates the percentage of total assets financed with borrowed money. Creditors prefer a low debt ratio. The *interest coverage ratio* is computed by dividing annual operating income by the annual interest expense. Creditors prefer a high interest coverage ratio.

50. Financing a business with debt is known as applying *leverage*. If the return on assets is *greater* than the costs of borrowing (interest rates paid to creditors), applying leverage will benefit stockholders by *increasing* the return on equity. But leverage can be a "double-edged sword." If the return on assets should fall *below* the cost of borrowing, large amounts of debt will dramatically *reduce* the return on equity.

51. In summary, a low debt ratio is a conservative capital structure. A high debt ratio creates the possibility of magnified returns to stockholders, but also the risk of negative returns.

52.* The term *estimated liabilities* refers to liabilities which appear in financial statements at estimated dollar amounts. Although the dollar amounts are estimated, these liabilities are (1) known to exist, and (2) the uncertainty is not so great as to prevent making a reasonable estimate and recording the liability.

53.* *Loss contingencies* are similar to estimated liabilities, but involve much more uncertainty. A loss contingency is a *possible* loss (or expense) stemming from past events, that will be resolved by some future event. An example is a lawsuit pending against a company. Loss contingencies may relate to the possible *impairment of assets*, as well as to the possible existence of liabilities.

54.* A loss contingency (and accompanying liability) is recorded in the accounting records at an estimated amount only when:

   a. It is *probable* that a loss has been incurred, and

   b. The amount of loss can be *reasonably estimated*.

---

* *Supplemental Topic A*, "Estimated Liabilities, Loss Contingencies, and Commitments."

Loss contingencies which do not meet both these conditions are *disclosed in footnotes* to the financial statements whenever there is a least a *reasonable possibility* that a loss has been incurred.

55.* A *commitment* is a contract, or agreement, to carry out future transactions. Although a liability is not recorded currently in most situations, commitments should be disclosed by footnotes to the financial statements if *material.*

56.** If at the date of issuance, the contract rate of interest for a bond issue were below par, the bonds could only be sold at a *discount*. If the contract rate were above market levels, the bonds could be sold at a *premium*.

57.** In practice, most bonds are issued *at* the current market rate of interest. Thus, the bonds will sell in the marketplace very close to their face amount. But an underwriter often buys the entire bond issue from the issuing company at a slight discount, and then resells the bonds to investors at par. Thus, many bonds are issued at a very slight discount.

58.** When bonds are issued at a discount, the borrower initially records a liability equal to the issue price. Over time, this liability increases to the maturity value (face amount) of the bonds. Accounting for bonds issued at a discount is described in 59 below.

59.** When bonds are issued, Cash is debited for the amount received, and Bonds Payable is credited for the *face amount* of the bond issue. Any discount is debited to a contra-liability account called Discount on Bonds Payable. In the balance sheet, the discount is subtracted from the balance in the Bonds Payable account, resulting in a "net liability" equal to the amount borrowed.

60.** Over the life of the bonds, the balance in the Discount account is gradually amortized into interest expense. These entries (debit Interest Expense, credit Discount on Bonds Payable) increase the periodic interest expense and also cause the net liability to gradually increase toward the bonds' maturity value.

61.** The discount should be viewed as part of the total interest expense which is not paid to the bondholders until the bonds mature. However, the discount is recognized as expense *over the life of the bonds*.

62.** Bonds seldom are issued at a premium. If they were, the amount of the premium would be credited to an account entitled Premium on Bonds Payable. In the balance sheet, bond premium is *added* to the face amount of the bonds to determine net liability.

63.** Over the life of the bonds, the premium is amortized by entries debiting Premium on Bonds Payable and *crediting* Interest Expense. Thus, amortization of a premium reduces the periodic interest expense and gradually *reduces* the net liability toward its maturity value.

TEST YOURSELF ON LIABILITIES

True or False

For each of the following statements, circle the T or the F to indicate whether the statement is true or false.

T F 1. Existing liabilities relate to *past* transactions or events, rather than to *future* transactions or events.

T F 2. Liabilities and owners' equity are similar in that both eventually mature.

T F 3. Obligations to pay interest stem from liabilities, not from owners' equity.

---

* *Supplemental Topic A*, "Estimated Liabilities, Loss contingencies, and Commitments."
** *Supplemental Topic B,* "Bonds issued at a Discount or a Premium."

T F 4. Some liabilities are recorded in accounting records at estimated amounts, rather than at the actual amount that will have to be paid.

T F 5. The balance of the account Accrued Interest Payable represents unpaid interest charges applicable to past periods.

T F 6. A company's wages and salaries expense is reduced by the amounts of income taxes and FICA taxes withheld from employees' pay.

T F 7. Unemployment taxes are levied directly upon employees.

T F 8. Social Security and Medicare taxes are levied equally upon the employee and the employer.

T F 9. The interest which must be paid on a long-term installment note payable during the next year is classified as a current liability.

T F 10. The principal amount of a long-term installment note payable that will be repaid within the next year is classified as a current liability.

T F 11. Income taxes payable do not become a liability until an income tax return is prepared and filed.

T F 12. A maturing obligation that will be refinanced on a long-term basis is classified as a long-term liability.

T F 13. The primary purpose of an amortization table is to record the gross pay, net pay, and amounts withheld for an individual employee during the year.

T F 14. An amortization table for an installment note payable probably will show increasing amounts of interest expense for each successive period.

T F 15. Unissued bonds may be reported as an asset in the balance sheet since they represent a potential source of cash.

T F 16. The time value of money concept means that the present value of a future payment is always less than the future amount.

T F 17. The lower the effective rate of interest required by investors, the lower the price at which a given bond should sell.

T F 18. If interest rates rise dramatically after bonds payable are issued, the fair market value of the bonds will rise and should be disclosed in notes to the financial statements.

T F 19. An investor who buys a bond at a premium is willing to earn a lesser rate of interest than the rate stated on the bond.

T F 20. Material gains and losses on the early retirement of bonds payable are reported in the income statement as extraordinary items.

T   F   21.   Leases which contain provisions indicating that they are in effect equivalent to a sale and purchase of assets are called **_operating leases_**.

T   F   22.   When lease payments are regarded as rent expense, no liability for the present value of future lease payments appears in the lessee's balance sheet.

T   F   23.   When the lessee records an asset and a liability equal in amount to the present value of the future lease payments, part of each lease payment is regarded as interest expense.

T   F   24.   A company must disclose in notes to its financial statements the specific terms of every long-term liability.

T   F   25.   The debt ratio and quick ratio are of interest primarily to long-term creditors.

T   F   26.   Creditors prefer a high debt ratio and a high interest coverage ratio.

T   F*   27.   Estimated liabilities are disclosed in footnotes to the financial statements but are not actually recorded in the accounting records.

T   F*   28.   Loss contingencies include all types of losses which may result from future events.

T   F*   29.   The manner in which loss contingencies are presented in financial statements depends upon the degree of certainty involved.

T   F*   30.   A three-year contract by a baseball team to pay a player a specified salary is classified partially as a current liability and partially as a long-term liability.

T   F**   31.   Total interest expense on a bond sold for less than its face value will be the cash paid as interest less the amortization of the discount.

T   F**   32.   If a company issues bonds payable at a discount, the rate of interest stated on the bond is greater than the effective rate.

T   F**   33.   Amortization of a discount on bonds payable increases interest expense and increases the carrying value of the liability.

T   F**   34.   Amortization of a premium on bonds payable reduces interest expense and reduces the carrying value of the liability.

Completion Statements

Fill in the necessary word to complete the following statements:

1.   Liabilities are _____ from _____ transactions.

---

* Supplemental Topic A, "Estimated Liabilities, Loss Contingencies, and Commitments."
** Supplemental Topic B, "Bonds Issued at a Discount or a Premium."

2. When an employer withholds income tax from an employee, the amount withheld will be credited to a _____ _____ account.

3. Most corporate bonds are issued in denominations of $_____ and pay interest _____ a year.

4. For each 9%, 30-year bond issued, Red Car Transport received $925. The market quotation as shown in the newspaper for these bonds would be _____.

5. The _____ _____ of a future payment is always (more, less) _____ than the future amount because money on hand today can be invested to become a _____ amount in the future.

6. Bonds payable reacquired by the issuing company through purchase on the open market at a price (less, greater) _____ than carrying value will cause the recording of a gain, whereas bonds reacquired at a price (less, greater) _____ than carrying value will cause the recording of a loss.

7. The lessee accounts for the monthly payments on an operating lease by debiting _____ _____. The type of lease is often called _____ _____-_____ financing because the lessee records no _____ for future lease payments.

8. In accounting for a capital lease used to finance the sale of merchandise, the lessor debits _____ _____ _____ and credits _____ for the _____ _____ of the future lease payments. When lease payments are received, the lessor recognizes part of each payment as _____ _____ and the remainder as a reduction in _____ _____ _____.

9. * Chrysler Corp. sells automobiles with a five-year limited warranty. At the end of each accounting period, Chrysler records a liability for the estimated cost of performing warranty repairs on cars sold during the period. The liability for warranty repairs is an example of a(n) _____ liability, and recording the related warranty repairs expense in the period in which the cars were sold is required by the _____ principle of accounting.

10. ** In the accounts of the issuing company, the carrying value of bonds equals the face value plus any _____ or minus any _____.

11. ** As the discount on bonds payable is amortized, the amount of the net bond liability (increases, decreases) _____; as the premium on bonds payable is amortized, the amount of the net bond liability (increases, decreases) _____.

*_Supplemental Topic A,_ "Estimated Liabilities, Loss Contingencies, and Commitments."
**_Supplemental Topic B,_ " Bonds Issued at a Discount or a Premium."

Multiple Choice

Choose the best answer for each of the following questions and enter the identifying letter in the space provided.

___ 1. In December, Fallbrook Lumber Co. received an invoice for legal fees rendered in November, payable by January 31. The invoice was not recorded until January 12. As a result of this delay:

    a. Liabilities are overstated at the end of December.

    b. Legal fees expense is overstated for December.

    c. The cost principle is violated.

    d. The matching principle is violated.

___ 2. Which of the following is not included among the current liabilities of a manufacturing company?

    a. The portion of a 10-year capital lease obligation that will be paid in the next 12 months.

    b. The estimated liability for warranty repairs on products sold.

    c. The liability for income taxes withheld from employees.

    d. The contingent liability for an unresolved lawsuit pending against the company, to be determined within the next year.

___ 3. The bookkeeper failed to classify a note payable as a current liability in preparing Burbank Corporation's balance sheet. As a result of this error:

    a. Burbank Corporation's working capital is understated.

    b. Burbank Corporation's current ratio is overstated.

    c. Burbank Corporation's liabilities are understated.

    d. Burbank Corporation's interest expense is understated.

___ 4. The amounts withheld from employees' gross earnings are recorded by the employer as:

    a. Payroll taxes expense.

    b. Current assets.

    c. Contra-asset accounts.

    d. Current liabilities.

___ 5. Which of the following would not be classified as a long-term liability as of December 31, 2002?

    a. Deferred income taxes.

    b. Portion of a 30-year mortgage to be paid off in the next 12 months.

    c. Unfunded liability for nonpension retirement benefits.

    d. Debt maturing in March of 2003 which has been refinanced on a long-term basis.

6. Albertson Company purchased a parcel of land for $15,000 and in exchange issued a 10-year installment note for this amount, plus interest at 12% per year. The note is fully amortizing and will be paid in 120 monthly installments of $215 each. With regard to this installment note, each of the following is true, except:

    a. Albertson's payments on this installment note total $25,800.

    b. Albertson's first payment includes $150 of interest expense.

    c. Over the 10-year period, Albertson will pay $10,800 interest.

    d. Over the 10-year period, Albertson will pay $18,000 interest.

7. Which of the following is not a characteristic of a corporate bond?

    a. Is a highly liquid, transferable investment.

    b. Has a specified maturity date.

    c. Represents ownership of the issuing corporation.

    d. Pays interest, usually semiannually.

8. The principal tax advantage of raising capital by issuing bonds instead of capital stock is that:

    a. More investors will be interested in purchasing bonds because they can be issued at a discount and the price will be less than the price of capital stock.

    b. Interest payments are deductible for income tax purposes; dividends are not.

    c. SEC approval is required for issuance of capital stock but not for bonds.

    d. The issuing corporation must pay income taxes whenever capital stock is sold, but only when bonds are sold at a premium.

9. On June 1, 2002, Eads Corporation issued $2,000,000 of 10-year, 12% bonds payable. Interest is payable semiannually, each April 1 and October 1. The bonds are issued at par plus accrued interest for the months since the last interest date. The journal entry to record the issuance of the bonds includes:

    a. A debit to Bond Interest Expense of $40,000.

    b. A debit to Cash of $2,040,000.

    c. A credit to Premium on Bonds Payable of $40,000.

    d. A credit to Bond Interest Payable of $80,000.

10. Refer to the data in question 9 above. How much bond interest expense should be reported in Eads Corporation's income statement for the year ended December 31, 2002, with respect to the bonds payable?

    a. $120,000.

    b. $ 80,000.

    c. $160,000.

    d. $140,000.

_ 11. A corporation that wishes to retire its bonds payable:

    a. Must wait until the maturity date.

    b. Must pay bondholders a price equal to the carrying value of the bonds payable.

    c. Will recognize an extraordinary loss on the retirement if the price paid is greater than the *face value* of the bonds payable.

    d. Will recognize an extraordinary gain on the retirement if the price paid is less than the *carrying value* of the bonds.

_ 12. Assume that a capital lease is erroneously treated as an operating lease in the accounting records of the lessee. One effect of this error will be:

    a. An overstatement of assets and liabilities

    b. An overstatement of rent expense and understatement of interest expense and depreciation expense.

    c. An understatement of rent expense and an overstatement of liabilities.

    d. None of the above.

_ 13. Which of the following would be perceived as *most favorable* by holders of a corporation's debt maturing in seven years?

    a. High current ratio.

    b. Low debt ratio.

    c. Low inventory turnover ratio.

    d. Low interest coverage ratio.

_ 14. * A *loss contingency* is recorded in the accounts when:

    a. It is reasonably possible that a loss has been incurred and the amount of loss can be estimated.

    b. It is probable that a loss has been incurred.

    c. All uncertainty surrounding the loss situation is resolved.

    d. It is probable that a loss has been incurred and the amount of loss can be reasonably estimated.

_ 15. * Loss contingencies relating to pending litigation usually are:

    a. Disclosed in notes to the financial statements.

    b. Shown as current liabilities in the balance sheet.

    c. Shown as extraordinary items in the income statement.

    d. Not disclosed or recorded until the litigation has been settled.

---

* *Supplemental Topic A,* "Estimated Liabilities, Loss Contingencies, and Commitments."

_____ 16. ** The discount on bonds payable is best described as:

    a. An element of interest expense on borrowed funds that will be paid by the issuing corporation at maturity.

    b. The payment of periodic interest at less than the rate called for in the bond contract.

    c. An amount below par which the bondholder may be called upon to make good.

    d. An asset representing interest that has been paid in advance.

_____ 17. ** The account Premium on Bonds Payable is best classified in the balance sheet as:

    a. An addition to bonds payable.

    b. A restriction of retained earnings.

    c. A deduction from bonds payable.

    d. An asset.

Exercises

1. Listed below are twelve technical accounting terms emphasized in this chapter.

Unfunded pension liability	*Loss contingency*
Deferred income taxes	*Commitment*
Bond premium	*Unemployment tax*
Bond discount	*Interest coverage rate*
Present value of future cash flows	*Capital lease*
Principal amount	*Applying leverage*

Each of the following statements may (or may not) describe one of these technical terms. In the space provided below each statement, indicate the accounting term described, or answer "None" if the statement does not correctly describe any of the terms.

a. An element of interest expense included in the maturity value of bonds payable.

_____

b. The valuation concept applied to capital lease obligations.

_____

c. The portion of a loan payment representing repayment of the original amount borrowed.

_____

d. A liability that appears in the balance sheet of every company which offers its workers a pension plan.

_____

** *Supplemental Topic B, "Bonds Issued at a Discount or a Premium."*

e. Financing a business with equity capital.

_____

f. A liability that results from using straight-line depreciation in financial statements and MACRS in income tax returns.

_____

g. The risk that losses in future business operations may result in net losses.

_____

h. A payroll tax shared jointly by employers and employees.

_____

i. A measure of debt paying ability used primarily by short-term creditors.

_____

j. A lease agreement in which the lessee treats the lease payments as rental expense.

_____

2. Shown below is a summary of the annual payroll data for Carter Company:

Wages and salaries expense (gross pay)............................		$500,000
Amounts withheld from employees' pay:		
Income taxes	$60,000	
Social Security and Medicare	45,000	105,000
Payroll taxes expenses:		
Social Security and Medicare	45,000	
Unemployment taxes..	12,000	57,000
Workers' compensation premiums		15,000
Group health insurance premiums (paid by employer)		75,000
Contributions to employees' pension plan (paid by employer and fully funded)		30,000
Cost of other postretirement benefits:		
Funded	$16,000	
Unfunded	$18,000	34,000

a. Compute Carter's total payroll-related expense for the year.

$_____

b. Compute the company's cash outlays during the year for payroll-related expenses (assume all short-term obligations such as insurance premiums and payroll taxes have been paid).

$_____

c. Compute the annual "take home pay" of Carter's employees.

$_____

3.   On October 31, year 1, Conrad Township signed a five-year installment note payable in the amount of $60,000 in exchange for two school buses. The note is fully amortizing and payable in equal monthly installments of $1,335, which include interest computed at an annual rate of 12%. The first monthly payment is made on November 30, year 1. Complete the amortization table following for the first three payments, and then answer the following questions.

a.   Compute the amount of interest expense on this note recognized by Conrad Township in **year 1:** $_____

b.   Conrad's balance sheet at December 31, year 1, includes a total liability for this note payable of $_____. (Do not separate into current and long-term portions.)

c.   Over the five-year life of the note, how much interest will Conrad Township pay? $_____.

Payment Date	Monthly Payment	Interest Expense	Repayment of Principal	Unpaid Balance
Issuance	----	----	----	$60,000
11/30/year 1	$1,335	$_____	$_____	$_____
12/31/year 1	$1,335	$_____	$_____	$_____
1/31/year 2	$1,335	$_____	$_____	$_____

4.   On March 1, year 1, Bestek Corporation issued at par $8 million of 12%, 10-year bonds payable. Interest is payable semiannually each March 1 and September 1.

a.   The amount of cash paid to bondholders for interest in year 1 is $_____.

b.   Show adjusting entry (if any) necessary at December 31, year 1, regarding this bond issue.

c.   Interest expense on this bond issue reported in Bestek's year 1-**income statement** is _____.

d.   Bestek's balance sheet at December 31, year 1 includes bonds payable of $_____ and interest payable of $_____. (Indicate $0 or "None" if the item is not reported.)

5.**   On July 1, year 1, Caldwell Company issued $600,000 of 10%, 10-year bonds with interest payable on March 1 and September 1. The company received cash of $614,200, including the accrued interest from March 1, year 1.

Bond discount or premium is amortized at each interest payment date and at year-end using the straight-line method. Place the correct answer to each of the following questions in the space provided. (Use the space provided below for computations.)

     a.   What was the amount of accrued interest on July 1, year 1? $_____.

     b.   What amount of discount or premium was associated with these bonds on the day they were issued? $_____. (indicate discount or premium)

     c.   What was the amount of cash paid to bondholders on September 1, year 1? $_____.

     d.   What amount of accrued interest payable should appear on the balance sheet on December 31, year 1? $_____.

     e.   What was the amount of the unamortized discount or premium on December 31, year 1? $_____.

     f.   What was the total interest expense for year 1 relating to this bond issue? $_____

Computations:

6.**   From the data in Exercise 5, prepare journal entries required on each of the following dates:

     a.   July 1, year 1 (issuance of bonds).

     b.   September 1, year 1 (payment of interest and amortization for two months).

     c.   December 31, year 1 (accrual of interest and amortization from 9/1 to 12/31).

Note: A general journal working paper is provided at the top of the following page.

** *Supplemental Topic B*, "Bonds Issued at a Discount or a Premium."

a.	July 1			
b.	Sept 1			
c.	Dec. 31			

157

7.** Listed below are 10 transactions of Marshall-Thomas, Inc.

 a. On April 1, issued at a discount 20-year bonds payable dated March 1.

 b. On September 1, made the first semiannual interest payment on the bonds described in a, above, and amortized the discount for five months.

 c. Made a year-end adjusting entry to recognize interest expense on bonds payable issued at a premium. (These bonds are due in seven years.)

 d. Immediately following an interest payment date, called bonds issued at a premium at a price above the original issue price, but below current market value. (Assume that all interest expense has been recognized through the date of the call.)

 e. Due to an increase in interest rates, the market value of the bonds described in a, above, declined substantially.

 f. Made a monthly payment on an operating lease.

 g. Made a monthly payment on a capital lease. (Assume all remaining principal payments on this lease are classified as a current liability.)

 h. Recorded pension expense on a fully funded pension plan, including the remittance of cash to the trustee.

 i. Recorded expenses relating to postretirement costs other than pensions. Fifty percent of these costs are funded immediately and another 25% will be funded in each of the next two years.

 j. Made an adjusting entry to record income taxes expense for the current year, a portion of which is deferred. (Assume that all deferred taxes arise from the methods used in depreciating plant assets.)

Indicate the effects of these transactions upon the elements of financial statements listed below. (Assume the accounts are closed only at year end.) Use the following code letters: I = Increase, D = Decrease, NE = No effect.

	Income Statement			Balance Sheet			
Transactions	Revenue & Gains	Expense & Losses	Net Income	Total Assets	Current Liabilities	Long-term Liabilities	Stockholders' Equity
a							
b							
c							
d							
e							
f							
g							
h							
i							
j							

** *Supplemental Topic B,* "Bonds Issued at a Discount or a Premium."

SOLUTIONS TO CHAPTER 9 SELF-TEST

True or False

1. **T** Liabilities are *existing* obligations stemming from *past* transactions or events. Obligations relating to future transactions are called *commitments* rather than liabilities. Commitments often are disclosed in notes to financial statements, but are not yet considered liabilities.

2. **F** Liabilities mature, but owners' equity *does not*. In fact, this is perhaps the greatest *difference* between liabilities and equity.

3. **T** Interest is compensation paid to *creditors* for the use of borrowed capital, not to owners for the use of equity capital.

4. **T** Many liabilities can only be estimated at the time that they are recorded. Examples include the amount of income taxes payable and a manufacturer's liability to perform warranty work on products sold.

5. **T** Accrued interest payable is recorded by an adjusting entry recognizing the interest expense accruing over past periods.

6. **F** Amounts withheld from employees reduce the amount *paid directly to employees*, but do not reduce the employer's wages and salaries expense. The portions of wage and salaries expense withheld simply must be paid to tax authorities instead of to the employees.

7. **F** Unemployment taxes are levied upon *employers*, not directly upon employees.

8. **T** The social security and Medicare programs are funded half by amounts withheld from employees and half by payroll taxes levied upon employers.

9. **F** No liability exists at present for interest applicable to *future* periods.

10. **T** The principal amount of an installment note all represents a liability. That portion which is scheduled to be repaid within the next year is classified as a *current* liability.

11. **F** A liability for income taxes accrues as *profits are earned*.

12. **T** If the liability will be refinanced on a long-term basis, *it will not be paid from current assets*. Therefore, it is not classified as a current liability.

13. **F** The purpose of an amortization table is to determine how installment payments are allocated between interest and principal. It has nothing to do with payrolls.

14. **F** A portion of each installment payment usually reduces the principal amount owed. As the liability is reduced, the interest expense of each successive period usually will decrease.

15. **F** When bonds are *issued* (sold), the company receives an asset and records a liability for the bonds payable.

16. **T** Money received today can be invested to earn interest and grow to a larger amount in the future.

17. **F** The selling price of bonds paying a fixed rate of interest varies inversely with the investors' required rate of interest (market rate).

18. **F** Bond prices fluctuate *inversely* with interest rates. If interest rates rise after bonds are issued, the market price of the bonds should *fall*.

19. **T** The investor receives interest checks equal to the stated rate of interest, but at maturity he will get back only the face amount of the bond, not the higher price he paid for the bond.

20. **T** Regardless of whether a corporation purchases its own bonds on the open market or exercises a call provision, the FASB requires that material gains or losses on retirement of debt be reported as extraordinary items.

21. **F** *Capital* leases are regarded as essentially equivalent to a sale of property.

22.   **T** For such *operating* leases, the lessee does not record any long-lived asset.

23.   **T** The balance of each lease payment reduces the recorded lease payment obligation.

24.   **F** It would not be feasible for a large business to disclose the terms of *every* long-term liability. Rather, the liabilities are grouped into categories of similar obligations, and the *range* of interest rates and maturity values is disclosed for each category.

25.   **F** The quick ratio (quick assets divided by current liabilities) is a measure of *short-term* solvency, of interest primarily to *short-term* creditors. Long-term creditors use primarily the debt ratio and the *interest coverage ratio* in evaluating the safety of their claims.

26.   **F** Creditors prefer a *low* debt ratio and a high interest coverage ratio. A low debt ratio indicates that owners have a large financial stake in the business.

27.*   **F** The amounts of estimated items, such as future warranty repairs or income taxes, *are* entered in the accounts and appear in financial statements both as an expense and as a liability.

28.*   **F** Loss contingencies refer to losses which already may have occurred *as a result past events*.

29.*   **T** If the existence of a loss is *probable* and the amount can be *reasonably estimated*, the loss contingency is recorded in the accounts at the estimated amount. If these conditions are not both met, the loss contingency is not recorded, but it must be disclosed if the existence of loss is *reasonably possible*. If the probability of a loss having been incurred is deemed remote, loss contingencies need not be recorded or disclosed.

30.*   **F** This contract is for *future* services; therefore, it is a commitment rather than a liability.

31.**   **F** Interest expense over the life of the bond equals cash interest payments *plus* amortization of the discount.

32.**   **F** Bonds sell at a discount when investors require a rate of return (effective rate of interest) *greater* than that paid by the bonds (stated rate of interest).

33.**   **T** Since the unamortized discount is subtracted from the maturity value of the bonds, the carrying value of the bonds increases as this contra liability is amortized.

34.**   **T** Unamortized premium is added to maturity value of bonds; as this premium is amortized, the sum of maturity value plus unamortized premium (carrying value) decreases.

Completion Statements

1. obligations, past. 2. current liability. 3. $1,000; twice. 4. 92 1/2 5. present value, less, larger. 6. less, greater. 7. rent expense, off-balance-sheet, liability. 8. lease payments receivable, sales, present value, interest revenue, lease payments receivable. *9. estimated, matching. **10. premium, discount. **11. increases, decreases.

Multiple Choice

1.   Answer **d**—liabilities and legal fees expense are both *understated*. The matching principle requires that Fallbrook recognize in each period all the expenses incurred in producing the revenue of that period. By failing to record the invoice for legal fees, Fallbrook omitted the legal fees expense that is to be matched with revenue of December. The cost principle would not be violated as long as Fallbrook valued the liability for legal fees at the cost of the service received, usually the invoice amount.

2.   Answer **d**—the contingent liability due to the unresolved lawsuit against the company would be disclosed in a footnote to the financial statement, unless it is known, or probable, that the manufacturing company will lose or settle the suit. At that point, the liability would be recorded

---

* *Supplemental Topic A,* "Estimated Liabilities, Loss Contingencies and Commitments."
** *Supplemental Topic B,* "Bonds Issued at a Discount or a Premium."

in the accounts and actually appear on the balance sheet as a liability. Answers **a, b,** and **c** are examples of current liabilities—obligations that must be paid within one year or within the operating cycle, whichever is longer.

3.   Answer **b**—by failing to classify a liability as current, current liabilities are understated. This results in a current ratio (current assets divided by current liabilities) that is overstated. Although Burbank's total liabilities are correct, working capital (current assets minus current liabilities) is overstated. Burbank's interest expense is not affected by this classification error.

4.   Answer **d**—the amounts withheld must be remitted to the appropriate taxing authorities or other organizations by the employer and therefore constitute current liabilities from the employer's point of view.

5.   Answer **b**—the portion of long term debt to be paid off in the next year or operating cycle is considered a current liability. Answers **a, c,** and **d** are typically all long-term liabilities.

6.   Answer **d**—total payments of $25,800 (120 months x $215) less amount toward principal of note ($15,000) equals interest paid of $10,800. Interest included in the first payment is computed as $15,000 (unpaid principal) x 1% (monthly rate), or $150.

7.   Answer **c**—an investor in bonds is a *creditor* of the issuing corporation. Answers **a, b,** and **d** are all characteristics of corporate bonds.

8.   Answer **b**—the deductibility of interest payments is a strong incentive for financing with debt rather than equity.

9.   Answer **b**—the amount received is $2,040,000 ($2,000,000 face amount plus *two months' accrued interest* of $40,000). The entry would consist of a debit to Cash for $2,040,000, a credit to Bonds Payable for $2,000,000 and a credit to Bond Interest Payable for $40,000. Since the bonds were issued at par, there is no discount or premium.

10.   Answer **d**—Eads' Year 1 income statement should report *seven months'* interest expense on the bonds (June 1 through December 31). The interest expense computation is $2,000,000 x 12% x 7/12.

11.   Answer **d**—if a corporation can eliminate a liability by paying *less* than the carrying value of that liability, the corporation recognizes a *gain* on the transaction. Answer c is incorrect because the price paid to retire the bonds is compared to the *face value*; it should have been compared to the *carrying value* to determine gain or loss. Corporations may retire their bonds payable by purchasing them on the open market if the bonds are not callable, or if the call price is higher than the market price.

12.   Answer **b**—if the lessee records an operating lease, it recognizes rent expense and shows no asset or liability in its accounting records. Upon entering a capital lease, the lessee records both an asset and a liability; it must record interest expense relating to the liability, and depreciation expense relating to the asset. Answer **a** would be correct if worded *understatement* instead of overstatement of assets and liabilities. The error would result in the reverse of answer **c** also—an *overstatement* of rent expense and *understatement* of liabilities.

13.   Answer **b**—long-term creditors evaluate the safety of their claims against a company's assets by examining statistics such as debt ratio and interest coverage ratio. Long-term creditors prefer a *low* debt ratio, and a *high* interest coverage ratio; thus, answer **b** is more favorable than answer **d**. Current ratio and inventory turnover ratio are measures of short term liquidity, and of interest primarily to short term creditors.

14.*   Answer **d**—loss contingencies are recorded in the accounting records only when *both* of the following criteria are met: (1) it is *probable* that a loss has been incurred, and (2) the amount of

---

* *Supplemental Topic A*, "Estimated Liabilities, Loss Contingencies, and Commitments."

loss can be *reasonably estimated*. If it is only reasonably possible that a loss has been incurred, footnote disclosure is appropriate. All uncertainty surrounding the situation need not be resolved.

15. * Answer **a**—contingent liabilities are disclosed in notes to the financial statements whenever there is at least a reasonable possibility that a loss has been incurred—often this is the situation before the litigation has been settled. If it is probable that a loss has been incurred and the amount can be reasonably estimated, the loss contingency and related liability can then, and only then, be recorded in the accounting records.

16. ** Answer **a**—the issuing corporation receives less than the face amount for bonds payable issued at a discount but must repay full face amount at maturity. This "extra" amount that must be repaid for the use of the investor's money represents *interest expense* (in addition to the cash interest paid semiannually).

17. ** Answer **a**—Premium on Bonds Payable is a credit balance account which is added to bonds payable in order to show the current carrying value of the liability on the balance sheet. Discount on Bonds Payable would be *deducted* from bonds payable.

Solutions to Exercises

1.

a. Bond discount

b. Present value of future cash flows

c. Principal amount

d. None (Many companies have funded pension plans and, therefore, show no liability for pension obligations.)

e. None (Applying leverage generally means financing the business with debt, rather than equity.)

f. Deferred income taxes

g. None (Loss contingencies are possible losses stemming from past events, not future operations.)

h. None (Unemployment taxes are borne entirely by the employer. "Shared" payroll taxes include Social Security and Medicare.)

i. None (The interest coverage rate is used primarily by long-term creditors.)

j. None (This statement describes an operating lease, not a capital lease.)

2.

a. $711,000   ($500,000 + $57,000 + $15,000 + $75,000 + $30,000 + $34,000)

b. $693,000   (All $711,000 from a, less unfunded postretirement benefits of $18,000)

c. $395,000   ($500,000 gross pay, less $105,000 withheld)

3.

Payment Date	Monthly Payment	Interest Expense	Repayment of Principal	Unpaid Balance
Issuance	----	----	----	$60,000
11/30/year 1	$1,335	$ 600	$ 735	$59,265
12/31/year 1	$1,335	$ 593	$ 742	$58,523
1/31/year 2	$1,335	$ 585	$ 750	$57,773

a. $ 1,193 ($600 + $593) (see amortization table)

---

* *Supplemental Topic A*, "Estimated Liabilities, Loss Contingencies, and Commitments."
** *Supplemental Topic B*, "Bonds Issued at a Discount or a Premium."

b. $58,523 (from amortization table)

c. $20,100 5 yrs. x $1,335 = $80,100 total paid

        $80,100 ($60,000 principal = $20,100 interest

4.

a. $480,000 $8,000,000 x 12% x 6/12 (Sept. 1 payment)

b.   Bond Interest Expense   ... $320,000

            Bond Interest Payable $320,000

        To accrue 4 months' interest.

c. $800,000

        $8,000,000 x 12% x 10/12 (bonds outstanding 10 months)

d.   Bonds payable........$8,000,000

        Interest payable......$ 320,000

        (4 mos. Interest accrued since payment date of September 1)

5.**

a. $20,000 ($600,000 x 10% x 4/12)

b. $ 5,800 **discount** [($600,000 ($614,200 $20,000)]

c. $30,000 ($600,000 x 10% x 6/12)

d. $20,000 ($600,000 x 10% x 4/12)

e. $ 5,500 unamortized discount [$5,800 less amortization of $50 ($5,800 / 116 months) per month
        for six months]

f. $30,300 (interest on $600,000 at 10% for six months, $30,000, plus amortization of the discount
        for six months, $300)

** *Supplemental Topic B,* "Bonds Issued at a Discount or a Premium."

6.**

Year 1		General Journal		
a.	July 1	Cash	614,200	
		Discount on Bonds Payable	5,800	
		Bonds Payable		600,000
		Bond Interest Payable		20,000
		To record issuance of bonds.		
b.	Sept 1	Bond Interest Payable	20,000	
		Bond Interest Expense	10,000	
		Cash		30,000
		To record payment of interest for six months, including		
		$20,000 which was accrued on date bonds were issued.		
	1	Bond Interest Expense	100	
		Discount on Bonds Payable		100
		To amortize discount for July and August at $50 per month		
		($5,800/116).		
c.	Dec. 31	Bond Interest Expense	20,000	
		Bond Interest Payable		20,000
		To accrue interest for four months.		
	31	Bond Interest Expense	200	
		Discount on Bonds Payable		200
		To amortize discount for four months at $50 per month		

7.**

	Income Statement			Balance Sheet			
Transactions	Revenue & Gains	Expense & Losses	Net Income	Total Assets	Current Liabilities	Long-term Liabilities	Stockholders' Equity
a	NE	NE	NE	I	I	I	NE
b	NE	I	D	D	D	I	D
c	NE	I	D	NE	I	D	D
d	NE	I	D	D	NE	D	D
e	NE	NE	NE	NE	NE	NE	NE
f	NE	I	D	D	NE	NE	D
g	NE	I	D	D	D	NE	D
h	NE	I	D	D	NE	NE	D
I	NE	I	D	D	I	I	D
j	NE	I	D	NE	I	I	D

** *Supplemental Topic B*, "Bonds Issued at a Discount or a Premium."

164

10

STOCKHOLDERS' EQUITY: PAID-IN CAPITAL

HIGHLIGHTS OF THE CHAPTER

1. The dominant form of business organization in the United States is the corporation. A *corporation* is an "artificial being" which is regarded as a legal person, having a continuous existence apart from its owners. Literally thousands or even millions, of individuals may be the owners of a single corporation; thus the corporation is an ideal means of amassing a great deal of investment capital.

2. Ownership in a corporation is evidenced by transferable *shares of stock,* and owners are called *stockholders*.

3. A corporation offers certain advantages not found in other forms of business organizations:

   a. The liability of individual stockholders for the debts of a corporation is *limited to the amount of their investment*.

   b. Large amounts of capital may be gathered by issuing stock to many investors.

   c. Shares of stock are easily transferable.

   d. A corporation is a separate legal entity with a perpetual existence.

   e. Corporations are usually run by professional management.

4. Some disadvantages of the corporate form of organization are:

   a. A corporation is a *taxable entity* and must pay a high rate of tax on its net income.

   b. Corporations are subject to a considerable degree of regulation and disclosure of their business and financial affairs.

   c. The separation of ownership and management (effective control of corporate affairs) may result in management practices which are detrimental to stockholders.

5. Corporations whose stock can be bought and sold through organized securities exchanges are called *publicly owned corporations*. Publicly owned corporations are subject to far more government regulation than are *closely held corporations*. For example, they must file financial statements and other financial information with the Securities and Exchange Commission. This information is referred to as *public information*.

6. A corporation is organized by filing an application with the appropriate state agency. The application contains the articles of incorporation and the list of stockholders and directors. Costs of organizing a corporation are recorded in an *Organization Costs* account and generally are written off as expense over a five-year period.

7. Corporate stockholders have certain basic rights:

   a. To vote for directors (voting rights generally are granted only to holders of common stock).

   b. To share in profits by receiving dividends (distributions of earnings to the stockholders) declared by the board of directors.

   c. To share in the distribution of assets if the corporation is liquidated. Stockholders *do not* have the right to intervene in the management of a corporation or to transact corporation business.

8. The primary functions of the *board of directors* are to manage the corporation and protect the interests of the stockholders. The directors formulate general policies, declare dividends, and review the actions of corporate officers. The board of directors is elected by the stockholders and often includes *outside* directors who are not officers of the corporation.

9. The corporate officers are the active, full-time professional managers of a corporation. Corporate officers usually include a president or chief executive officer (CEO), several vice presidents, a controller, a treasurer, and a secretary.

10. The owners' equity section of a corporation's balance sheet is called the *stockholders' equity* section. Stockholders' equity includes at least two classifications: (a) capital contributed by stockholders (*paid-in capital*) and (b) capital accumulated and retained through profitable operations (*retained earnings*).

11. Capital contributed by stockholders comes from the sale of shares of stock. In order to appeal to a large number of investors, a corporation may issue more than one class of stock. When only one class of stock is issued, it is generally referred to as *capital stock;* when two or more classes of stock are outstanding, they usually consist of *common stock* and various types of *preferred stock*.

12. The articles of incorporation specify the number of shares of capital stock which a corporation is authorized to issue and the *par value* (if any) per share. Par value (or stated value) represents *legal capital*—the amount below which stockholders' equity cannot be reduced except by losses. A dividend cannot be declared if it would reduce total stockholders' equity below the par value of the outstanding shares.

13. Capital stock is generally issued for a sum greater than the par (or stated) value; the excess is credited to *Additional Paid-in Capital*. Stock is almost never issued for less than par value. In the absence of a par or stated value, the entire proceeds are viewed as legal capital and are credited to the Capital Stock account.

14. Most *preferred stocks* have the following features: (a) full dividends to be paid before any dividends on common stock, (b) cumulative dividend rights, (c) preferred claim to assets in case of liquidation, (d) callable at the option of the corporation, and (e) no voting power.

15. The dividend preference of most preferred stocks is *cumulative*. This means if any preferred dividends are omitted, these dividends must be *made up* before any dividend can be paid to common stockholders. Omitted dividends on preferred stock are called *dividends in arrears*.

16. Dividends in arrears are not listed as liabilities because no liability to pay a dividend exists unless the dividend has been declared by the directors.

17. A share of *convertible preferred stock* can be exchanged for an agreed number of shares of common stock. A holder of convertible preferred stock has greater assurance of receiving regular dividends than does a holder of common stock, while at the same time sharing in any increase in the value of the common stock.

18. An *underwriter* may help a corporation sell a large stock issue. The underwriter guarantees the issuing company a specific price for the stock and makes a profit by selling the stock to the public at a higher price.

19. When stock is issued for assets other than cash, the *fair market value* of the noncash assets or the *market value* of the stock should be used as a basis for recording the transaction.

20. Small corporations sometimes allow investors to *subscribe* to stock by agreeing to pay for the stock in installments or at a future date. When the subscription contract is signed, the issuing corporation debits Subscriptions Receivable for the subscription price, credits Capital Stock Subscribed for the par value of subscribed shares, and credits Additional Paid-in Capital for the excess of subscription price over par value. When the subscribed shares are paid for and issued, the par value is transferred into appropriate Capital Stock accounts.

21. If assets are donated to a corporation, total assets and total stockholders' equity are increased by the fair market value of the assets received. The receipt of the gift is recorded by debiting the appropriate asset accounts and crediting *Donated Capital.* Donated Capital appears in the stockholders' equity section as an element of paid-in capital. No profit is recognized when a gift is received.

22. Cash flows from transactions with owners of a business are classified as *financing activities* in the statement of cash flows. The issuance of capital stock for cash constitutes a cash *receipt* from financing activities. Payment of cash dividends is reported as cash *used* in financing activities. Exchange of a corporation's capital stock in exchange for a noncash asset, such as a building, has no *effect* upon cash flows. However, this type of noncash transaction is included in a special schedule accompanying the statement of cash flows (to be discussed in Chapter 12).

23. The amount of capital accumulated and retained through the profitable operation of a corporation is shown in the stockholders' equity account called *Retained Earnings.* Retained earnings are increased by profitable operations and decreased by net losses and dividends. Thus, the balance of the Retained Earnings account is the accumulated earnings of the corporation since the business began minus any losses and minus all *dividends* distributed to stockholders. Remember, Retained Earnings is an owner's equity account; *it is not an asset and is not a fund of cash.*

24. Corporations may obtain funds by issuing capital stock, by borrowing money, and by retaining the resources generated from profitable operations. The stockholders' equity in a corporation consists of the capital invested by stockholders (paid-in capital), and the capital acquired through profitable operations (retained earnings).

25. Ownership of stock is evidenced by a *stock certificate* showing the name of the stockholder and the number of shares owned. At the time of issue, the stock certificate is signed by the president and secretary of the issuing corporation and delivered to the stockholder.

26. The balance sheet accounts relating to capital stock are actually control accounts. In order to know who the individual stockholders are, the corporation usually maintains a *stockholders subsidiary ledger*. This ledger is continually updated for changes in identity of stockholders.

27. For large corporations, a bank or trust company may serve as a *stock transfer agent* and perform the task of updating the stockholders' ledger. Another bank may act as a *stock registrar* who assumes responsibility for issuing stock certificates to stockholders.

28. When only a single class of stock is outstanding, the *book value* per share is computed by dividing the total stockholders' equity by the number of shares outstanding. When both preferred and common stock are outstanding, the book value per share of common stock is computed by dividing the number of shares of common stock into the common stockholders' equity (total stockholders' equity less the redemption value of preferred stock and any dividends in arrears.)

29. After shares of stock have been issued, they are sold by one investor to another at the stock's current market price. The market value of an investment in stock depends on the expected future return on the investment (dividends and appreciation) and the risk that those returns will not be realized.

30. Investors buy preferred stock primarily to receive the dividends these shares pay; therefore, the dividend rate is one important factor in determining market price of *preferred stock.* The market price of preferred stock also varies *inversely* with interest rates. As interest rates rise, preferred stock prices decline; as interest rates fall, preferred stock prices rise.

31. The dividends paid to common stockholders are not fixed in amount. Although the dividend rate and current interest rates affect the market price of a common stock, the most important factor in the market price of *common stock* is *investors' expectations* as to the profitability of future operations.

32. When the markets price of a corporation's stock appreciates in value so much that it becomes too expensive for many investors, the corporation may propose a *stock split.*

33. A stock split may take the form of any desired ratio. Ratios of 2 for 1, 3 for 2, and 3 for 1 are common stock split ratios.

34. The effect of a stock split is to reduce the stock's par value in proportion to the stock split ratio. In a 2 for 1 split, for example, a $10 par value is reduced to $5, and a shareholder who owned 100

shares prior to the split would own 200 shares after the split. A stock split *does not change* the balance of any ledger accounts.

35.   If a corporation acquired shares of its own stock from its stockholders, the reacquired stock is referred to as *treasury stock*. Treasury stock may be held indefinitely or may be reissued; shares of treasury stock are not entitled to dividends and do not have voting rights.

36.   Treasury stock is generally reported as a deduction from total stockholders' equity in the balance sheet. *Treasury stock is not an asset*. If treasury stock is reissued, the Treasury Stock account is credited for the cost of the shares sold, and a separate paid-in capital account is debited or credited for the difference between the cost and the resale price. Regardless of the resale price, *no gain or loss is recognized on treasury stock transactions.*

37.   The purchase of treasury stock involves a distribution of cash to stockholders. If the company is to keep its paid-in capital intact, it must not pay out to its stockholders more than it earns. Thus, retained earnings equal to the cost of treasury stock purchases is usually *not available* to distribute as a cash dividend.

38.   Cash transactions between the corporation and its owners are reported in the statement of cash flows as *financing activities*. The purchase of treasury stock represents an *outflow* of cash from financing activities. The reissuance of treasury stock provides an *inflow* of cash from financing activities.

TEST YOURSELF ON FORMS OF BUSINESS ORGANIZATION

True or False

For each of the following statements, circle the T or the F to indicate whether the statement is true or false.

T F   1.   Any individual stockholder in a corporation may personally be held liable for all debts incurred by the corporation.

T F   2.   A corporation has continuity of existence which permits the business to continue regardless of changes in ownership or the death of a stockholder.

T F   3.   A stockholder in a corporation does not have the right to transact corporate business or to intervene in the management of the business.

T F   4.   Stockholders of a corporation elect the board of directors, who in turn appoint the top officers of the corporation.

T F   5.   Retained earnings is a fund of cash accumulated from profitable operation of the business.

T F   6.   Dividends are a contractual obligation of the corporation, which must be paid at regular time intervals.

T F   7.   When capital stock is sold for a price higher than par value, the Capital Stock account is credited only for the par value of the shares sold.

T F   8.   In reference to question 7, any amount received in excess of the par value of the stock sold is recorded as a credit to the Retained Earnings account.

T F   9.   Dividends usually cannot be paid on common stock unless the regular dividend has been paid to preferred stockholders.

T F   10.   The expression *double taxation* refers to the fact that the net income of a corporation is taxed both by the state in which it is incorporated and by the federal government.

T F   11.   Dividends in arrears refer to bypassed preferred dividends which must be made up before any dividends may be paid on common stock.

T F   12.   In case of liquidation, the claims of the preferred stockholders are given preference over the claims of creditors.

T F   13.   Common stock of Corporation X pays an annual $1 per share dividend and sells for $15 per share on the open market. The corporation's $1.80 convertible preferred stock is selling for $37 per share and is convertible into two shares of common stock. The holder of 100 shares of the convertible preferred stock should exchange his holdings for 200 shares of common stock because this action will increase his annual dividend revenue from $180 to $200.

T F 14.   An underwriter guarantees the issuing corporation a set price for a new issue of stock and then resells the stock to the investing public at a higher price.

T F 15.   Retained earnings represents stockholders' equity generated from profitable business operations.

T F 16.   The book value of a share of common stock usually approximates the market price of the stock, particularly for growth companies like Microsoft.

T F 17.   In determining whether to extend credit to a business, the balance sheet of a corporation would be more important to the lending decision than would the balance sheet of a sole proprietorship.

T F 18.   The purpose of a stock split is to decrease the market price per share.

T F 19.   A corporation's total stockholders' equity accounts do not change as a result of a stock split.

T F 20.   The purchase of treasury stock reduces both assets and stockholders' equity.

T F 21.   The reissuance of treasury stock for an amount in excess of its cost results in a gain to be reported in the income statement.

T F 22.   The reisssuance of treasury stock for an amount less than its cost results in a financing cash inflow reported in the statement of cash flows.

Completion Statements

Fill in the necessary word to complete the following statements:

1.   The owners of a corporation are _____, and their ownership of shares of stock is evidenced by a stock _____.

2.   Among the disadvantages of the corporate form of organization are _____ _____ and _____ _____.

3.   The two major sources of *equity* capital in a corporation are (a) the sale of _____ and (b) _____ earnings.

4.   When common stock is issued at a price above par value, the _____ _____ of the shares issued is _____ to the _____ _____ account, and the excess is _____ to an account called _____ _____ _____ _____.

5.   Par value represents _____ _____, which cannot be paid as dividends to stockholders.

6. Most preferred stocks are _____ at the option of the corporation at a stipulated price.

7. The conversion of preferred stock into common generally requires a debit to _____ _____ and credits to _____ _____ and _____ _____ _____ _____.

8. A corporation had total assets of $400,000 and total liabilities of $150,000 at the beginning of the current year. At the end of this year it reported total assets of $600,000 and total liabilities of $200,000. During the year it paid dividends of $48,000, representing 60% of its ending earnings. The total stockholders' equity at the end of the current year amounted to $_____.

9. A stock split reduces both the _____ value and the _____ price of a corporation's capital stock.

10. The purchase of treasury stock represents a cash _____ from financing activities, whereas the reissuance of treasury stock represents a cash _____ from financing activities.

Multiple Choice

Choose the best answer for each of the following questions and enter the identifying letter in the space provided.

___ 1. One of the following is *not* a characteristic of the corporate form of organization:
    a. Limited liability of shareholders.

    b. Mutual agency.

    c. Centralized authority.

    d. Continuous existence.

___ 2. Title to the assets of a corporation is legally held by:
    a. The stockholders, jointly and severally.

    b. The corporation, as a legal entity.

    c. The president of the corporation in trust for the stockholders.

    d. The board of directors, as trustees.

___ 3. The *directors* of a corporation are responsible for:
    a. Declaring dividends.

    b. Maintaining stockholder records.

    c. The day-to-day managing of the business.

    d. Preparation of accounting records and financial statements.

___ 4.   One of the following is *not* an officer of a corporation:
    a.   Stock registrar.

    b.   Controller.

    c.   Secretary.

    d.   Treasurer.

___ 5.   For which of the following types of organizations would a creditor consider the balance sheet of the business most important to making a lending decision?
    a.   A sole proprietorship.

    b.   A general partnership.

    c.   A limited partnership.

    d.   A corporation.

___ 6.   Which of the following is most relevant in determining the cost of assets acquired in exchange for capital stock?
    a.   Par or stated value of the stock.

    b.   Market value of the stock.

    c.   Issuance price of stock already outstanding.

    d.   Estimated useful life of the assets.

___ 7.   Which of the following is *not* a characteristic of most preferred stock issues?
    a.   Preference as to dividends.

    b.   Participating clause.

    c.   Preference as to assets in event of liquidation.

    d.   No voting power.

___ 8.   Which of the following is *least* important in determining the fair market value of a share of stock?
    a.   Dividend rate per share.

    b.   Book value per share.

    c.   Investors' expectations as to future profitability of the company.

    d.   The par of stated value per share.

___ 9.   Which of the following does *not* increase the number of shares of capital stock outstanding?
    a.   A stock split.

    b.   The reissuance of treasury stock.

    c.   A new public offering of capital stock by an underwriter.

    d.   The purchase of treasury stock.

Exercises

1. Listed below are eight technical accounting terms emphasized in this chapter.

   Double taxation   *Legal capital*
   Preferred stock   *Corporation*
   Common stock   *Stock Split*
   Treasury stock   *Underwriter*

   Each of the following statements may (or may not) describe one of these technical terms. In the space provided below each statement, indicate the accounting term described, or answer "None" if the statement does not correctly describe any of the terms.

   a. Shares of a corporation's stock which have been issued and reacquired, but not canceled.

   _____

   b. An amount equal to the par value or stated value of capital stock issued.

   _____

   c. A disadvantage of the corporate form of organization.

   _____

   d. A bank or trust company retained by a corporation to maintain its records of capital stock ownership and make transfers from one investor to another.

   _____

   e. A classification of stock without voting rights.

   _____

   f. A classification of stock with voting rights.

   _____

   g. An increase in the number of shares outstanding with a corresponding decrease in the par value per share.

   _____

   h. A business organized as a legal entity separate from its owners.

   _____

2. Eastern Corporation has outstanding 10,000 shares each of two classes of $100 par value stock: 5% cumulative preferred stock and common stock. The corporation reported a deficit of $20,000 at the beginning of Year 2, and preferred dividends for Year 1 were in arrears. During Year 2 the corporation earned $180,000. How large a dividend per share did the corporation pay on the common stock if the balance in retained earnings at the end of Year 2 amounted to $25,000? Use the space below for computations.

   Dividends per share $_____

3. Complete the stockholders' equity section from the account balances shown below:

Organization costs	$ 7,000
Retained earnings	128,000
Additional paid-in capital: preferred stock	10,000
Common stock, no-par value, 50,000 shares	200,000
$9 preferred stock, $100 par, 1,000 shares	100,000
Receivable from underwriters (from sale of stock)	40,000
Plant and equipment	315,000
Accumulated depreciation	125,000
Notes payable	100,000
Donated capital	65,000

Stockholders' equity:	
$9 preferred stock, $100 par value, 1,000 shares issued and outstanding	$
Total paid-in capital	$
Total stockholders' equity	$

4. The book value of a share of capital stock is $10 per share. For each of the independent events listed below, use a check mark to indicate whether the transaction or event will increase, decrease, or have no effect on the book value per share of stock.

	Transaction or Event	Increase	Decrease	No Effect
a	Declaration of cash dividend			
b	Net income is reported for latest year			
c	Additional stock is sold at $8 per share			
d	Additional stock is sold at $14 per share			

5. Finday Corporation had total stockholders' equity of $12,000,000 at January 1, 2001. During the year, the company engaged in the following activities:

    April 19   Announced a 2 for 1 stock split on the 1,000,000 shares of its $4 par value stock outstanding

    June 12   Purchased 5,000 shares of treasury stock at $25 per share.

    July 18   Reissued 2,000 shares of treasury stock at $15 per share.

    December 31   Reported income for the year of $5,000,000.

    Finday declared no dividends during 2001.
    Total stockholders' equity reported in Finday's balance sheet dated December 31, 2001 will be:

    $_____

SOLUTIONS TO CHAPTER 10 SELF-TEST

True or False

1. **F** Creditors of a corporation have a claim against the assets of the corporation only.
2. **T** The continuous life of a corporation despite changes in ownership is made possible by the issuance of transferable shares of stock.
3. **T** The stockholders own the corporation but do not manage it on a daily basis; the corporate officers appointed by the board of directors manage the business.
4. **T** The owners (stockholders) elect a board of directors who select the president and other corporate officers to manage the company.
5. **F** Retained earnings is an element of stockholders' equity and is not an asset. The total amount of cash owned by a corporation is shown by the balance of the Cash account, which appears in the asset section of the balance sheet.
6. **F** Dividends are paid to stockholders only when (and if) declared by the board of directors; there is no contractual obligation to pay dividends to common stockholders on a regular basis.
7. **T** Regardless of the issue price, the Capital Stock account is credited with only the *par value* of the shares issued.
8. **F** The amount of sales proceeds received that *exceeds* par value is credited to the Additional Paid-in Capital account.
9. **T** Preferred stock is entitled to receive each year a specified dividend amount before any dividend is paid to the common stockholders.
10. **F** *Double taxation* refers to the fact that corporations are subject to income taxes on their income when earned; when that income is distributed to stockholders in the form of dividends, the stockholders must also pay income tax on the amount of dividends received.
11. **T** All dividends in arrears as well as the preferred dividend requirement for the current year must be paid before any dividend can be paid on common stock.
12. **F** Creditors are given preference in liquidation over all stockholders.

13. **F** Although the annual dividend will increase as mentioned, the market values of the two types of stock do not warrant conversion. The preferred stock has a market value of $3,700 (100 shares at $37); the common stock after conversion has a market value of $3,000 (200 shares at $15). The investor could sell the preferred stock and buy *more* than 200 shares of common stock at this time instead of converting.

14. **T** Use of an underwriter assures the corporation that the entire stock issue will be sold promptly and that the entire amount of funds to be raised will be available on a specified date.

15. **T** Retained earnings is an element of *owner's equity*, representing the accumulated profits, less dividends, since incorporation.

16. **F** Book value is a historical concept; the market price of shares reflects the investors' expectations of the firm's profitability.

17. **T** In deciding whether to lend money to a corporation, a lender must rely on the corporation to repay the loan. The stockholders are not personally liable for the debts of the business.

18. **T** A stock split increases the number of shares outstanding, and decreases the market value of those shares in proportion to the split.

19. **T** A stock split is recorded by memorandum only. There are no journal entries associated with a stock split.

20. **T** The purchase of treasury stock reduces both cash (an asset), and total stockholders' equity by the cost of the treasury stock acquired.

21. **F** The reissuance of treasury stock for an amount other than its cost never results in a gain or a loss reported in the income statement.

22. **T** The reissuance of treasury stock for any amount always results in a cash inflow from financing activities to be reported in the statement of cash flows.

Completion Statements

1. stockholders, certificate. 2. double taxation, high regulation. 3. stock, retained. 4. par value, credited, capital stock, credited, additional paid-in capital. 5. legal capital. 6. callable. 7. preferred stock, common stock, additional paid-in capital. 8. $400,000. 9. par, market. 10. outflow, inflow.

Multiple Choice

1. Answer **b**—the concept of mutual agency does not apply to corporations; an individual stockholder has no right to participate in the management of the business unless he or she has been hired as a corporate officer.

2. Answer **b**—a corporation is a legal entity having an existence separate and distinct from that of its owners or management. A corporation, as a separate legal entity, may own property in its own name. The assets of a corporation belong to the corporation itself, not to the stockholders.

3. Answer **a**—an independent fiscal agent (bank or trust company) maintains stockholder records for large corporations; the corporate secretary (one of the officers) may keep stockholder records for a small closely held corporation. The officers are responsible for the day-to-day running of the business; the controller (an officer) is responsible for accounting records and financial statements.

4. Answer **a**—the stock registrar for large publicly held corporations must be an independent fiscal agent, usually a bank or trust company. (In a small closely held corporation, the duties of maintaining stockholder records may be performed by the corporate secretary.)

5. Answer **d**—the corporation is the only type of business organization that is solely responsible for its debts. A sole proprietorship, a general partnership, and a limited partnership all have owners that are personally liable for the debts of the business.

6. Answer **b**—the cost recorded should be the current market value of the asset *received*. However, *if* an appraised value of the asset received is not available, the best evidence of market value of the asset is the market value of the shares issued in exchange. Par value and issuance price of shares already outstanding have no bearing on the current market value of shares to be issued in the transaction.

7. Answer **b**—the majority of preferred stock issues are nonvoting, and have preference over common stock issues as to dividends and assets in the event of liquidation.

8. Answer **d**—par (or stated value) represents the legal capital per share and is no indication of a stock's market value. To some extent, book value may be used in evaluating the reasonableness of the market price of a common stock; however, common stock may sell at a price well above or below book value, depending upon investors' confidence in company management. Answer **a** (and also current interest rates) are major factors affecting the market price of a preferred stock. Answer **c** is one of the most important factors in determining the market price of common stock.

9. Answer **d** –The purchase of treasury stock reduces the number of shares outstanding. A stock split, a new public offering, and the reissuance of treasury stock all increase the number of shares outstanding.

Exercises

1.
a. Treasury stock.
b. Legal capital.
c. Double taxation.
d. None (The statement describes a transfer agent.)
e. Preferred stock.
f. Common stock.
g. Stock split.
h. Corporation.

2.

Net income for Year 2	$180,000
Less: Deficit at beginning of Year 2	20,000
Retained earnings available for dividends	$160,000
Less: Dividends on preferred stock for 2 years	
(10,000 shares x $10)	100,000
Available for common stock	$ 60,000
Less: Balance in retained earnings at end of Year 2	25,000
Dividends paid on common stock	$ 35,000
Dividends per share: $35,000/10,000 shares	$3.50

3.

Stockholders' equity:

$9 preferred stock, $100 par, 1,000 shares issued and outstanding	$100,000
Common stock, no par value, 50,000 shares issued and	
outstanding	200,000
Additional paid-in capital: preferred stock	10,000
Donated capital	65,000
Total paid-in capital	$375,000
Retained earnings	128,000
Total stockholders' equity	$503,000

4.

	Transaction or Event	Increase	Decrease	No Effect
a	Declaration of cash dividend		√	
b	Net income is reported for latest year	√		
c	Additional stock is sold at $8 per share		√	
d	Additional stock is sold at $14 per share	√		

5.

$16,905,000 ($12,000,000 + $0 - $125,000 + $30,000 + $5,000,000)

11

INCOME AND CHANGES IN RETAINED EARNINGS

HIGHLIGHTS OF THE CHAPTER

1. To assist users of an income statement in estimating the income likely to occur in future periods, the results of unusual and nonrecurring transactions are shown in a separate section of the income statement after the income or loss from normal business activities has been determined. Current accounting practice recognizes three categories of "unusual" transactions and accords each one a different treatment in the income statement. These categories are: (1) the operating results of a segment of the business which has been discontinued during the current year, (2) extraordinary items, and (3) the cumulative effects of changes in accounting principles.

2. A *segment* of a business is a component of a company whose activities represent a major line of business or class of customer. The assets and operating results of a segment of a business should be clearly identifiable from other assets and operating results of the company.

3. The operating results of a segment discontinued during the current period are reported separately in the income statement *after* developing the subtotal, *Income from Continuing Operations*. This subtotal presumably is a better indicator of the earning power of continuing operations than is the net income figure.

4. The revenue and expenses shown in the income statement for the year in which a segment of a business is eliminated include *only the revenue and expenses from continuing operations*. The net income or loss from discontinued operations is reported separately; the total revenue from the discontinued segment is disclosed in the notes to the financial statements. Any gain or loss on the disposal of a segment should be reported with the results of the discontinued operations.

5. When an income statement includes sections for both continuing and discontinued operations, the company's income tax expense should be *allocated* between these sections. Only the income tax expense applicable to continuing operations should be deducted as an expense in arriving at Income from Continuing Operations. Any income tax expense (or tax savings) related to the discontinued operations should be considered along with other expenses of the discontinued segment in computing the income (or loss) from discontinued operations.

6. *Extraordinary items* are *material* transactions and events that are *both unusual in nature and occur infrequently in the operating environment of a business*. Examples of extraordinary items include:

    a. Effects of major casualties, such as an earthquake.

    b. Expropriation (seizure) of assets by foreign governments.

    c. Effects of prohibition of a product under a newly enacted law or regulation.

7. When a company has an extraordinary gain or loss in its income statement, *Income before Extraordinary Items* is developed as a subtotal before presentation of the extraordinary items. The extraordinary item is then subtracted from (or added to) Income before Extraordinary Items to arrive at net income.

8. Extraordinary items are shown in the income statement net of income taxes—the amount of the extraordinary item is adjusted for any related income taxes or income tax savings.

9. Items which qualify as extraordinary losses are rare and extraordinary gains are almost nonexistent. Such things as gains and losses from disposal of plant assets and losses from strikes or lawsuits *do not qualify* as extraordinary items because they are not considered both unusual and infrequent in the environment of a business. These items may be separately identified in the

income statement to focus attention on their *nonoperating* nature, but they should be included in Income from Continuing Operations.

10.   One important type of "unusual" loss relates to restructuring of operations. ***Restructuring charges*** consist of items such as losses on write-downs or sales of productive assets, severance pay for employees, and expenses related to relocation of facilities. Restructuring charges are presented in the income statement as a single item in determining *operating* income. However, if the restructuring involves discontinuing a segment of the business, the related expenses are included in the discontinued operations section.

11.   When a company makes a change in accounting principle, such as a change in the method used to compute depreciation, the new method usually is applied retroactively. The cumulative effect of the change upon the income of prior years is shown as a special item in the ***income statement in the year of the change***. This "cumulative effect of an accounting change" is shown net of any related income tax effects.

12.   If an income statement includes several of the special items described above, discontinued operations are shown before any extraordinary items. Thus, Income before Extraordinary Items includes the income or loss from discontinued operations. The cumulative effect of an accounting change upon the income reported in prior years always is shown last among the special items.

13.   Perhaps the most widely used of all accounting statistics is ***earnings per share*** of common stock. To compute earnings per share, the net income ***available to the common stock is divided by the weighted-average*** number of common shares outstanding during the year. Net income available to the common stock is total net income ***less the current year's dividends on preferred stock***. Earnings per share is intended to show the claim of each share of common stock to the earnings of the company.

14.   Convertible preferred stock and other securities convertible into common stock may pose a special problem in computing earnings per share.

15.   Earnings per share based upon reported net income is shown at the bottom of the income statement. If the income statement includes Income from Continuing Operations and/or Income before Extraordinary Items, these subtotals also are shown on a per-share basis.

16.   A *dividend* is generally understood to mean a pro rata cash distribution by a corporation to its stockholders. Dividends are declared by the board of directors after giving careful consideration to such factors as the balance in retained earnings and the company's cash position. Four dates are usually involved in the distribution of a dividend:

   a.   Date of declaration.

   b.   Date of record.

   c.   Ex-dividend date.

   d.   Date of payment.

17.   Dividends paid in a form other than cash, such as securities of other corporations or merchandise, are called *property* dividends. A *liquidating dividend* usually takes place when a corporation pays a dividend that exceeds the balance in the Retained Earnings account. A *stock dividend* is a distribution to stockholders of additional shares of the corporation's own stock.

18.   A *stock dividend* causes no change in assets or in the total amount of the stockholders' equity. The only effect of a stock dividend is the transfer of a portion of the retained earnings into the Capital Stock and the Additional Paid-in Capital: Stock Dividends accounts. A stock dividend increases the number of common shares outstanding and decreases the book value per share. Each stockholder owns a larger number of shares after the stock dividend, but his or her total equity in the corporation remains unchanged.

19. A "small" stock dividend may range from 1% of the outstanding stock to a maximum of 20 to 25%. Stock dividends of this size are recorded by a debit to Retained Earnings equal to the total *market value* of the additional shares being distributed, a credit to Stock Dividend to Be Distributed equal to the par or stated value of the additional shares, and a credit to Additional Paid-in Capital: Stock Dividends equal to the excess of market value over par (or stated) value of the "dividend" shares. When the shares are distributed, Stock Dividend to Be Distributed is debited and Capital Stock is credited.

20. Stock dividends in excess of, say, 20 to 25% are not considered small and are subject to different accounting treatment. They should be recorded by transferring only the *par or stated value* of the dividend shares from Retained Earnings to the Capital Stock account.

21. Assume that a company discovers that a material error was made in the measurement of the net income of a prior year. How should this error be corrected? Since the net income of the prior year has been closed into Retained Earnings, the error is corrected by adjusting the balance of the Retained Earnings account. Such adjustments are called *prior period adjustments*. A prior period adjustment has no effect upon the net income of the current period and does not appear in the income statement; it is shown in the statement of retained earnings.

22. The *statement of retained earnings* is a vehicle for reconciling the beginning balance in retained earnings with the ending balance. The usual format of the statement is to combine any prior period adjustments with the beginning balance as originally reported. The restated beginning balance is then increased by the net income for the current year and reduced by the amount of dividends declared in arriving at the ending balance.

23. Retained earnings of a corporation are either unrestricted and available for dividends or restricted (earmarked) for some specific purpose, such as to finance an expansion of plant facilities. Most companies disclose restrictions upon the availability of retained earnings for dividends in a note to their financial statements.

24. Cash transactions between the corporation and its owners are reported in the statement of cash flows as *financing activities*. Thus, the payment of cash dividends is reported in the statement of cash flows as an *outflow* of cash from financing activities. Stock dividends and property dividends have no effect upon cash flow.

25. Many companies prepare an expanded version of the statement of retained earnings called a *statement of stockholders' equity*. This financial statement contains all of the information showing all changes in stockholders' equity during the period. While widely used, the statement of stockholders' equity is not a required financial statement.

26. Certain items that change a company's financial position do not enter into the determination of net income. The increase in market value of a portfolio of marketable securities is an example. Such items are described as elements of other comprehensive income. *Comprehensive income* is a term used to identify the total of net income plus or minus these *other* elements. Comprehensive income may be displayed in the financial statements in a separate income statement, in a single income that includes net income and these *other* components, or reported separately in the statement of stockholders' equity.

TEST YOURSELF ON UNUSUAL EVENTS AND SPECIAL EQUITY TRANSACTIONS

True or False

For each of the following statements, circle the T or the F to indicate whether the statement is true or false.

T F 1.   A basic purpose of developing income statement subtotals such as Income from Continuing Operations is to assist the users of financial statements in predicting future earnings.

T F 2.   Assume Rite-Price owns nine grocery stores and two restaurants. The disposal of two grocery stores during the current year should be reported in the income statement as "discontinued operations."

T F 3.   Assume Rite-Price owns nine grocery stores and two restaurants. The disposal of the two restaurants during the current year should be reported in the income statement as "discontinued operations."

T F 4.   Assume that Pepsico, the soft drink company, sells its Taco Bell chain of fast food restaurants. The resulting gain or loss is an example of an extraordinary item.

T F 5.   Assume that a new federal law outlaws use of one ingredient in Weight Begone's product, "Slim Lunch." The company therefore destroys a $12 million inventory of this product. This loss is an example of an extraordinary item.

T F 6.   There is no such thing as an extraordinary gain.

T F 7.   If a company discontinues a segment of its operations during the current year, the amount of Income from Continuing Operations will always be greater than the amount of net income.

T F 8.   Discontinued operations appear in the published financial statements of large corporations more frequently than do extraordinary items.

T F 9.   The "cumulative effect of a change in accounting principle" is actually computed by recalculating the net income of prior years.

T F 10. The income statement of a corporation should always include the subtotal Income from Continuing Operations.

T F 11. Income tax effects should be ignored in reporting the income or loss from a discontinued segment of the business.

T F 12. The statistic "earnings per share" relates to a corporation's common stock.

T F 13. When a company reports discontinued operations, the earnings per share figure appearing in the income statement is based upon Income from Continuing Operations, rather than net income.

T F 14. The investor who purchases shares of the X Co. on the ex-dividend date will not receive the next dividend paid by X Co.

T F 15. A 10% stock dividend decreases the total stockholders' equity of the issuing corporation by 10%.

T F 16. A 10% stock dividend increases the market value of each stockholders' investment by 10%.

T F 17. A 10% stock dividend increases the number of shares outstanding by 10% but does not cause any change in total stockholders' equity.

T F 18. A 100% stock dividend has the same effect upon the number of shares outstanding as does a 2 for 1 stock split.

T F 19. A corporation's stockholders' equity accounts will be the same whether it declares a 100% stock dividend or splits its stock 2 for 1.

T F 20. Prior period adjustments are shown net of income taxes in a special section of the income statement.

T F 21. A statement of stockholders' equity contains all of the information shown in a statement of retained earnings and also explains the changes in the other stockholders' equity accounts.

Completion Statements

Fill in the necessary word to complete the following statements:

1. Large unexpected losses from inability to collect accounts receivable or from the shrinkage in the value of inventories should be taken into account in computing _____ before _____ _____

2. Companies use the _____ _____ number of common shares outstanding to compute earnings per share.

3. The correction of an error in the measurement of the net income of a prior year is called a _____ _____ _____ and is reported in the _____ _____ _____ _____ as an adjustment to the balance of _____ _____ at the _____ of the current period.

4. On January 1, the Avery Corporation had 100,000 shares of capital stock with a par value of $10, additional paid-in capital of $300,000, and retained earnings of $700,000. During the year the company split its stock 2 for 1 (reducing the par value of $5 per share) and subsequently declared a 2% stock dividend (its first) when the market value of the stock was $40. It earned $200,000 during the year and paid no cash dividends. (a) At the end of the year the balance in the Capital Stock account will be $_____; (b) the balance in Additional Paid-in Capital will be $_____; and (c) the balance in Retained Earnings will be $_____.

5. A _____ _____ _____ _____ includes all of the information found in a statement of _____ _____ and also explains the changes in the balances of all other stockholders' equity accounts.

6.   Cash dividends are reported in the statement of cash flows as _____
        _____. Cash dividends have no effect upon _____
        _____. Stock dividends and stock splits have no effect upon
        _____ _____, as well as no effect upon _____
        _____.

Multiple Choice

Choose the best answer for each of the following questions and enter the identifying letter in the space provided.

___ 1.   Which of the following would not be shown in a separate section of the income statement, after the determination of the income from normal, ongoing activities?

        a.   The operating results of a segment of the business discontinued during the year.

        b.   The cumulative effect of a change in accounting principles upon the income reported in prior years.

        c.   An extraordinary item.

        d.   A prior period adjustment.

___ 2.   Revenue and expenses relating to a segment of business discontinued during the year are:

        a.   Netted and reported as an extraordinary item.

        b.   Included in total revenue and expenses as reported in the income statement.

        c.   Netted and reported as a separate item following income from continuing operations.

        d.   Netted and reported as a prior period adjustment.

___ 3.   Which of the following qualifies as an extraordinary item?

        a.   Gain on sale of unprofitable consumer goods division.

        b.   A large loss due to restructuring of the corporation's operations.

        c.   A write-off and abandonment of goods in process inventory because of a new government regulation prohibiting the use of one of the ingredients.

        d.   Additional depreciation recorded because of reduction in useful life of assets.

_____ 4.   The financial statements of Fields Corporation reported earnings of $4,000,000 from continuing operations, a $700,000 loss (net of income tax benefit) from a segment of the business discontinued during the year, a $300,000 decrease (net of related tax effects) in retained earnings as a result of a prior period adjustment, and a $500,000 extraordinary loss (net of income tax benefit). The amount appearing in the income statement as Income before Extraordinary Items was:

  a. $4,000,000.

  b. $3,300,000.

  c. $3,000,000.

  d. Some other amount.

_____ 5.   The *cumulative effect of a change* in accounting principle may best be described as:

  a. A correction of an error in the measurement of the income of prior periods.

  b. A material and unusual event that is not expected to recur in the foreseeable future.

  c. The adjustment to the amount of income reported in prior accounting periods as a result of retroactively applying a different accounting method; this effect is reported in the *current year* income statement.

  d. The income or loss associated with the disposal of a segment of the business.

_____ 6.   Boston Office Supplies reported net income of $2,000,000. The company had outstanding 100,000 shares of $5 preferred stock and 100,000 shares of common stock. Earnings per share amount to:

  a. $15.

  b. $20.

  c. $25.

  d. None of the above.

_____ 7.   The distribution of a 20% stock dividend on common stock:

  a. Reduces the market price per share of common stock outstanding.

  b. Does not change the number of shares of common stock outstanding.

  c. Decreases total stockholders' equity.

  d. Increases the net assets of the corporation.

_____ 8.   In recording a large stock dividend, say 50% or 100%, the amount of retained earnings transferred to paid in capital is generally measured by:

  a. The market value of the stock on the date of declaration.

  b. The book value of the stock on the date of declaration.

  c. The par (or stated) value of the additional shares issued.

  d. The amount authorized by the board of directors to be transferred from the Retained Earnings account.

9. Which of the following is most likely to increase the market price per share of common stock?

    a.   A large stock dividend.

    b.   A 2 for 1 stock split.

    c.   Higher than expected earnings per share.

    d.   The arrival of the "ex-dividend" date.

10. *A prior period adjustment:*

    a.   Is shown in a separate section of the income statement.

    b.   Results in a change in the amount of paid-in capital.

    c.   Shows the retroactive effect upon the income of the prior periods of switching to a different account period.

    d.   Is shown in the statement of retained earnings as a correction to retained earnings at the beginning of the period.

11. A statement of retained earnings could properly disclose each of the following except:

    a.   The declaration of a 10% stock dividend.

    b.   The cumulative effect of a change in accounting principle.

    c.   Net loss incurred by the corporation in the current year.

    d.   A prior period adjustment.

12. Which of the following would effect McGill Corporation cash flows from financing activities?

    a.   The payment of a cash dividend.

    b.   A small stock dividend of 5%.

    c.   A large stock dividend of 50%.

    d.   A 2 for 1 stock split.

13. Which of the following items would never be disclosed in a statement of stockholders' equity?

    a.   The correction of an error in the amount of income reported in a prior year.

    b.   Comprehensive income.

    c.   Cash dividends during the period.

    d.   The cumulative effect of a change in accounting principle upon the income of prior years

Exercises

1.   Listed below are eight technical accounting terms emphasized in this chapter.

Comprehensive income	*Statement of retained earnings*
Date of record	*Prior period adjustment*
Stock dividend	*Extraordinary item*
Earnings per share	*Ex-dividend date*

Each of the following statements may (or may not) describe one of these technical terms. In the space provided below each statement, indicate the accounting term described, or answer "None" if the statement does not correctly describe any of the terms.

a.   Net income plus or minus certain changes in financial position, such as changes in the value of available-for-sale marketable securities.

_____

b.   The date before which you must purchase stock if you want to receive the most recently declared dividend.

_____

c.   Net income applicable to common stock, divided by the weighted average number of shares outstanding during the year.

_____

d.   The effect upon the income of prior periods of retroactively applying a different accounting method.

_____

e.   A financial statement which summarizes all of the changes to stockholders' equity accounts during the year.

_____

f.   A distribution of cash to stockholders in proportion to the number of shares owned.

_____

g.   An event that is shown separately in the income statement because it is unusual, material in amount, and not expected to recur in the foreseeable future.

_____

2.   The Axel Company had issued 105,000 shares of capital stock, of which 5,000 shares were reacquired and held in the treasury throughout the year. During the year, the company reported income from continuing operations of 5% of sales, and a loss from a segment of the business discontinued during the year of $300,000 (net of the income tax benefit). Sales from continuing operations were $4,200,000, gross profit rate on sales amounted to 30%, and income taxes were 40% of income before taxes. In the space below prepare the income statement for Axel Company, including the earnings per share figures.

AXEL COMPANY
Income Statement for the Current Year

Sales	$
Cost of goods sold...	_____
Gross profit on sales (30%)	$
Operating expenses...	_____
Operating income (before taxes)......................	$
Income taxes (40% of operating income)	_____
Income from continuing operations.................	$
Loss from discontinued operations, net of	
income tax benefit.............................	_____
Net loss	$_____
Per share of capital stock:	
Income from continuing operations....	$
Loss from discontinued operations	_____
Net loss	$_____

3.   The income statement of Windjammer Company shows income from continuing operations of $490,000 and income from a segment of the business discontinued near year end of $182,000 (net of income taxes). The company had 100,000 shares of common stock and 10,000 shares of $6 preferred stock outstanding throughout the year. Compute the following earnings per share figures for Windjammer Company:

Earnings from continuing operations:

$_____

Net earnings:

$_____

4.   At the beginning of the year, Bender Mfg. Company had 250,000 shares of $5 par value common stock outstanding. In the space provided below, prepare journal entries to record the following selected transactions during the year:

Mar. 1   Declared a cash dividend of 80 cents per share, payable on Mar. 21.
Mar. 21   Paid cash dividend declared on Mar. 1.
Aug. 10   Declared 5% stock dividend. The market price of the stock on this date was $40 per share.
Sept. 2   Issued 12,500 shares pursuant to 5% stock dividend declared on Aug. 10.

20__	General Journal		
Mar 1	Dividends		
	Declared cash dividend of $0.80 per share on 250,000 shares.		
21			
Aug 10			
Sept. 2			

SOLUTIONS TO CHAPTER 11 SELF-TEST

True or False

1. **T** Unusual and nonrecurring activities are shown in a separate section of the income statement after a subtotal for results of normal business activities.

2. **F** Rite-Price is not disposing of the entire segment of its grocery business.

3. **T** Since the restaurants service a distinct category of customers and the entire segment has been disposed of, this situation should be reported as "discontinued operations."

4. **F** The sale of Taco Bell by Pepsico is shown separately in the income statement as "discontinued operations."

5. **T** This loss is material in amount, unusual in nature, and not expected to recur.

6. **F** Gains *and losses* that meet the three criteria are classified as extraordinary items.

7. **F** In cases where the disposal of a segment produces a gain, the net income will be greater than Income from Continuing Operations.

8. **T** Corporate restructuring, often accompanied by the disposal of segments, has become commonplace.

9. **T** Although the cumulative effect is reported in the *current year* income statement, the amount is determined as the difference between restated net income and originally reported net income for all prior years.

10. **F** The subtotal Income from Continuing Operations is reported only when a segment of the business has been discontinued during the year. In this situation, the income statement includes sections for both continuing and discontinued operations.

11. **F** The income or loss from operating the segment prior to its disposal and the gain or loss on disposal are each shown net of income tax effect in the "discontinued operations" section of the income statement.

12. **T** Preferred stockholders have no claim to earnings beyond the stipulated preferred stock dividends.

13. **F** In this situation, earnings per share figures are required for both the subtotal Income from Continuing Operations and Net Income.

14. **T** An investor who purchases the stock *before* the ex-dividend date is entitled to receive the dividends.

15. **F** In a stock dividend, no assets are distributed; there is no change in total stockholders' equity.

16. **F** Since assets, liabilities, and stockholders' equity of the issuing corporation are the same amounts as before, the market value per share *should* fall in proportion to the number of shares issued. (For small stock dividends, the decrease in market value per share might not be proportional to the percentage increase in shares.)

17. **T** The market value of the shares is transferred from retained earnings to paid-in capital accounts, but total stockholders' equity is not changed.

18. **T** Both double the number of shares outstanding.

19. **F** A 100% stock dividend causes a transfer from the Retained Earnings account to the Common Stock account equal to the par or stated value of the dividend shares, whereas the stock split does not change the dollar balance of any account. Both double the number of outstanding shares without changing the total amount of stockholders' equity.

20. **F** Prior period adjustments are shown net of taxes in the statement of retained earnings as an adjustment to beginning retained earnings.

21. **T** A statement of stockholders' equity is often substituted for a statement of retained earnings because it presents a more complete description of transactions affecting stockholders' equity.

Completion Statements

1. income, extraordinary items. 2. weighted-average. 3. prior period adjustment, statement of retained earnings, retained earnings, beginning. 4(a). $1,020,000; (b) $440,000; (c) $740,000. 5. statement of stockholders' equity, retained earnings. 6. financing activities, net income, net income, cash flows.

Multiple Choice

1. Answer **d** — prior period adjustments are shown in the statement of retained earnings as adjustments to the balance of retained earnings at the beginning of the period.

2. Answer **c** — revenue and expenses relating to a segment of business discontinued during the year are shown separately in the "discontinued operations" section of the income statement.

3. Answer c — an extraordinary item must be material in amount, unusual in nature, and not expected to recur in the foreseeable future. Answers a, b, and d describe items classified as discontinued operations, continuing operations, and a change in accounting estimate, respectively.

4. Answer **b** — the subtotal Income before Extraordinary Items would reflect Fields Corporation's earnings of $4,000,000 from continuing operations and its $700,000 loss from discontinued operations.

5. Answer **c** — the "cumulative effect" of an account change is the effect upon the income of prior periods of retroactively applying the new accounting method. Answers **a, b**, and **d,** respectively, describe a prior period adjustment, an extraordinary item, and discontinued operations.

6. Answer **a** — [$2,000,000 - (100,000 preferred shares x $5)]/(100,000 shares common shares, = $15 per share.

7.   Answer **a** — the market value of stock *should* fall in proportion to the number of new shares issued; however, many factors besides number of shares outstanding influence market prices of stock.

8.   Answer **c** — large stock dividends are recorded by transferring only the par value of the dividend shares from the Retained Earnings account to the Common Stock account.

9.   Answer **c** — stock price is closely related to stockholders' expectations of future earnings. Answers **a**, **b**, and **d** should all cause the market price of the stock to decline.

10.   Answer **d** — a prior period adjustment is a correction of an error in the amount of net income reported in a prior period. As the Income Summary account for the prior period was closed into the Retained Earnings account, the error is corrected by adjusting the balance of retained earnings at the beginning of the period when the error is discovered. This adjustment is reported in the statement of retained earnings, not in the income statement. The adjustment affects retained earnings, not paid-in capital. Answer **c** describes the cumulative effect of a change in accounting principle.

11.   Answer **b** — a cumulative effect of an accounting change upon the income of prior years is shown in the *income statement* of the year of the change.

12.   Answer **a** — cash transactions between the corporation and its stockholders are reported in the statement of cash flows as financing activities. A cash dividend is an example of a cash transaction with stockholders. Stock dividends and stock splits do *not* involve cash.

13.   Answer **d** — a statement of stockholders' equity explains the changes in stockholders' equity accounts. The cumulative effect of an accounting change is shown as a separate item in the *income statement*. Although net income causes a change in the Retained Earnings account, the statement of stockholders' equity does not disclose the individual components of net income which resulted in the change to Retained Earnings.

Solutions to Exercises

1.

a.   Comprehensive income

b.   Ex-dividend date

c.   Earnings per share

d.   None (The statement describes the cumulative effect of a change in accounting principle.)

e.   None (The statement describes the statement of stockholders' equity.)

f.   None (The statement describes a cash dividend, not a stock dividend.)

g.   Extraordinary item

2.

AXEL COMPANY
Income Statement for the Current Year

Sales	$4,200,000
Cost of goods sold	2,940,000
Gross profit on sales (30%)	$1,260,000
Operating expenses	910,000
Operating income (before taxes)	$ 350,000
Income taxes (40% of operating income)	140,000
Income from continuing operations	210,000
Loss from discontinued operations, net of income tax benefit	$(300,000)
Net loss	$ (90,000)
Per share of capital stock:	
Income from continuing operations	$2.10
Loss from discontinued operations	(3.00
Net loss	$(.90)

3.   Earnings from continuing operations:

        ($490,000 - $60,000) / 100,000 shares $4.30

    Net earnings:

        ($672,000 - $60,000) / 100,000 shares $6.12

4.

		General Journal		
20___				
Mar. 1	Dividends		200,000	
	Dividends Payable			200,000
	Declared cash dividend of $0.80 per share on 250,000 shares.			
21	Dividends Payable		200,000	
	Cash			200,000
	Paid dividend declared Mar. 1.			
Aug 10	Retained Earnings		500,000	
	Stock Dividend to Be Distributed			62,500
	Additional Paid-in Capital: Stock Dividends			437,500
	Declared 5% stock dividend on 250,000 shares of $5 par value stock.			
Sept. 2	Stock Dividend to Be Distributed		62,500	
	Common Stock			62,500
	Distributed 12,500-share stock divided.			

12

STATEMENT OF CASH FLOWS

HIGHLIGHTS OF THE CHAPTER

1. We have seen how the income statement measures the profitability of a business. But profitability alone does not assure success; a business must also have enough liquid resources to pay its maturing obligations and to take advantage of new investment opportunities. To some extent, a balance sheet shows whether or not a business is solvent at a particular date. To assist investors in assessing a company's ability to remain solvent, companies prepare a third major financial statement called the *statement of cash flows*.

2. The basic purpose of a statement of cash flows is to provide information about the *cash receipts* and *cash payments* of a business during the accounting period. A second purpose is to provide information about all *investing* and *financing* activities of the business. The statement helps assist investors, creditors, and others in assessing such factors as:

   a. The ability of the company to generate positive cash flows.

   b. The ability of the company to meet its obligations and to pay dividends.

   c. The company's need for external financing.

   d. The reasons for differences between reported profits and the related cash flows.

   e. The cash and noncash aspects of the company's investing and financing activities during the period.

   f. The causes of the change during the period in the company's cash balance.

3. A statement of cash flows shows separately the cash flows from (a) *operating activities*, (b) *investing activities*, and (c) *financing activities*. Each section shows the nature and amounts of cash receipts and cash payments relating to that type of activity during the period. All cash transactions that do not relate to investing or financing activities are included in the operating activities section. Thus, the statement of cash flows summarizes *all types* of cash receipts and cash payments during the period.

4. The major cash receipts from *operating activities* are collections from customers (including cash sales and collections on accounts receivable) and receipts of investment income, such as interest and dividends. Cash payments include cash paid to suppliers of goods and services, and payments of interest and taxes.

5. Cash receipts from *investing activities* include the proceeds from selling investments or plant assets, and the principal amounts collected on loans. (Receipts of interest are classified as operating activities.) Cash payments include purchases of investments and plant assets, and amounts advanced to borrowers.

6. Cash receipts from *financing activities* include proceeds from borrowing and from issuing stock. Cash payments include repayment of amounts borrowed, and distributions to owners, such as dividends or purchases of treasury stock.

7. Some investing and financing activities *do not involve cash flows*. For example, land might be purchased by issuing a long-term note payable. One purpose of the statement of cash flows is to disclose all investing and financing activities during the period. Therefore, the noncash aspects of these transactions should be *disclosed in a supplementary schedule* to the statement of cash flows. (See Highlight 17.)

8. Receipts and payments of *interest* are classified as *operating activities*, not as investing or financing activities. The reason is that the FASB wants net cash flow from operating activities to reflect the cash effects of those transactions entering into the determination of net income.

9. In the long-run, a company must generate positive cash flows from operating activities if the business is to survive. A business with negative cash flows from operations will not be able to raise cash from other sources (investing and financing activities) indefinitely.

10. In a statement of cash flows, "cash" is defined as including not only currency and bank accounts, but also all cash equivalents. *Cash equivalents* are short-term, highly liquid investments, such as money market accounts, Treasury bills, and commercial paper. Transfers of cash between bank accounts and cash equivalent are *not* viewed as cash receipts or cash payments. However, any interest earned from a cash equivalent is considered a cash receipt from operating activities.

11. Captions and amounts appearing in a statement of cash flows are not the titles and balances of specific ledger accounts. This financial statement summarizes cash transactions, but accounting records usually are maintained on the *accrual basis* of accounting, not the cash basis.

12. In most situations, it usually is more practical to prepare a statement of cash flows by analyzing an income statement and the changes during the period in all of the balance sheet accounts *except for Cash*. To illustrate, consider the changes during the period in the Marketable Securities account. Debits to this account indicate purchases of securities, while credits indicate sales. Both types of transactions involve cash flows which should appear in the investing activities section of a statement of cash flows. Of course the credit entries to the Marketable Securities account represent only the cost of the securities sold. This dollar amount must be *adjusted for any gain or loss* appearing in the income statement to determine the cash proceeds from the sale.

13. To determine cash flow from operations, we convert the company's accrual-basis measurements of revenue and expenses to the cash basis.

    a. *Net sales* can be converted to cash received from customers by adding any decrease (or subtracting any increase) in accounts receivable. A similar approach may be used to convert interest revenue from the accrual basis to the amount of cash received.

    b. The *cost of goods sold* can be converted to cash payments to suppliers by adding any increase (or subtracting any decrease) in inventory, and then adding any decrease (or subtracting any increase) in accounts payable to suppliers.

    c. *Expenses* are converted to the cash basis as follows: first, deduct any noncash expenses, such as depreciation; next, add any increase (or subtract any decrease) in short-term prepayments. Finally, add any decrease (or subtract any increase) in related accrued liabilities.

14. The computations described above may be used to compute the major operating cash flows, such as "Cash received from customers." This approach is called the *direct method* of determining the cash flow from operations. An acceptable alternative is the indirect method. Instead of listing cash outflows and cash inflows, the *indirect method* shows a reconciliation of net income to the net cash flow from operating activities.

15. Differences between net income and cash flow from operations are caused by:

    a. *Depreciation and other noncash expenses* Depreciation and amortization reduce net income, but do not affect cash flows of the period.

    b. *Short-term timing differences* Under the accrual basis of accounting, revenue is recognized when it is earned and expenses are recognized when the goods and services are used. In either case, this may differ from the period in which cash is received or paid.

    c. *Nonoperating gains and losses* Nonoperating gains or losses do affect cash flows, but, by definition, do not affect cash flows from operating activities. Most nonoperating gains and losses affect the amount of cash received from investing activities.

16.   The direct and indirect methods result in exactly the same net cash flow from operations. The FASB has stated its preference for the direct method. However, either method is acceptable. The indirect method is covered in the *Supplemental Topic A* in this chapter and in later accounting courses.

17.   Two supplementary schedules accompany a statement of cash flows. The first reconciles the *net income* for the period to the *net cash flow reported from operating activities*. The second supplementary schedule reports *noncash investing and financing activities*, such as the issuance of capital stock in exchange for land.

18.   Of the three categories in the statement of cash flows, the net cash flow from *operating activities* is of most interest to users of financial statements. Even more important than the dollar amount of net cash flow from operating activities in any one year is the *trend* of this cash flow, and *consistency* of the trend, over a period of years.

19.   *Free cash flow* is a statistic used by some analysts to put a company's cash flows into perspective. Free cash flow represents the cash flow available to management for discretionary purposes, *after* the company has met all of its basic business obligations. As there is disagreement as to what constitutes "basic business obligations," different analysts compute free cash flow different ways. One common method of computing free cash flow is to start with net cash flow from operating activities and subtract any net cash used for investing activities as well as any dividends paid.

20.*   Net cash flows from *operating activities* may be reported using either the *direct* or the *indirect* method. Although the FASB encourages use of the direct method, the indirect method is a permissible alternative and remains in widespread use.

21.*   The two methods of computing net cash flow from operating activities are based upon the same accounting data and result in the *same amount of net cash flow*. Both methods convert accrual-based income statement amounts into cash flows by adjusting for changes in related balance sheet accounts.

22.*   The difference between the two methods lie only in *format*. The *direct method* describes the nature and dollar amounts of the specific cash inflows and outflows comprising the operating activities of the business. The *indirect method* reconciles net income (as shown in the income statement) with net cash flow from the operating activities.

23.*   Net cash flow from operating activities differs from net income for three major reasons:

   a.   *"Noncash" expenses* Some expenses, such as depreciation, reduce net income but require no cash outlay during the current period.

   b.   *Timing differences* Net cash flow reflects the effects of current period cash transactions. Revenue and expenses are measured using the concepts of accrual accounting and may be recognized in an accounting period other than that in which a related cash flow occurs.

   c.   *"Nonoperating" gains and losses* By definition, net cash flow from operating activities shows only the effects of those cash transactions classified as "*operating activities.*" Net income, however, includes gains and losses relating to investing and financing activities as well.

24.*   The adjustments involved in reconciling net income with net cash flow from operating activities are determined using a working paper or computer program and do *not* appear in the company's accounting records.

25.*   *Adjusting for noncash expenses* To reconcile net income with net cash flow, we add back the amount of depreciation and any other "noncash" expenses, such as amortization, depletion, etc.

_____

* *Supplemental Topic A*, "The Indirect Method."

26.* **Adjusting for timing differences** Timing differences between net income and net cash flow arise whenever revenue or expense is recognized by debiting and crediting either an asset account (*other than cash*) or a liability account. Accounts giving rise to these timing differences include accounts receivable, inventories, prepaid expenses, accounts payable, and accrued expenses payable.

    a. **Changes in accounts receivable** A net *increase* in accounts receivable indicates that revenue from credit sales exceeds collections from customers. Thus, this increase is *deducted* from net income in order to arrive at net cash flow from operations. A net *decrease* in receivables is *added* to net income.

    b. **Changes in inventory** A net increase in inventory indicates that purchases during the period *exceed* the cost of goods sold. To reconcile net income with net cash flow from operations, we *deduct the net increase* from net income. A net *decrease* in inventory is *added* to net income.

    c. **Changes in prepaid expenses** A net *increase* indicates that cash payments made for items such as insurance or rent exceed the amounts recognized as expense; this increase is *deducted* from net income in order to arrive at net cash flow from operations. A net *decrease* in prepaid expenses is *added* to net income.

    d. **Changes in accounts payable** A net *increase* indicates that the accrual-based figure for purchases (included in the cost of goods sold) is *greater* than the cash payments made to suppliers. The increase is added to net income to arrive at net cash flow from operations. A net *decrease* is *subtracted* from net income.

27.* A **helpful hint** for all related asset and liability accounts that explains timing differences—a net **credit change** in the account's balance is always added to net income; a net **debit change** is always subtracted from net income to arrive at net cash flow from operating activities.

28.* **Adjusting for nonoperating gains and losses** "Nonoperating" gains and losses do not affect operating activities but do enter into the determination of net income. In converting net income to net cash flow from operating activities, we add back any nonoperating losses and deduct any nonoperating gains included in net income.

29.* Nonoperating gains and losses include gains and losses from sales of investments or plant assets, gains and losses on discontinued operations, and gains and losses on the early retirement of debt.

30.* **The indirect method appears in all statements of cash flows**. If the **indirect** method is used to compute cash flows from operating activities, it will appear either in the body of the statement of cash flows or in a supplementary schedule. However, companies using the **direct** method to compute cash flows from operating activities are required to provide as well a **supplementary schedule** showing a reconciliation of net income with net cash flows from operating activities (that is, the indirect presentation.)

31.** A **worksheet** is often used to prepare a statement of cash flows. The worksheet develops the information for the statement by analyzing the changes in the balance sheet accounts.

TEST YOURSELF ON CASH FLOWS

True or False

For each of the following statements, circle the T or the F to indicate whether the statement is true or false.

---

* *Supplemental Topic A*, "The Indirect Method."
** *Supplemental Topic B*, " A Worksheet for Preparing a Statement of Cash Flows."

T   F   1.   A statement of cash flows generally is organized into three major sections: cash receipts, cash payments, and noncash investing and financing activities.

T   F   2.   All cash receipts and cash payments not classified as investing or financing activities are classified as operating activities.

T   F   3.   One purpose of a statement of cash flows is to provide information about financing and investing activities, even if these activities do not involve cash receipts or cash payments.

T   F   4.   Accounts receivable from large corporations are considered cash equivalents.

T   F   5.   A statement of cash flows provides more information about the profitability of a business than does an income statement.

T   F   6.   In a statement of cash flows, the transfer of cash from a bank account to a money market fund is shown among the investing activities.

T   F   7.   In a statement of cash flows, payments of dividends are classified as operating activities.

T   F   8.   Cash payments to purchase merchandise are classified as investing activities.

T   F   9.   In a statement of cash flows, receipts and payments of interest are both classified as operating activities.

T   F   10.   A growing, successful company will usually show a positive net cash flow from operations.

T   F   11.   A growing, successful company will usually show a positive net cash flow from investing activities.

T   F   12.   The easiest way to prepare a statement of cash flows is by analyzing the debit and credit entries in the Cash account.

T   F   13.   Credits to the Notes Receivable account normally represent cash receipts from investing activities.

T   F   14.   Debits to the Notes Payable account normally represent cash payment relating to financing activities.

T   F   15.   If accounts receivable are increasing over the period, cash received from customers probably exceeds net sales.

T   F   16.   Large increases in inventory tend to cause cash payments to suppliers to exceed the cost of goods sold.

T   F   17.   Depreciation expense increases the net cash flow resulting from operating activities.

T   F   18.   Depreciation expense decreases the net cash flow resulting from operating activities.

T   F   19.   The amount of net cash flow from operating activities will be the same, regardless of whether this amount is computed by the direct method or the indirect method.

T   F   20.   Depreciation expense reduces net income but has no effect on net cash flow from operating activities.

T   F   21.   If unexpired insurance decreases over the period, the cash paid to the insurance agency probably exceeds the amount recognized as insurance expense.

T   F   22.   A loss on the sale of a plant asset is an example of a noncash expense.

T   F   23.*   Although the FASB requires that net cash flows from operating activities be reported using the direct method, the indirect method is widely used.

T   F   24.*   Both the indirect and the direct method result in the same net dollar amount of cash flow from operating activities.

T   F   25.*   The indirect method describes the nature and dollar amounts of the specific cash inflows and outflows comprising the operating activities of the business.

T   F   26.**   A worksheet may be used to prepare a statement of cash flows using the direct method but not the indirect method.

T   F   27.**   A worksheet for preparing a statement of cash flows is developed by systematically analyzing changes in balance sheet accounts.

Completion Statements

Fill in the necessary word to complete the following statements:

1.   There are three major financial statements: The _____ _____ measures the profitability of a business, the _____ _____ shows the financial position of the business at the end of the period, and the _____ _____ _____ _____ summarizes _____ transactions.

2.   In a statement of cash flows, cash transactions are classified into the categories of (a) _____ activities, (b) _____ activities, and (c) _____ activities.

3.   In a statement of cash flows, the payment of interest is classified as a (an) _____ activity, and the payment of a dividend is classified as a (an) _____ activity.

---

* *Supplemental Topic A,* "The Indirect Method."
** *Supplemental Topic B,* "A Worksheet for Preparing a Statement of Cash Flows."

4. Of the three major classifications of cash flows, it is most important for a business to show a positive cash flow from _____ activities over the long run.

5. For purposes of preparing a statement of cash flows, "cash" includes currency, bank deposits, and _____ _____, such as money market funds, Treasury bills, and commercial paper.

6. The proceeds from short-term borrowing are equal to the sum of the (debit, credit) _____ entries in the Notes Payable account.

7. The amount of cash received from customers is equal to the amount of net sales, plus any (increase, decrease) _____ in _____ _____ over the period.

8. Net cash flow from operating activities may be computed in either of two ways: the _____ method identifies the major operating cash flows, whereas the _____ method reconciles the reported amount of _____ _____ with the net cash flow from operating activities.

9. The cash flow available to management after basic business obligations have been met is termed _____ _____ _____.

10. * Net cash flow from operating activities differs from net income as a result of (a) _____ _____, (b) _____ _____, or (c) _____ _____ _____ ____ _____.

11. * Depreciation is an example of a _____ _____. Depreciation expense reduces _____ _____ with no corresponding cash _____. Under the indirect method, in reconciling net income with _____ _____ _____ _____ _____, the amount of depreciation is _____ _____ net income.

12. * _____ _____ may arise as the result of revenue and/or expense recognition in an accounting period different from that in which a related _____ _____ occurs.

13. * To reconcile net income with net cash flow from operating activities, the _____ _____ in accounts receivable is deducted from net income, and a _____ _____ in inventory is added to net income.

14. * By definition, nonoperating gains and losses do not affect operating activities. In converting net income to net cash flow from operating activities, we add back any _____ _____ and deduct any _____ _____ included in net income.

---

* Supplemental Topic A, "The Indirect Method."

15. [*] A company which computes the cash flow from operating activities by the direct method must still show a reconciliation of net income to net cash flow from operating activities in a _____ _____.

Multiple Choice

Choose the best answer for each of the following questions and enter the identifying letter in the space provided.

___ 1. A statement of cash flows is *not* intended to provide readers with information about:

    a. The profitability of a business.

    b. Noncash investing and financing transactions.

    c. The ability of a business to continue paying dividends.

    d. The net cash flow from operating activities.

___ 2. Which of the following captions should *not* appear in a statement of cash flows?

    a. Net cash provided by financing activities.

    b. Proceeds from sales of plant assets.

    c. Net income.

    d. Net cash used by investing activities.

___ 3. A successful, growing business is *most likely* to show a negative cash flow from:

    a. Operating activities.

    b. Investing activities.

    c. Financing activities.

    d. Transactions with customers.

___ 4. Which of the following cash flows is *not* classified as a financing activity in a statement of cash flows?

    a. Payment of a cash dividend.

    b. Payment of interest.

    c. Short-term borrowing.

    d. Issuance of capital stock in exchange for plant assets.

___ 5. Which of the following indicates a cash *receipt*?

    a. A decrease in accounts receivable.

    b. An increase in accumulated depreciation.

    c. An increase in prepaid rent.

    d. A decrease in accounts payable.

---

[*] *Supplemental Topic A*, "The Indirect Method."

6. Which of the following indicates a *cash payment*?

    a. A credit change in the Capital Stock account.

    b. A debit change in the Notes Payable account.

    c. A credit change in the Accounts Receivable account.

    d. A debit change in the Cash account.

7. Which of the following will cause cash payments to suppliers of goods and services to *exceed* the amount of expense recorded on the accrual basis?

    a. Depreciation expense.

    b. An increase in accrued expenses payable.

    c. An increase in prepaid insurance.

    d. Payment of a cash dividend declared in a prior period.

8. Dexter Corporation reported net income in excess of its net cash flow from operating activities. A possible explanation for this is:

    a. Depreciation expense.

    b. Nonoperating gains.

    c. Nonoperating losses.

    d. An increase in accounts payable over the period.

9. The accounting records of Tiger Corp. include a $200,000 debit to the Land account. This transaction should appear in a statement of cash flows as a:

    a. Cash inflow from investing activities.

    b. Cash outflow from financing activities.

    c. Cash inflow from financing activities.

    d. Cash outflow from investing activities.

10. During the current year, the Marketable Securities account of Trend Co. was debited for $150,000 and credited for $200,000. The income statement includes a gain on sales of marketable securities of $45,000. Based upon this information, the investing activities section of the company's statement of cash flows should include a cash receipt of:

    a. $245,000.

    b. $155,000.

    c. $195,000.

    d. None of the above.

___ 11.   MedVac, Inc., purchased land by issuing a long-term note payable. No cash down payment was made. In the company's statement of cash flows, this transaction should appear:

      a.   Among the cash flows from financing activities.

      b.   Among the cash flows from investing activities.

      c.   In a supplementary schedule.

      d.   Nowhere, as no cash was received or paid.

___ 12.   Which of the following would *increase* the net cash flow from operating activities?

      a.   Sale of capital stock for cash.

      b.   Issuance of a note payable for cash.

      c.   Sale of goods on credit.

      d.   Sale of goods for cash.

___ 13. *   In a comparison of the direct and indirect methods of computing net cash flow from operating activities, which of the following is *not* correct?

      a.   Both methods begin with items reported in an accrual-based income statement.

      b.   Both methods provide readers of the cash flow statement with amounts of specific cash inflows and outflows comprising operating activities.

      c.   Both methods result in the same amount of net cash flow from operating activities.

      d.   Both methods focus upon net changes during the period in related balance sheet accounts.

___ 14. *   Navarro Corporation uses the indirect method in preparing its statement of cash flows. Under this approach, depreciation expense is added to net income because depreciation expense:

      a.   Represents amounts deposited in a reserve fund maintained for the replacement of plant assets.

      b.   Reduces net income, but results in an inflow of cash.

      c.   Reduces net income, but does not involve an outflow of cash.

      d.   Is a source of cash.

___ 15. *   The debit and credit entries to record several common transactions are shown in answers **a** through **d**. Which situation would *not* give rise to a timing difference in preparing the statement of cash flows using the *indirect method*?

      a.   A debit to Accounts Receivable accompanied by a credit to Sales Revenue.

      b.   A debit to Interest Expense accompanied by a credit to Interest Payable.

      c.   A debit to Inventory accompanied by a credit to Cash.

      d.   A debit to Rent Expense accompanied by a credit to Prepaid Rent.

---

* *Supplemental Topic A*, "The Indirect Method."

___ 16. * The balance sheet of Pickering, Inc., shows a net increase in receivables of $520 and a net decrease in inventory of $280. To arrive at net cash flow from operating activities, net income should be:

    a. Reduced by $240.

    b. Increased by $240.

    c. Reduced by $800.

    d. Increased by $800.

___ 17. * At the beginning of the year, NTA Corporation bought equipment for $1,500 by issuing a note payable. The equipment was assumed to have a 10-year life and was depreciated using the straight-line method. To arrive at net cash flow from *operating activities*, net income should be:

    a. Increased by $150.

    b. Increased by $1,350.

    c. Reduced by $1,350.

    d. No adjustment is necessary as no cash was received or paid.

___ 18. * At the end of the first year of operation, Wilbur Showers, Inc., had the following account balances: Accounts Receivable, $200; Accounts Payable, $300; Inventory, $500. The corporation reported net income of $650 for the year. Net cash flow from *operating activities* should be reported as:

    a. $1,050.

    b. $ 850.

    c. $1,650.

    d. $ 250.

___ 19. * The Jayne Corporation is preparing its statement of cash flows using the indirect method. The following information has been gathered for the current period:

Loss on sale of equipment	$ 7,500
Common stock issued for cash	200,000
Net income	76,000
Depreciation expense	32,000
Cash received from sale of equipment	60,000
Increase in inventory	4,500

Based only upon the above information, Jayne's net cash flow from operating activities is:

    a. $120,000.

    b. $111,000.

    c. $371,000.

    d. $171,000.

---

* *Supplemental Topic A,* "The Indirect Method."

Exercises

1. Listed below are eight technical accounting terms emphasized in this chapter.

   Operating activities   *Solvent*
   Financing activities   *Cash equivalent*
   Investing activities   *Net cash flow*
   Statement of cash flows   *Balance sheet*

   Each of the following statements may (or may not) describe one of these technical terms. In the space provided below each statement, indicate the accounting term described, or answer "None" if the statement does not correctly describe any of the terms.

   a. The financial statement that best describes the profitability of a business.

   _____

   b. Cash receipts during the period, less cash payments made during the period.

   _____

   c. The classification in a statement of cash flows that includes investments made by a business in plant assets.

   _____

   d. The condition of consistently earning revenue in excess of expenses.

   _____

   e. A short-term, highly liquid investment, such as a money market fund.

   _____

   f. The classification of cash flows for which it is most important for cash flows to be positive over the long-run.

   _____

   g. The category within a statement of cash flows that includes investments made by owners in the capital stock of a business.

   _____

2. Indicate how each of the events should be classified in a statement of cash flows for the current year. Use the following code: **O** = Operating activities, **I** = Investment activities, **F** = Financing activities. If the event does not cause a cash flow to be reported in the statement, enter an **X** in the space provided.

_____ a. Collected accounts receivable originating from sales in the prior year.
_____ b. Paid the interest on a note payable to First Bank.
_____ c. Paid the principal amount due on the note payable to First Bank.
_____ d. Received a dividend from an investment in AT&T common stock.
_____ e. Paid a dividend to stockholders.
_____ f. Recorded depreciation expense for the current year.
_____ g. Sold a segment of the business to another corporation.
_____ h. Transferred cash from a money market fund into a checking account.
_____ i. Purchased marketable securities.
_____ j. Made a year-end adjusting entry to record accrued interest payable on bonds payable.

3. The financial statements of Canyon Street Galleries provide the following information:

	End of Year	Beginning of Year
Accounts receivable	$ 29,000	$ 25,000
Inventory	35,000	28,000
Prepaid expenses	500	1,500
Accounts payable (for merchandise)	17,000	14,000
Accrued liabilities	2,000	750
Net sales	320,000	
Cost of goods sold	200,000	
Operating expenses (including depreciation of $8,000)	90,000	
Net income	30,000	

Using these data, compute:

a. Cash received from customers.

b. Cash payments for purchases of merchandise.

c. Cash paid for operating expenses.

4. From the following information, complete the statement of cash flows (direct method) for Tycor Distributors for the year ended December 31, 20___.

Purchases of plant assets	$ 520,000
Proceeds from sales of plant assets	50,000
Proceeds from issuing capital stock	400,000
Proceeds from short-term borrowing	100,000
Payments to settle short-term debt	70,000
Interest and dividends received	40,000
Cash received from customers	1,800,000
Dividends paid	200,000
Cash paid to suppliers and employers	1,400,000
Interest paid	60,000
Income taxes paid	120,000
Cash and cash equivalents, beginning of the year	84,000
Cash and cash equivalents, end of the year	?

TYCOR DISTRIBUTORS
Statement of Cash Flows
For the Year Ended December 31, 20___

Cash flows from operating activities:
    Cash received from customers .... $

    Cash provided by operating activities.................. $
    Cash paid to suppliers and employees .... $(   )

    Cash disbursed for operating activities................   (_____)
Net cash flow from operating activities....................... $
Cash flows from investing activities: $

Net cash used by investing activities............................ $(   )
Cash flows from financing activities:
    Proceeds from short-term borrowing.................... $

Net cash provided by financing activities ....
Net increase (decrease) in cash.................................... $
Cash and cash equivalents, beginning of the year ....
Cash and cash equivalents, end of year .... $

5.*   Listed below are eight technical accounting terms emphasized in *Supplemental Topic A.*

Noncash expense	*Operating activities*
Indirect method	*Direct method*
Net cash flow	*Timing difference*
Nonoperating gains and losses	*Net cash flow from operating activities*

Each of the following statements may (or may not) describe one of these technical terms. In the space provided below each statement, indicate the accounting term described, or answer "None" if the statement does not correctly describe any of the terms.

a.   Amounts reported in the income statement that relate to investing and/or financing activities.

    _____

b.   A method of reporting net cash flow from operations by listing specific types of cash inflows and outflows.

    _____

_____
* *Supplemental Topic A*, "The Indirect Method."

c. The category of expense which reduces net income, yet requires no cash outflow.

_____

d. Amount determined by application of either the direct method or the indirect method.

_____

e. Cash receipts during the period, less cash payments made during the period.

_____

f. The result of recognizing either a revenue or an expense with no corresponding cash flow during the same accounting period.

_____

g. A measurement of a company's performance reflecting both operating and nonoperating transactions on an accrual basis.

_____

6.* In the computation of net cash flow from operating activities by the **indirect method**, determine whether each of the following items would be added to net income, deducted from net income, or omitted from the computation. Indicate your answer in the space provided by using the following symbols: + (added to net income), − (deducted from net income), or **O** (omitted from computation).

_____ a. Depreciation for the year amounted to $500.

_____ b. Dividends were declared in December, to be paid early next year.

_____ c. Accounts receivable increased by $400 during the year.

_____ d. Dividends, declared at the end of last year, were paid to shareholders during the current year.

_____ e, Gain was recognized when equipment was sold in exchange for a note receivable.

_____ f. Accounts payable decreased during the year.

_____ g. Prepaid expenses increased during the year.

---

* *Supplemental Topic A*, "The Indirect Method."

7.* The data below was take from the financial statements of the Stilwell Company:
Income statement:

	2002
Net income	$65,000
Depreciation expense	23,000
Amortization of patents	7,000
Loss on sale of investments	15,000
Gain on sale of land	6,000

Balance sheet:	**12/31/02**	**12/31/01**
Accounts receivable	$55,000	$62,000
Inventory	78,000	82,000
Prepaid advertising	4,000	2,000
Accounts payable (to supplier)	58,000	61,000
Accrued expenses payable	27,000	21,000

Compute the partial statement of cash flows for the year ended December 31, 2002, showing the computation of *net cash flow from operating activities by the indirect method:*

STILWELL COMPANY
Partial Statement of Cash Flows
For the Year Ended December 31, 2002

Cash flow from operating activities:
Net income.. $
Add:

_____

Subtotal.. $
Less:

_____

Net cash flow from operating activities.................................... $_____

SOLUTIONS TO CHAPTER 12 SELF-TEST

True or False

1. **F** The three major categories of cash flows are (a) operating activities, (b) investing activities, and (c) financing activities.

2. **T** If a transaction does not fall into either the financing or investing category, by default it is considered an operating activity.

3. **T** The FASB requires that a supplementary schedule disclosing any "noncash" investing and financing activities accompany the statement of cash flows.

---

* *Supplemental Topic A*, "The Indirect Method."

4.	F Cash equivalents are short-term, highly liquid investments, such as money market funds, commercial paper, and Treasury bills.

5.	F The income statement measures profitability, whereas the statement of cash flows provides information about cash flows from operating, investing, and financing activities.

6.	F Cash in a money market account is considered a cash equivalent.

7.	F Payments to owners, such as dividends, are classified as financing activities.

8.	F Payments to purchase merchandise are classified as operating activities.

9.	T The FASB wanted net cash flow from operating activities to reflect the cash effects of those transactions entering into the determination of net income.

10.	T In the long-run, a business must generate positive cash flows from operations if the business is to survive.

11.	F A growing business is generally investing in plant assets and acquiring other investments; these activities could lead to a negative cash flow from investing activities.

12.	F It is easier to prepare the statement of cash flows by examining the income statement and the *changes* in all balance sheet accounts except Cash.

13.	T A credit to Notes Receivable usually represents cash received. Investing activities can include cash receipts as well as cash disbursements.

14.	T Debit entries to long-term debt accounts usually indicate cash payments. Borrowing and repayment of borrowing constitute financing activities.

15.	F If accounts receivable are increasing, some of the credit sales have not been collected from customers.

16.	T If the company is increasing its inventory, it is buying more merchandise than it is selling. If accounts payable are not increasing by the same amount as the inventory increase, the payments to suppliers are greater than the cost of goods sold.

17.	F Depreciation is a noncash expense that does not affect cash flows from operation activities.

18.	F Depreciation is a noncash expense; it has no effect on cash flows from operating activities.

19.	T The indirect method is simply an alternative approach to determine net cash flow from operations.

20.	T Depreciation is a noncash expense, requiring no cash outlay during the current period.

21.	F A net decrease in unexpired insurance indicates that the company exhausted a portion of the insurance it had paid for *previously*. In this case, the amount recognized as insurance expense would exceed the current period cash outlay.

22.	F A loss on the sale of a plant asset is an example of a nonoperating loss.

23.*	F While the FASB encourages the use of the direct method, it *does not require* use of this method and permits use of the indirect method.

24.*	T The direct method and the indirect method of computing net cash flow from operating activities differ only in format—both methods result in the same amount of net cash flow from operating activities.

25.*	F The indirect method begins with reported net income and reconciles this figure to the net cash flow from operating activities.

26.**	F A worksheet may be used to prepare a statement of cash flows under either method.

27.**	T The worksheet analyzes assets and liabilities other than cash.

---

* Supplemental Topic A, "The Indirect Method."
** *Supplemental Topic B*, " A Worksheet for Preparing a Statement of Cash Flows."

Completion Statements

1. income statement, balance sheet, statement of cash flows, cash. 2(a). operating, (b) investing, (c) financing 3. operating, financing. 4. operating. 5. cash equivalents. 6. credit. 7. decrease, accounts receivable. 8. direct, indirect, net income. 9. free cash flow. *10(a). noncash expenses, (b) timing differences, (c) nonoperating gains and losses. *11. noncash expense, net income, outlay, net cash flow from operating activities, added to. *12. timing differences, cash flow. *13. net increase, net decrease. *14. nonoperating losses, nonoperating gains. *15. supplementary schedule.

Multiple Choice

1. Answer **a** — A statement of cash flows provides information about the *solvency* of a business; the income statement provides information about *profitability*. A statement of cash flows also provides information about *noncash* investing and financing activities.

2. Answer **c** — income is an accrual concept, not a cash flow.

3. Answer **b** — investing activities include purchases and sales of plant assets and of investments. A growing company is likely to be purchasing greater quantities of plant assets and of investments than it is selling. Thus, a growing company is likely to show a negative cash flow from investing activities.

4. Answer **b** — payment of interest is classified as an operating activity.

5. Answer **a** — accounts receivable decrease when cash is collected from customers. Answers **c** and **d** indicate cash payments. Answer **b** occurs when depreciation expense is recorded and involves no cash receipt or payment.

6. Answer **b**—a debit change in the Notes Payable account indicates that payment has been made on a note payable. Answer **a** indicates the issuance of capital stock, answer **c** indicates collection of an account receivable, and answer **d** indicates an increase in the Cash account. Thus, answers **a**, **c**, and **d** all indicate receipts of cash.

7. Answer **c** — an increase in a prepaid expense requires a cash outlay that is not recognized as expense in the current period. Answers **a** and **b** cause expenses recorded in the period to exceed the amount of cash payments. Answer **d** does not involve a cash payment to suppliers of goods or services.

8. Answer **b**—nonoperating gains increase net income and *total* net cash flow they do not, however, increase the net cash flow from *operating* activities.

9. Answer **d** — a debit to the Land account indicates a purchase of land, which is an investing activity requiring a cash outflow.

10. Answer **a** — the credits to the Marketable Securities account indicate that marketable securities costing $200,000 were sold during the period. The $45,000 gain in the income statement means that the sales price must have been $45,000 above cost, or $245,000.

11. Answer **c** — the FASB requires that *noncash* investing and financing activities be disclosed in a supplementary schedule accompanying the statement of cash flows. As the transaction does not involve a cash receipt or a cash payment, it would not appear among the cash flows from financing or investing activities.

12. Answer **d** — the sale of goods for cash reflects a cash receipt from operating activities. Answer **c** does not result in a cash flow, while answers **a** and **b** are examples of financing activities (nonoperating activities).

13.* Answer **b** — the *direct* method discloses amounts of specific cash inflows and outflows comprising operating activities. The *indirect* method reconciles reported net income with net cash flow from operating activities.

14.* Answer **c** — because the computation of net cash flow from operating activities begins with reported net income under the indirect method, noncash expenses such as depreciation are added back to net income in order to arrive at the net cash flow from operations. Depreciation expense does not generate an inflow of cash, nor is there a fund of cash set aside as a result of recording depreciation expense.

15.* Answer **c** — a timing difference arises when a revenue or expense is recognized by debiting or crediting either an asset account (*other than cash*), or a liability account.

16.* Answer **a** — both a net increase in accounts receivable and a net decrease in inventory represent timing differences. The $520 net increase in accounts receivable is deducted from net income, while the $280 net decrease in inventory is added to net income—a net $240 reduction of net income to arrive at net cash flow from operating activities.

17.* Answer **a** — depreciation of $150 ($1,500 (10 years) is an example of a noncash expense which reduces net income yet does not entail a current period cash outlay.

18.* Answer **d** — since this is Wilbur Showers, Inc.'s first year of operations, the account balances reflect net increases. An increase in accounts payable is added to net income; the increases in accounts receivable and in inventory are deducted from net income to arrive at net cash flow from operating activities. ($650 + $300 – $200 – $500 = $250 net cash flow from operating activities.)

19.* Answer **b**—

$ 76,000	net income
32,000	depreciation expense
(4,500)	increase in inventory
7,500	nonoperating loss
$111,000	net cash flow from operating activities

The issuance of common stock is classified as a financing activity; the sale of equipment is classified as an investing activity.

Solutions to Exercises

1.

a. None (The statement describes the *income statement*.)

b. Net cash flow

c. Investing activities

d. None (Statement describes *profitable*, not *solvent*.)

e. Cash equivalent

f. Operating activities

g. Financing activities

2.

a. O

b. O

c. F

---

* *Supplemental Topic A*, "The Indirect Method."

d.   <u>O</u>

e.   <u>F</u>

f.   <u>X</u>

g.   <u>I</u>

h.   <u>X</u>

i.   <u>I</u>

j.   <u>X</u>

3.

a. $316,000 ($320,000 - $4,000)

b. $204,000 ($200,000 + $7,000 - $3,000)

c. $79,750 ($90,000 - $8,000 - $1,000 - $1,250)

4.

TYCOR DISTRIBUTORS
Statement of Cash Flows
For the Year Ended December 31, 20__

Cash flows from operating activities:		
Cash received from customers	$ 1,800,000	
Interest and dividends received	<u>40,000</u>	
Cash provided by operating activities		$1,840,000
Cash paid to suppliers and employees	$(1,400,000)	
Interest paid	(60,000)	
Income taxes paid	<u>(120,000)</u>	
Cash disbursed for operating activities		<u>(1,580,000)</u>
Net cash flow from operating activities		$ 260,000
Cash flows from investing activities:		
Cash paid to acquire plant assets	$ (520,000)	
Proceeds of sales from plant assets	<u>50,000</u>	
Net cash used by investing activities		(470,000)
Cash flows from financing activities:		
Proceeds from short-term borrowing	$ 100,000	
Payments to settle short-term debt	(70,000)	
Proceeds from issuing capital stock	400,000	
Dividends paid	<u>(200,000)</u>	
Net cash provided by financing activities		<u>230,000</u>
Net increase (decrease) in cash		$ 20,000
Cash and cash equivalents, beginning of the year		<u>84,000</u>
Cash and cash equivalents, end of year		<u>$ 104,000</u>

5.

a.   Nonoperating gains and losses

b.   Direct method

c.   Noncash expense

d.   Net cash flow from operating activities

e.   Net cash flow

f.   Timing difference

g.   None (The statement describes *net income*.)

6.[*]

a.   +

b.   O (Cash payment of a dividend is classified as a *financing* activity; in addition, no cash was paid
        in this transaction.)

c.   -

d.   O (Cash payment of a dividend is classified as a *financing* activity.)

e.   -

f.   -

g.   -

7.[*]

STILWELL COMPANY
Partial Statement of Cash Flows
For the Year Ended December 31, 2002

Cash flow from operating activities:

Net income			$ 65,000
Add:	Depreciation expense	$23,000	
	Amortization of patents	7,000	
	Decrease in accounts receivable	7,000	
	Decrease in inventory	4,000	
	Increase in accrued expenses payable	6,000	
	Nonoperating loss of sale of investments	15,000	62,000
Subtotal			$127,000
Less:	Increase in prepaid advertising	$ 2,000	
	Decrease in accounts payable	3,000	
	Nonoperating gain on sale of land	6,000	(11,000)
Net cash flow from operating activities			$116,000

---

[*] Supplemental Topic A, "The Indirect Method.

216

13

FINANCIAL STATEMENT ANALYSIS

Highlights of the Chapter

1. *Financial statements* represent a report on a company's performance. Financial statements are of interest to many groups, each with a different set of needs. In order to interpret the information contained in financial statements, the user should understand the workings of the accounting system.

2. The published financial statements of corporations have been audited by CPA firms and reviewed in detail by governmental agencies such as the Securities and Exchange Commission. Consequently, users of these financial statements may have confidence that the information in the statements is reasonable, reliable, and is presented in accordance with generally accepted accounting principles.

3. Critics of business often blame "excessive" corporate profits for rising prices and other economic problems. In evaluating the reasonableness of corporate profit, we must relate the dollar amount of net income to the volume of sales and the value of the economic resources necessary to produce that profit. Also, we must consider the need for profits as a means of financing expansion, creating jobs, and increasing the supply of goods and services.

4. Some sources of financial data available to users of financial statements include:

    a. Annual reports of corporations.

    b. Data filed with the Securities and Exchange Commission.

    c. Investment advisory services and stock brokerage firms.

    d. Organizations such as Moody's Investors Service, Standard & Poor's Corporation, and Dun & Bradstreet, Inc.

5. A given figure contained in financial statements is seldom significant to the reader; the *relationships* among figures, or the *changes* over time, generally are much more useful.

6. Four techniques commonly used in the analysis of financial statements are:

    a. Dollar and percentage changes.

    b. Trend percentages.

    c. Component percentages.

    d. Ratios.

7. *Dollar and percentage changes* relate a financial statement item to the same item in the last year's statements. This analysis indicates whether things are getting better or worse in the short-term.

8. *Trend percentages* show the tendency of a financial statement to change over a series of years. This type of analysis gives clues to long-run growth patterns and other important trends.

9. A *component percentage* is the percentage between a financial statement item and a total (such as total assets or net sales) which includes that item. The analysis indicates the relative importance of the item.

10. A *ratio* measures the relationship of one item to another. Ratios may be used to identify unusual relationships, such as a high rate of return. By computing ratios for several years, we can also see whether key financial indicators, such as the current ratio, are improving or deteriorating.

11. In interpreting the significance of percentage changes, component percentages, and ratios, some *standards of comparison* should be used. Two widely used *standards* are:

  a. The past performance of the company.

  b. The performance of other companies in the same industry or the performance of the industry as a whole.

12. Comparison of data over time (*horizontal* analysis) gives some idea of the company's performance compared with its past record and may be helpful in forecasting future performance.

13. Comparison of a company's performance with that of other companies similarly situated or with the aggregate results for an industry offers valuable clues relating to a company's ability to compete and perhaps to surpass the industry's performance.

14. The key objectives of financial analysis are to determine a company's *future earnings performance* and the *soundness of its financial position*. To evaluate earnings performance and financial soundness, we are interested not only in the amount of earnings and assets, but also in the *quality of earnings*, the *quality of assets*, and the *amount of debt*.

15. The quality of earnings depends upon the *source* and *stability* of those earnings. The quality of earnings helps us to evaluate how likely it is that earnings will continue to grow and whether future earnings are likely to fluctuate widely. An analysis of the accounting principles and methods used by a company is helpful in evaluating the quality of earnings reported by the company.

16. A company may become insolvent even though it is profitable. The health and even the survival of the company may therefore be dependent not only on earnings, but also on the quality of assets and the *amount of liabilities* outstanding. A firm with an inadequate cash position, slow moving inventories, past due receivables and large amounts of short-term liabilities may be facing serious financial difficulties.

17. It is also important to remember that during periods of inflation statements based upon historical cost tend to overstate the profitability of a business by failing to recognize the current value of the resources consumed in the production of revenue. The FASB *recommends* that companies include in their annual reports supplementary schedules showing the effects of inflation upon their financial statements. Inclusion of these supplementary disclosures is voluntary, *not* mandatory.

18. *Stockholders and potential investors* in the common stock of a company are primarily interested in the following:

  a. Earnings per share.

  b. Price-earnings ratio.

  c. Dividends paid and the yield based on the market value of the stock.

  d. Revenue and expense analysis (the increase or decrease in specific revenue and expense items.)

  e. The rate of return on assets used in the business.

  f. The rate of return on common stockholders' equity.

  g. Debt ratio (the proportion of total assets financed by borrowing).

19. The concept of return on investment (called *ROI*) is a measure of management's efficiency in using the resources under its control. The ROI concept is used in many situations such as evaluating the performance of a company, product line, or particular investment. ROI is computed several different ways, depending upon the circumstance; two common measures of ROI are *return on assets* and *return on stockholders' equity*.

a. **Return on assets** "Return" is defined as **operating income**, since interest expense and income taxes are determined by factors other than the manner in which assets are used.

$$\text{Return on Assets} = \frac{\text{Operating Income}}{\text{Average Total Assets}}$$

b. **Return on equity** "Return" to stockholders is the net income of the business. Therefore:

$$\text{Return on Assets} = \frac{\text{Net Income}}{\text{Average Total Stockholders' Equity}}$$

20. Financing a business with fixed-return securities (bonds and notes payable and preferred stock) is knows as using **leverage**. If the rate earned on total assets is **greater** than the rate paid on the fixed-return securities (the cost of borrowing), the common stockholders will gain from the use of leverage. Common stockholders will gain because the capital provided by issuing the fixed-return securities is being invested to earn more than the amount which must be paid to the providers of that capital. The excess of the earnings generated by that capital over the fixed return paid out belongs to the common stockholders.

21. If the return earned on total assets is **less** than the cost of borrowing the common stockholder will **lose** by using leverage.

22. The **debt ratio** (total liabilities ÷ total assets) measures the degree to which a company is financed with debt. A **high** debt ratio means that a high percentage of the total assets are financed by creditors and that the company is making use of leverage. A high debt ratio may be profitable to common stockholders in periods of prosperity (when return on assets is greater than cost of borrowing) but can lead to serious trouble in a period of low earnings if return on asset falls **below** the cost of borrowing.

23. **Long-term creditors** are primarily interested in the following measurements:

    a. The rate of return on investment, known as the yield on bonds.

    b. The firm's ability to meet periodic interest requirements.

    c. The firm's ability to repay the principal.

24. The **yield** on bonds is the **effective interest rate** that an investor will earn by buying the bond at their current market price and holding them to maturity. The yield varies **inversely** with changes in the market price of a bond. The safety of an investment in bonds depends on the ability of a firm to meet the interest and principal payments. An indication of the ability to pay **interest** is the **number of times** that the interest obligation was earned. This **interest coverage ratio** is computed by dividing the income from operations by the annual interest expense. The safety of **principal** is, to some extent, measured by the **debt ratio**. The lower the debt ratio, the safer the position of creditors.

25. **Short-term creditors** are primarily concerned with the relationship of **liquid assets** to current liabilities and the **turnover** of accounts receivable and inventories. These are usually analyzed by computing the following:

    a. Working capital: the excess of current assets over current liabilities.

    b. Current ratio: current assets divided by current liabilities.

    c. Quick ratio: quick assets (cash, marketable securities, and receivables) divided by current liabilities.

    d. Turnover of accounts receivable: credit sales for the year divided by the average receivables for the year.

26. Short-term creditors consider the quality of working capital as well as the dollar amount. Factors affecting the quality of working capital include (a) the nature of the assets comprising the

working capital and (b) the length of time required to convert these assets into cash. Turnover ratios give an indication of how rapidly inventory and receivables can be converted into cash.

27. The inventory turnover and accounts receivable turnover may be expressed in **days** by dividing 365 (days in a year) by the number of times the average inventory or receivables have turned over in one year. The total result is the number of days necessary to turn inventory into receivables and receivables into cash.

28. Adding the days required to turn over (sell) Inventory to the days required to turn over (collect) receivables gives the days necessary to convert inventory into cash. This is the **operating cycle** for a merchandising business (for firms that manufacture their inventory, this would be only part of the operating cycle). An operating cycle that lengthens from one period to the next may indicate that the firm is having trouble selling its inventory or collecting its accounts receivable.

29. No analysis of financial position is complete without cash flow analysis. A company's ability to generate sufficient cash flow from **operating activities** is of importance to both stockholders and creditors. The specific items comprising cash flow from operations, as well as the dollar amount and trend of this statistic can be determined by examining the statement of cash flows for the successive years.

30. An integral part of a corporation's financial statements are the **notes**, which contain information essential to proper interpretation of those statements. Summary of accounting methods, material loss contingencies, current market value of financial instruments, unused lines of credit and post balance sheet events are but a few of the items disclosed in the **notes to the financial statements**.

TEST YOURSELF ON ACCOUNTING INFORMATION

True or False

For each of the following statements, circle the T or the F to indicate whether the statement is true or False.

T   F   1.   The dollar amount of a change during a period in a certain item appearing in financial statement is probably less significant than the change measured as a percentage.

T   F   2.   Percentage changes are usually computed by using the latest figure as a base.

T   F   3.   It is possible that a decrease in gross profit rate may be more than offset by a decrease in expenses, thus resulting in an increase in net income.

T   F   4.   In a common size income statement each item is expressed as a percentage of net sales.

T   F   5.   Industry standards tend to place the performance of a company in a more meaningful perspective.

T   F   6.   Two earnings per share figures frequently appear in an income statement: earnings per share before taxes and earnings per share after taxes.

T   F   7.   Dividing the market price of a share of common stock by the dividends per share gives the price-earnings ratio.

T F 8. If some expenses are fixed (do not fluctuate in proportion to change in sales volume), net income should increase by a greater percentage than the increase in sales volume.

T F 9. Dividing net sales by average inventory, gives the inventory turnover rate, which is a measure of how quickly inventory is selling.

T F 10. If the rate of return on assets is substantially higher than the cost of borrowing, the common stockholder should want the company to have a low debt ratio.

T F 11. The common stockholder will lose from the use of leverage when the cost of borrowing exceeds the return on assets.

T F 12. A high current ratio may indicate that capital is not productively used and that inventories and receivables may be excessive.

T F 13. It is possible to improve many balance sheet ratios by completing certain transactions just before the close of the fiscal period.

T F 14. Certain account balances at the end of the accounting period may not be representative for the entire year, and as a result the ratios (or turnover figures) may be misleading.

Completion Statements

Fill in the necessary word to complete the following statements:

1. The four most widely used analytical techniques are _____ and _____ changes, _____ _____, _____ _____ and _____.

2. The four groups that supply capital to a corporation are _____-_____ _____,_____-_____ _____,_____ _____, and _____ _____.

3. The market price of common stock divided by earnings per share is known as the _____-_____ _____.

4. The current ratio is 3 to 1; working capital amounts to $100,000, and the quick ratio is 1.5 to 1. Compute the following: (a) current assets, $ _____; (b) current liabilities, $ _____; (c) total investment in inventories and short-term prepayments, $_____.

5. The interest coverage ratio is primarily important to _____-_____ _____ and may be found by dividing _____ _____ _____ by the annual _____ _____.

6. When the _____ _____ _____ is less than the cost of borrowing, common stockholders should prefer a _____ debt ration.

7. Cost of goods sold during a year divided by the average cost of _____ gives the _____ _____ _____ for the year.

8. The _____-turnover plus the _____ _____ turnover, expressed in *days*, measured the length of the _____ _____ of merchandising business.

Multiple Choice

Choose the best answer for each of the following questions and enter the identifying letter in the space provided.

___ 1. An investor wants to evaluate the relative profitability of several companies of different size. In order to put the earnings into perspective, the investor would be *least* likely to compare the net income of each company with that company's:

    a. Stockholders' equity.

    b. Total assets.

    c. Working capital.

    d. Net sales.

___ 2. Which of the following sources of financial information is *not* generally available to an individual considering investing in a large publicly held corporation?

    a. Data published by Standard and Poor's Corporation and other investors' services.

    b. The company's accounting records.

    c. Audited financial statements for the current and prior years.

    d. Financial information that has been filed with the Securities and Exchange Commission (SEC).

___ 3. An income statement showing only component percentages is known as a:

    a. Common dollar statement.

    b. Condensed income statement.

    c. Common size income statement.

    d. Comparative income statement

___ 4. Which of the following is *not* a valuable standard of comparison in analyzing financial statements of a company engaged in the manufacture of mobile homes?

    a. Past performance of the company.

    b. Performance of another company engaged in the manufacture of mobile homes.

    c. Performance of all companies engaged in manufacture of mobile homes.

    d. Performance of companies engaged in construction of apartment buildings.

5.　Maxwell Corporation and Nardo, Inc. each report net income of $500,000 for 2001. If the companies are of similar size and other aspects of their operations are equal, which of the following *independent* additional pieces of information would indicate that Maxwell's earnings are of *higher* "*quality*" than Nardo's?

    a.　Maxwell uses the FIFO method of inventory valuation; Nardo uses LIFO (assume rising prices).

    b.　Maxwell depreciation vehicles over a useful life of seven years; Nardo depreciates vehicles over a three-year life.

    c.　Maxwell has had a history of increasing earnings; Nardo's earnings have been erratic over the past several years.

    d.　Maxwell's financial statements are audited by a large prestigious CPA firm; Nardo's are audited by a smaller CPA firm.

6.　*Common stockholders* would be *least concerned* with which of the following?

    a.　Earnings per share of stock.

    b.　Revenue and expense analysis.

    c.　Return on equity.

    d.　Number of times interest earned (interest coverage ratio).

7.　A company has a current ratio of 2 to 1 at the end of the current. Which of the following transactions will *increase* this ratio?

    a.　Sale of bonds payable at a discount.

    b.　Declaration of 50% stock dividend.

    c.　Collection of a large account receivable.

    d.　Borrowed cash from bank, using a six-month note.

8.　*Bondholders* would be *most* interested in which of the following?

    a.　Quick ratio.

    b.　Inventory turnover.

    c.　Times interest earned (interest coverage ratio).

    d.　Operating cycle.

9.　If we added the average number of days required to turn the inventory over and the average age of receivables (in number of days), we would have an estimate of:

    a.　The company's fiscal period.

    b.　The sales volume of the business.

    c.　The company's operating cycle.

    d.　Nothing meaningful.

_____ 10. In projecting the future profitability of a merchandising company, ***investors,*** will be ***least*** concerned with changes in :

     a.   The gross profit rate.

     b.   The rate earned on total assets.

     c.   The quick ratio.

     d.   Sales volume.

_____ 11. If sales increase by 10%, from 2000 to 2001, and cost of goods sold increases only 6%, the gross profit on sales will increase by:

     a.   4%.

     b.   10%.

     c.   6%.

     d.   Some other percentage.

_____ 12. Carlisle Corp. has both common and preferred stock outstanding. In computing return on common stockholders' equity for Carlisle Corp., the "return" that is divided by average common stockholder's equity consists of:

     a.   Net income.

     b.   Net income minus preferred dividends.

     c.   Operating income.

     d.   Net income minus the call price of all preferred shares outstanding.

_____ 13. A positive net cash flow from ***operating activities*** of $100,000:

     a.   Represents cash flow remaining after payment of interest and dividends.

     b.   Is generally viewed as sufficient by stockholders and creditors.

     c.   Means that the company is both profitable and solvent.

     d.   May be viewed as unsatisfactory if dividends annually are $300,000.

Exercises

1. Listed below are eight technical accounting terms emphasized in this chapter.

Current ratio	***Component percentage***
ROI	***Horizontal analysis***
Debt ratio	***Price-earnings ratio***
Leverage	***Operating cycle***

Each of the following statements may (or may not) describe one of these technical terms. In the space provided below each statement, indicate the accounting term described, or answer "None" if the statement does not correctly describe any of the terms.

a. An indication of the relative size and importance of each item in a total.

_____

b.   Comparison of the change in a financial statement item during two or more accounting periods.

_____

c.   A measurement of management's efficiency in using available resources

_____

d.   Current assets divided by current liabilities.

_____

e.   A measurement of the proportion of total assets financed by creditors.

_____

f.   A measurement of the cash return earned by stockholders, based on current price for a share of stock.

_____

g.   Buying assets with money raised by borrowing.

_____

2.   There are 10 transactions or events listed below. Opposite each item is listed a particular ratio used in financial analysis. Indicate the effect of each transaction or event on the ratio listed opposite it. Use the following symbols: Increase – **I**, Decrease = **D**, NO Effect = **NE** (Assume that the current ratio and the quick ratio are higher than 1 to 1.)

	Transaction or Event	Ratio	Effect
a	Purchased inventory on open account.	Quick ratio	
b.	A larger physical volume of goods was sold at reduced prices	Gross profit percentage	
c.	Declared a cash dividend of $1 per share.	Current ratio	
d.	An uncollectible account receivable was written off against the allowance account.	Current ratio	
e.	Issued additional shares of common stock and used proceeds to retire long-term debt.	Rate earned on total assets (before interest and income taxes)	
f	Distributed a 20% stock dividend on common stock.	Earnings per share of common stock	
g.	Operating income increase 25%; interest expense increased 10%.	Interest coverage ratio	
h.	During period of rising prices, company changed from FIFO to LIFO method of inventory pricing.	Inventory turnover	
i.	Paid previously declared cash dividend.	Debt ratio	
j	Issued shares of common stock in exchange for plant assets.	Debt ratio	

3.   From the following comparative balance for the Gulfstream Company, compute the dollar and percentage changes form 2001 to 2002:

GULFSTREAM COMPANY
Comparative Balance Sheet
2001 and 2002

Assets	2002	2001	Increase (or Decrease) Amount	Percentage
Current assets	$150,000	$120,000	$	
Investments	160,000	80,000		
Plant and equipment (net)...............................	360,000	300,000		
Intangibles	80,000	100,000		
Total assets	$750,000	$600,000	$	
Liabilities & Stockholders' Equity				
Current liabilities...	$76,000	$80,000	$	
Long-term debt...	116,000	100,000		
Capital stock, $5 par..	250,000	200,000		
Retained earnings	308,000	220,000		
Total liabilities & stockholders' equity	$750,000	$600,000	$	

4.   The balance sheet of the Olympia Corporation at the beginning and end of 2002 and the income statement for 2002 presented below and at the top of the following page:

OLYMPIA CORPORATION
Comparative Balance Sheet
2001 and 2002

Assets	Dec 31 2002	Dec 31 2001
Cash	$ 60,000	$ 45,000
Marketable securities.......................................	30,000	40,000
Accounts receivable (net)................................	50,000	70,000
Inventory	140,000	130,000
Plant and equipment (net of accumulated depreciation).......................................	420,000	330,000
Total assets	$700,000	$615,000
Liabilities & Stockholders'Equity		
Accounts payable	$ 95,000	$ 30,000
Accrued liabilities..	10,000	15,000
7% bonds payable, due in 2008.......................	80,000	100,000
Capital stock, $5 par..	300,000	300,000
Retained earnings*	215,000	170,000
Total liabilities & stockholders' equity...	$700,000	$615,000

---

* Dividends paid amounted to $0.65 per share.

OLYMPIA CORPORATION
Income Statement
For Year Ended December 31, 2002

Net sales (all on credit)...................................	$800,000
Cost of goods sold	490,000
Gross profit on sales...	$310,000
Operating expenses (includes depreciation of $25,000).......	160,000
Income from operations.......................................	$150,000
Other expense: bond interest expense	7,000
Income before income taxes..	$143,000
Income taxes	59,000
Net income	$ 84,000
Earnings per share	$ 1.40

On the basis of the information in the Olympia Corporation financial statements, fill in the blanks below with the appropriate amounts (do not compute the ratios):

a. The *current ratio* at the end of 2002 would be computed by dividing $ _____ by $_____.

b. The *quick ratio* at the end of 2002 would be computed by dividing $_____ by $_____.

c. The *average turnover of receivables* during the year would be computed by dividing $ _____ by $ _____.

d. The *average turnover of inventories* during the year would be computed by dividing $_____ by $_____.

e. The *interest coverage ratio* during 2002 (before income taxes) would be determined by dividing $_____ by $_____.

f. The *rate earned on average investment* in assets would be determined by dividing $ _____ by $_____.

g. The *debt ratio* at the end of 2002 would be determined by dividing $_____ by $_____.

h. The *rate of return on the average stockholders' equity* would be determined by dividing $_____ by $_____.

i. The *earnings per share* of capital stock would be determined by dividing $_____ by _____ shares outstanding.

j. If the capital stock has a market value at the end of the year $42 per share, the *price-earnings ratio* would be determine by dividing $_____ by $_____.

k. The *yield* on the stock, assuming a market value of $42, is computed by dividing $_____ by $_____.

l. The *gross profit percentage* would be computed by dividing $_____ - by $_____.

SOLUTIONS TO CHAPTER 13 SELF-TEST

True or False

1. **T** The percentage change allows better comparison between years and shows the growth or decline of the company.

2. **F** Percentage changes are computed by dividing the dollar amount of change between the comparison year and a base year by the amount for the base year. The base year is usually the prior year.

3. **T** Net income is computed as gross profit minus expenses; a large decrease in expenses can more than offset a decrease in gross profit, resulting in higher net income.

4. **T** By definition a common size income statement is one in which all items are expressed as a percentage of net sales.

5. **T** Industry standards provide one method of comparing operating results of one company with those of its competitors.

6. **F** Earnings per share is determined from net income (after income taxes have been subtracted).

7. **F** The price-earnings ratio is computed by dividing the market price of common stock by the earnings per share.

8. **T** If sales volume increases, causing net sales to increase, while certain expenses remain unchanged, net income should increase by a greater percentage than the increase in sales volume.

9. **F** The inventory turnover ratio, which tells the number of times the inventory is sold each year, is computed by dividing the *cost of goods sold* by the average inventory.

10. **F** If borrowed capital can be used to generate a greater return than the cost of borrowing, the common stockholders would want the company to have a high debt ratio.

11. **T** When the cost of borrowing exceeds the return on assets, there is a reduction in net income and a decrease in the return on common stockholders' equity.

12. **T** A high current ratio could indicate excessive amounts of inventory, poor collection of accounts receivable, or excessive current assets that could be invested for a greater return.

13. **T** Many balance sheet ratios are determined using figures in existence at balance sheet date; thus, it is possible to manipulate these amounts by strategic timing of certain transactions.

14. **T** In determining turnover ratios, it would be best to have a running average balance for accounts throughout the period.

Completion Statements

1. dollar, percentage, trend analysis, component percentages, ratios. 2. short-term creditors, long-term creditors, preferred stockholders, common stockholders. 3. price-earnings ratio. 4(a) $150,000; (b) $50,000; (c) $75,000 5. long-term creditors, income from operations, interest expense. 6. return on assets, low. 7. inventory, inventory turnover rate. 8. inventory, accounts receivable, operating cycle.

Multiple Choice

1. Answer **c** – to compare relative profitability of several companies, each company's earnings can be compared with its total assets and with its invested capital, as well as with sales. Total assets and invested capital are the resources utilized by management to generate earnings. Sales are the source of income generated, and the amount of profit *per dollar of sales* is a more useful indicator of profitability than the absolute dollar amount of net income. Working capital measures short-run debt-paying ability and bears no direct relationship to net income.

2. Answer **b** – answers **a, c,** and **d** are all available to stockholders, potential investors and creditors, and the general public. A company internal accounting records are not made public.

3. Answer **c** – a common size income statement is an application of component percentages where all items on the income statement are expressed as a percentage of net sales. Comparative income statements would have two or more years of data (in dollars) side by side in adjacent columns. Condensed and common dollar income statements would show dollar amounts, not percentages.

4. Answer **d** – in order for a ratio or a comparison to be useful, the two amounts being compared must be logically related. Answers **a, b**, and **c** are logically related in some way to the current year financial statements of a company engaged in the manufacture of mobile homes. Answer **d** refers to an unrelated industry.

5. Answer **c** – in assessing the quality of earnings, we look at the accounting principles selected by management as well as at the source and stability of earnings. Answers **a** and **b** describe situations in which **Nardo** is using the more conservative accounting policies (hence Narod's earnings would be judges of higher quality).

6. Answer **d** – number of times interest earned is a statistic of interest primarily to bondholders and other long-term creditors.

7. Answer **a** – the current ratio is computed as current assets divided by current liabilities. Sale of bonds, even at a discount, will increase current assets and have no effect on current liabilities – hence the ratio will increase. Answer **c** simply alters the composition of current assets, but has no effect on total current assets or current liabilities. Answer **d** increases both current assets and current liabilities by the same amount. Since the current ratio is 2 to 1 already, this transaction will cause the current ratio to decrease.

8. Answer **c** – answers **a, b**, and **d** are all statistics of interest primarily to short-term creditors.

9. Answer **c** – the operating cycle is defined as the average time period between the purchases of merchandise and the conversion of this merchandise back into cash. This period is the total time required to sell the inventory (turnover) *and* collect the accounts receivable (average age of receivables)

10. Answer **c** – the quick ratio is a measure of the *short-term liquidity* of the firm. Changes in the statistics in answers **a, b**, and **d** are of more significance in projecting the future profitability of a company.

11. Answer **d** – as sales are increasing faster than the cost of goods sold, gross profit will increase even faster than sales.

12. Answer **b** – return on common stockholders' equity is computed by dividing net income minus the *preferred dividends requirement* by the average common stockholders' equity.

13. Answer **d** – although positive, the $100,000 cash flow from operations is insufficient to cover current year dividends. Interest payments have already been deducted in arriving at the $100,000 figure, but dividends have not; therefore answer **a** is not correct. The $100,000 net cash flow from operations must be evaluated in comparisons to interest payments, net income prior years' cash flows, dividends requirements, etc., in order to determine whether it is "sufficient." A company

may operate at a loss and yet have a positive cash flow from operations. In addition, a company may generate cash flow from operations and have such substantial liabilities that it is insolvent.

Solutions to Exercises

1.

a.	Component percentage
b.	Horizontal analysis
c.	ROI
d.	Current ratio
e.	Debt ratio
f.	None (The statement describes *dividend yield*.)
g.	Leverage

2.

a.	D
b.	D
c.	D
d.	NE
e.	NE
f.	D
g.	I
h.	I
i.	D
j.	D

3.

GULFSTREAM COMPANY
Comparative Balance Sheet
2001 and 2002

Assets	2002	2001	Increase (or Decrease) Amount	Percentage
Current assets	$150,000	$120,000	$ 30,000	25%
Investments	160,000	80,000	80,000	100%
Plant and equipment (net)	360,000	300,000	60,000	20%
Intangibles	80,000	100,000	(20,000)	(20%)
Total assets	$750,000	$600,000	$150,000	25%
Liabilities & Stockholders' Equity				
Current liabilities	$76,000	$80,000	$ (4,000)	(5)%
Long-term debt	116,000	100,000	16,000	16%
Capital stock, $5 par	250,000	200,000	50,000	25%
Retained earnings	308,000	220,000	88,000	40%
Total liabilities & stockholders' equity	$750,000	$600,000	$150,000	25%

4.

a. $280,000 by $105,000

b. $140,000 by $105,000

c. $800,000 by $60,000 [($50,000 + $70,000)/2]

d. $490,000 by $135,000 [($140,000 + $130,000)/2]

e. $150,000 by $7,000

f. $150,000 by $657,500 [($700,000 + $615,000)/2]

g. $185,000 by $700,000

h. $84,000 by $492,500 [($515,000 + $470,000)/2]

i. $84,000 by 60,000 shares

j. $42 by $1.40

k. $0.65 by $42

l. $310,000 by $800,000

14

GLOBAL BUSINESS AND ACCOUNTING

Highlights of the Chapter

1. *Globalization* is a process by which managers become aware of the impact of international activities on their company's future. Globalization activities typically progress through a series of outward growth stages that include exporting, licensing, joint ventures, wholly owned subsidiaries, and global sourcing.

2. *Exporting*, at the simplest level, is selling a good or service to a foreign customer. Exporting enables the producing company to maintain control over product creation. Licensing, in contrast, gives up some control for a monetary return. *International licensing* is a contractual agreement between a company and a foreign party allowing the use of trademarks, patents, technology, etc. Many international companies are involved in some form of international product licensing. *International joint ventures*, are companies created by two or more companies from different countries, whereas *wholly owned international* subsidiaries are created when a single company purchases 100% equity control of another company in a different country. *Global sourcing* requires the coordination of numerous business activities, across international boundaries, and typically involves a combination of exporting, licensing, joint ventures, and wholly owned subsidiaries.

3. The strategic direction of planned globalization has implications for the type of accounting information gathered, created, and reported. For example, the type of information gathered and reported for a wholly owned international subsidiary must be more detailed and control oriented than the information required to monitor exporting and licensing activities.

4. Four related environmental forces shape globalization. They are: (1) political and legal systems, (2) economic systems, (3) culture, and (4) technology and infrastructure.

5. *Political risk* often occurs when governments take ownership or control over business assets and operations. When a foreign country nationalizes its industries, for example, companies must often give up ownership of their assets to the controlling country's government. Government may also intervene in business activities by enacting restrictive laws pertaining to taxes, licensing fees, or tariffs. Governments often create tariffs, duties, and special trade zones to encourage or discourage particular types of importing or exporting activities.

6. *Legal reporting* requirements vary significantly from country to country. Differences in accounting practices reflect the influences that shape business activity in a country, its legal environment, and the primary providers of capital for businesses. For example, in the United States, legal reporting requirements are based primarily on the need to provide information to private investors and creditors. In those countries where private capital is unavailable, reporting requirements are often oriented toward the needs of centralized government planning.

7. Differences in accounting and reporting practices among countries create problems in trying to analyze and compare accounting information. As long as a company operates solely within its own borders, differences in financial reporting practices are not as significant as they are if business activity extends across borders.

8. Reporting differences also present problems for companies that sell their securities in foreign markets. *Cross-border financing* activities have led to an interest in the *harmonization of accounting standards*, a phrase used to describe the standardization of accounting methods and principles throughout the world.

9. The *International Accounting Standards Committee* (IASC) is particularly interested in harmonization and is charged with the responsibility of establishing and gaining acceptance of international accounting standards.

10. The economic systems under which businesses operate significantly affect the form and availability of accounting information. In a *planned economy*, the government uses central planning to allocate resources and determine and output among various economic segments. In *market economies,* ownership of land and the means of production are private, and the market dictates the allocation of resources and the output among segments of the economy.

11. The way businesses are organized into industrial organizations contributes to differences in how capital is raised around the globe. In some Asian countries, for example, companies group themselves into conglomerates representing different industries. Within these cartels of companies, suppliers receive loans, investment capital, technology, and long-term supply agreements from customers. In the United States, antitrust and price-fixing laws often preclude these types of business relationships.

12. *Culture* may be thought of as the way in which individuals act and perceive each other's actions. U.S. cultural practices have significant affects on the way foreign companies conduct business in the United States. Likewise, many commonly accepted U. S. business practices would not be acceptable in other cultures.

13. Experts on culture have identified several variables that differ among international locations. Of the cultural differences identified, the variables with the most significant implications for management accounting and production include: (1) Individualism versus collectivism, (2) Uncertainty avoidance, (3) Short-versus long-term orientation, and (4) Large versus small power distance.

14. *Individualism versus collectivism* refers to the interdependence among individuals in a society or culture. High interdependence among individuals connotes collectivism, whereas low interdependence is connotes individualism.

15. *Uncertainty avoidance* refers to the extent to which members of a society or culture feel uncomfortable or threatened by unknown or uncertain situations.

16. *Short-versus long-term orientation* refers to the extent to which a society or culture values lasting relationships, social order, and personal stability.

17. *Large versus small power distance* refers to the extent to which a society or culture adheres to the idea that everyone is created equal and should have an equal voice.

18. Cultural differences pose problems regarding the design and administration of accounting systems. A budgeting system that is effective in one culture may be completely ineffective in another. Even within one culture or country, there are highly diverse groups in terms of religion, ethnic groups, language, and income level. These differences also have implications for effective business management.

19. Training and educational differences complicate cultural differences through variation in the infrastructure, educational level, and ability to transfer information and knowledge between and among various geographic locations and peoples. These differences create barriers to successful international business operations. Companies that create joint ventures or acquire wholly owned subsidiaries often find few employees with the education and technical training available in the U. S. workforce.

20. *Infrastructure impediments* also pose problems for globalization. Poor access to communications equipment, inadequate transportation systems, and unreliable power sources make establishing international business in some locations difficult.

21. In addition to environmental characteristics, companies with international business dealings also encounter problems from multiple securities and the exchange rates related to each. A currency *exchange rate* is the amount it costs to purchase one unit of currency with another currency. Thus, the exchange rate may be viewed as the price of buying one unit of foreign currency, as stated in terms of the domestic currency (which, for our purpose, is U. S. dollars).

22. Exchange rates may be used to determine how much of one currency is equivalent to a given amount of another currency. The process of restating an amount of foreign currency in terms of the equivalent number of dollars is called *translating* the foreign currency.

23. In the financial press, currencies are often described as strong or weak, or as rising or falling against another. A currency is described as strong when its exchange rate is falling. Exchange rates fluctuate due to changes in the environmental forces discussed earlier.

24. When a U. S. Company buys or sells merchandise in a transaction with a foreign company, the transaction can be stated in terms of dollars or in terms of the foreign currency. If the price of merchandise bought or sold is stated in terms of dollars, the U. S. company encounters no special accounting problems. Such is not the case if the transaction is stated in terms of the foreign currency.

25. If the transaction price is stated in terms of the foreign currency, the U. S. company encounters two problems. First, the transaction must be *translated* into dollars before the transaction can be recorded. Second, a problem arises if the purchase or sale is made on account, and the exchange rate *changes*, between the date of the transaction and the date that the account is paid or received. This fluctuation in exchange rates will cause the U. S. company to experience either a *gain* or *loss* in the settlement of the transaction.

26. Having an *account payable* that must be paid in a foreign currency results in a gain for the U. S. company if the exchange rate declines between the date of the transaction and the date of payment. A gain results because fewer dollars are needed to repay the debt than had originally been owed. An increase in the exchange rate causes the U. S. company to incur a loss because more dollars must be spent than originally owed in order to purchase the foreign currency needed to settle the account payable. U. S. companies that *import* foreign products often have large liabilities (accounts payable) that are fixed in terms of the foreign currency that must eventually be paid to settle the account.

27. Having an *account receivable* that will be collected in a foreign currency results in a loss for the U. S. company if the exchange rate declines between the date of transaction and the date of payment. A loss results because the amount of foreign currency collected in a settlement of the receivable will convert to fewer U. S. dollars than it would have on the day that the transaction originally transpired. An increase in the exchange rate results in a gain for the U. S. company because the amount of foreign currency collected in settlement of the receivable will convert into more U. S. dollars than it would have on the day that the transaction originally transpired. U. S. companies that *export* products to foreign countries often have large receivables that are fixed in terms of the foreign currency that will eventually be collected to settle the account.

28. Gains and losses resulting from exchange rate fluctuations are normally recorded at the time the related payable or receivable is settled. An exception to this practice occurs at the end of each accounting period. An *adjusting entry* is required at the end of each

accounting period to recognize gains or losses that have accumulated on foreign payables and receivables through the balance sheet date. These gains and losses are included in the income statement where they typically follow income from operations. They are presented in a manner much like interest expense and gains and losses on the sale of plant assets.

29. There are two basic approaches to avoiding losses from fluctuations in foreign exchange rates. One approach is to insist that receivables and payables be settled in terms of specified amounts of domestic currency. The other approach is called hedging.

30. *Hedging* is the strategy of taking off-setting positions in a foreign currency to avoid losses from fluctuations in foreign exchange rates. A company that has similar amounts of accounts receivable and accounts payable in the same foreign currency automatically has hedged position. A company that does not have similar dollar amounts of payable and receivables in the same foreign currency may create a hedged position by buying or selling *future contracts*, or *futures*.

31. A future contract is, in effect, an account receivable in foreign currency. A company with only foreign payables may hedge its position by *purchasing* a similar dollar amount of foreign currency future contracts. A company with only foreign receivables would hedge its position by *selling* future contracts, i.e., creating an offsetting liability payable in foreign currency.

32. Many corporations have subsidiaries organized and operating in foreign countries. These foreign subsidiaries should be included in the parent company's consolidated financial statements. Several complex technical issues are involved in preparing consolidated statements that include foreign subsidiaries. First, the accounting records of the subsidiary must be translated into U. S. dollars. Next, the accounting principles in use in the foreign country may differ from the generally accepted accounting principles (GAAP) used in the United States.

33. Readers of the financial statements of a U. S. corporation need not be concerned with these technical problems. Once accountants have completed the consolidation process, the consolidated financial statements are expressed in U. S. dollars and conform to the GAAP used in the United States.

34. Differences in exchange rates can create significant complexities for firms practicing global sourcing. These firms must estimate costs that will be incurred in multiple countries involved in producing the merchandise to be sold in the open market. The costs associated with various phases of production (including the cost of labor, materials, and shipping) are often stated in terms of different foreign currencies. Making accurate estimates of costs in a global value chain is one of the biggest challenges facing a company wishing to become more global.

35. In many countries, product costs also include expenses incurred to expedite official paperwork. In many countries, bribery is also a part of doing business and is not considered wrong or unethical. The Foreign Corrupt Practices Act (FCPA) prescribes fines and jail time for American managers violating its rules. The FCPA has implications for accounting in two specific areas: record keeping and internal control procedures.

TEST YOURSELF ON GLOBAL BUSINESS AND ACCOUNTING

True or False

For each of the following statements, circle the T or the F to indicate whether the statement is true or false.

T　F　1. Globalization typically progresses through a series of stages that include legal reporting, foreign currency transactions, and cultural sensitivity.

T　F　2. In the United States, banks provide most of the capital for international businesses.

T　F　3. In a planned economy, the government uses central planning to allocate resources and determine output among various industrial segments.

T　F　4. Culturally speaking, the industrial organization of Asian countries is characterized by individualism.

T　F　5. The International Accounting Standards Committee develops accounting standards that must be followed by all multinational companies.

T　F　6. An American company that buys from (or sells to) a foreign company may have gains and losses from fluctuations in currency exchange rates even if the American company does not have a foreign subsidiary.

T　F　7. Restating an amount of foreign currency in terms of the equivalent number of units of domestic currency is termed *translating* the foreign currency.

T　F　8. The *exchange rate*, for a foreign currency will fluctuate if the worldwide supply of currency exceeds demand.

T　F　9. If the U. S. dollar is strengthening in the world currency markets, an American company with large accounts payable due in specified amounts of foreign currencies will experience losses from exchange rate fluctuations.

T　F　10. If the exchange rate for a particular foreign currency is rising, an American company with receivables in this currency will recognize gains from the exchange rate fluctuations.

T　F　11. Large imports but small exports tend to weaken a country's currency.

T　F　12. High interest rates relative to the rate of inflation tend to weaken a country's currency.

T　F　13. The balance sheet of a multinational corporation has multiple money columns, showing the financial statement amounts in various currencies, such as dollars, yen, and pounds.

T　F　14. The accounting standards and principles used in the preparation of financial statements vary from one country to another.

T　F　15. A multinational corporation headquartered in the United States prepares consolidated financial statements which include its foreign subsidiaries and which comply with generally accepted accounting principles.

Completion Statements

Fill in the necessary word to complete the following statements:

1. _____ is the process of managers becoming aware of the impact of international activities on the future of their company.

2. In _____ _____, ownership of land and the means of production are private, and markets dictate the allocation of resources and the output among segments of the economy.

3. The mental mindset that affects the way individuals in a society act and perceive each other's actions may be viewed as a society's _____.

4. The close coordination of R & D, manufacturing, and marketing across national boundaries is typically referred to as _____ _____.

5. The _____ _____ _____ _____ is responsible for developing international accounting standards.

6. The process of restating an amount of foreign currency in terms of the equivalent number of U. S. dollars is termed _____ the foreign currency.

7. Assume that an American company purchases merchandise on account from a Japanese company at a price of ¥500,000. At the date of this purchase, the exchange rate is $.0106. The American company should record a liability of $_____.

8. Assume that the exchange rate for the British pound is falling relative to the U. S. dollar. American companies making credit sales to British companies will experience (gains, losses) _____ and American companies making credit purchases from British companies will experience (gains, losses) _____ as a result of the fluctuations in the exchange rate.

9. Assume that an American company incurs a liability for 100,000 French francs when the exchange rate is $0.1900 per franc, and that the company pays off this liability when the exchange rate is $0.2000 per franc. The company will report a (gain, loss) _____ of $_____ from the fluctuation in the exchange rate.

10. An American exporter with substantial amounts of contracts stated in a foreign currency may avoid loses from fluctuations in foreign exchange rates by _____ future contracts. This strategy of holding offsetting positions in the foreign currency is called _____.

Multiple Choice

Choose the best answer for each of the following questions and enter the identifying letter in the space provided.

___ 1.   Globalization typically progresses through a series of stages. The first stage of globalization often involves:

     a.   Exporting.

     b.   International joint ventures.

     c.   Wholly owned international subsidiaries.

     d.   International licensing.

___ 2.   Which of the following is *not* an environmental force affecting how accounting information is measured, reported, and created?

     a.   Political and legal systems.

     b.   Global sourcing.

     c.   Economic systems.

     d.   Culture.

___ 3.   The extent to which members of a society feel uncomfortable or threatened by unknown or uncertain situations is sometimes referred to as:

     a.   Power distance.

     b.   Long-term orientation.

     c.   Collectivism.

     d.   Uncertainty avoidance.

___ 4.   Fashion House, an American company, purchases merchandise on account from a French company at a price of 40,000 French francs. Payment is due in 90 days and the current exchange rate is $.1900 per French franc. On the date of this purchase, Fashion House should:

     a.   Record a liability of 40,000 French francs.

     b.   Record a liability of $7,600.

     c.   Record a liability of $235,294.

     d.   Disclose the obligation in a footnote to the financial statements, as the amount of the liability cannot be determined with certainty until the exchange rate at the payment date is known.

___ 5.   In the evening news, a newscaster made the following statement: "Today a weak U. S. dollar fell sharply against the German deutsche mark, but rose slightly against the British pound." This statement indicates that today:

     a.   The exchange rate for the deutsche mark, stated in dollars, is falling.

     b.   The exchange rate for the pound, stated in dollars, is rising.

     c.   The pound was a weaker currency than the dollar.

     d.   The pound was a stronger currency than the deutsche mark.

___ 6.   European Look purchased cashmere sweaters from England on account at a price of
          £10,000. On the purchase date the exchange rate was $1.61 per British pound, but
          when European Look paid the liability the exchange rate was $1.58 per pound.
          When this foreign account payable is paid. European Look should record a:

    a.   Liability of $300.

    b.   Loss of $300.

    c.   Receivable of $300.

    d.   Gain of $300.

___ 7.   Assume that the exchange rate for the British pound is rising relative to the U. S.
          dollar. An American company will incur *losses* from this rising exchange rate if the
          company is making:

    a.   Credit sales to British companies at prices stated in pounds.

    b.   Credit purchases from British companies with prices stated in U. S. dollars.

    c.   Credit sales to British companies at prices stated in U. S. dollars.

    d.   Credit purchases from British companies at prices stated in pounds.

___ 8.   Assume that the exchange rate for the German deutsche mark is *falling* relative to
          the U. S. dollar. An American company will incur *losses* from this falling exchange
          rate if it is making:

    a.   Credit sales to German companies at prices stated in deutsche marks.

    b.   Credit purchases from German companies at prices stated in U. S. dollars.

    c.   Credit sales to German companies at prices stated in U. S. dollars.

    d.   Credit purchases from German companies at prices stated in deutsche marks.

Exercises

1.   Listed below are eight technical accounting terms emphasized in this chapter.

Multinational company	*"Strong" currency*
"Weak" currency	*Translating*
International accounting	*Foreign currency*
Exchange rate	*Gain on fluctuations in foreign exchange rates*

Each of the following statements may (or may not) describe one of these technical
terms. In the space provided below each statement, indicate the accounting term
described, or answer "None" if the statement does not correctly describe any of the
terms.

a.   A business that is organized and operating in a different country from its parent
      company.

      _____

b. The process of restating an amount of foreign currency in terms of the domestic currency (dollars).

_____

c. Any unit of foreign currency worth more than one U. S. dollar.

_____

d. The ratio at which one currency may be converted into another.

_____

e. A condition of the domestic currency that helps companies that sell domestically produced products, either at home or abroad.

_____

f. Accounting for business activities that span national borders.

_____

g. A currency whose exchange rate is rising relative to that of most other currencies.

_____

2. Translate the following amounts of foreign currency into an equivalent number of U. S. dollars using the exchange rates in the table shown below.

Country	Currency	Exchange Rate
Britain	Pound (£)	$1.6295
France	French franc (FF)	.1991
Japan	Yen (¥)	.0106
Mexico	Peso ($)	.1586
Germany	Deutsche mark (DM)	.7022

a. DM15,000
b. £130,000
c. ¥300,000

3. Jill Adams owns a company that imports perfume from France. In the space provided on the following page, prepare journal entries to record the following events.

Nov. 24   Purchased perfume from St. Jean, a French company, at a price of 50,000 francs, due in 60 days. The current exchange rate is $.1913 per franc. (Adams uses the perpetual inventory method.)

Dec. 21   Adams made a year-end adjusting entry relating to the account payable to St. Jean. The exchange rate at year-end was $.1900 per franc.

Jan. 23   Issued a check for $9,540 (U. S. dollars) to Global Bank in full settlement of the liability to St. Jean. the current exchange rate is $.1908 per franc.

2002	General Journal		
Nov. 24	Inventory		
Dec. 31			
2003			
Jan. 23			

SOLUTIONS TO CHAPTER 14 SELF-TEST

True or False

1.   **F** Globalization typically progresses through a series of stages that include exporting, licensing, joint ventures, wholly owned subsidiaries, and global sourcing.

2.   **F** In the United States, most large international companies raise capital by selling their securities in well-developed capital markets.

3.   **T** In a planned economy, land and production facilities are government owned and controlled. The former Soviet Union and the Soviet Eastern Bloc countries used central planning and had planned economies. China continues to use central planning extensively.

4.   **F** Asian countries, such as South Korea and Japan, have collectivist types of industrial organization. Studies have shown that collectivist cultures place less emphasis upon the importance of control in business organizations.

5.   **F** The international Accounting Standards Committee has no enforcement power.

6.   **T** Whenever an American company buys or sells merchandise in a *credit* transaction with a foreign company, and the contract price is stipulated in the *foreign currency*, any fluctuations in the exchange rate will cause gains and losses.

7.   **T** Exchange rates are used to determine how much of one currency is equivalent to a given amount of another currency.

8.   **T** Exchange rates (the "price" of one currency stated in terms of another) fluctuate based upon supply and demand.

9.   **F** A *gain* results because fewer dollars are needed to repay the debt (stipulated in a foreign currency) than when the debt arose.

10. **T** An increase in the exchange rate causes a creditor to incur a gain on receivables in that currency, and a debtor to incur a loss on payables stipulated in that currency.

11. **T** With small exports, there is not a great demand by purchasers for the country's currency to pay for the goods exported. Low demand causes the exchange rate to decline relative to other countries' currencies.

12. **F** When a politically stable country offers high interest rates relative to inflation, foreign investors will want to invest funds in that country. To do this, they must obtain that country's currency; high demand strengthens a country's currency.

13. **F** A company's financial statements are presented in one currency; financial statement amounts for foreign subsidiaries are translated into that currency.

14. **T** Generally accepted accounting principles used in America are *not* in worldwide use.

15. **T** In addition to translating the accounting records of foreign subsidiaries to U. S. dollars, the parent company must adjust a foreign subsidiary's accounting records to U. S. GAAP.

Completion Statements

1. Globalization.
2. Market economies.
3. Culture.
4. Global sourcing.
5. International Accounting Standards Committee.
6. Translating.
7. $5,300.
8. Losses, gains.
9. Loss; $1,000.
10. Selling, hedging.

Multiple Choice

1. Answer **a** – Most companies begin globalization by exporting goods to foreign customers. While exporting maintains control over production, international licensing is a more complex relationship which gives up control for a monetary return. International joint ventures and wholly owned international subsidiaries are usually an outgrowth of exporting and licensing activities.

2. Answer **b** – Global sourcing is the close coordination of diverse business activities across international boundaries. Global sourcing represents the degree to which a company is engaged in globalization. It does not represent an environmental force. Economic systems, culture, technology, infrastructure, and political and legal systems are considered environmental forces which influence the way in which accounting is measured, reported, and created.

3. Answer **d** – Uncertainty avoidance is a to describe people's comfort in dealing with ambiguous situations. Power distance refers to perceptions regarding the distribution of power within and across institutions and organizations. Long-term orientations are associated with valuing highly perseverance, thriftiness, maintaining order, and lasting relationships. Collectivism refers to a high interdependence among members of a particular culture.

4.   Answer **b** – (40,000FF x $.1900 per franc = $7,600). Answer **d** is incorrect; the amount of the liability *is known* as the purchase date. Any changes in the amount of this liability will be *future* events and will be recorded if and when they occur.

5.   Answer **c** – if the dollar "rose slightly" against the pound, the exchange rate for the pound (stated in dollars) has declines. Thus, the pound was a weaker currency than the dollar.

6.   Answer **d** – European Look's liability to the English company originally was $16,100 (£10,000 x $1.61 per pound). However, European Look ultimately paid only $15,800 to settle this liability (£10,000 x $1.58 per pound), thus resulting in a $300 gain from the fluctuation in the exchange rate.

7.   Answer **d** – as a result of the rising exchange rate, the American company will have to pay *more dollars* to settle its liability (for a fixed number of pounds) at the settlement date than was required earlier, at the date of the initial purchase. This difference is a *loss* from exchange rate fluctuations. Answer **a** is incorrect, because the seller's receivable (which is fixed in pounds) becomes equivalent to more dollars as the exchange rate for the pound rises. Answers **b** and **c** are incorrect; if the receivables or payables are fixed in dollars, the American company will experience neither a gain nor a loss from exchange rate fluctuations.

8.   Answer **a** – if the exchange rate for the deutsche mark is falling, an American company with receivables of a fixed number of deutsche marks is seeing the value of this asset decline.

Solutions to Exercises

1.

a.   None (The statement describes a *foreign subsidiary*; a multinational company is one that does business in more than one country.)

b.   Translating

c.   None (The terms *strong currency* and *weak currency* refer to the direction of recent changes in the exchange rate, not to the absolute level of this rate.)

d.   Exchange rate

e.   "Weak" currency

f.   International accounting

g.   "Strong" currency

2.

a. $10,533 (DM 15,000 x $.7022 per deutsche mark.)

b. $211,835 (£130,000 x $1.6295 per pound)

c. $3,180 (¥300,000 x $.0106 per yen)

3.

2002	General Journal		
Nov. 24	Inventory	9,565	
	Accounts Payable – St. Jean		9,565
	Purchased perfume from St. Jean for 50,000 francs, exchange		
	rate, $.1913 per franc (50,000FF x $.1913 = $9,565)		
Dec. 31	Accounts Payable – St. Jean	65	
	Gain on Fluctuation in Foreign Exchange Rates		65
	To adjust liability to St. Jean based on year-end exchange rate:		
	Original balance $9,565		
	Adjusted balance (50,000FF x $.1900) $9,500		
	Gain through year-end $ 65		
2003			
Jan. 23	Accounts Payable – St. Jean	9,500	
	Loss on Fluctuation in Foreign Exchange Rates	40	
	Cash		9,540
	Paid 50,000 franc liability to St. Jean; exchange rate,		
	$.1908 per franc (50,000FF x $.1908 = $9,540)		

APPENDIX B
THE "TIME-VALUE" OF MONEY: FUTURE AMOUNTS AND PRESENT VALUES

HIGHLIGHTS OF THE APPENDIX

1. A very important consideration in investing is the concept of the time value of money. This concept is based on the idea that an amount of money received today has a present value that is always less than its future amount. This is because money on hand today can be invested to become equivalent to a larger *amount in the future*.

2. The difference between a future amount and its present value may be regarded as interest revenue (or expense) included in the future amount. The amount of the interest depends on two factors: (a) the rate of interest and (b) the length of time on which interest accumulates.

3. Typical applications of the time value of money include determining: (a) the amount to which an investment will accumulate over time, (b) the amount that must be invested every period to accumulate a required future amount, and (c) the present value of cash flows expected to occur in the future.

4. Table FA-1 in the text's appendix shows the amount to which $1 will accumulate over a given number of periods. By multiplying the factor from the table by the amount of the investment, the future amount of any present value can be calculated.

5. If the investor needs to determine how much to invest to accumulate a specified future value. The specified future value in Table FA-1 should be divided by the table value corresponding to the appropriate interest rate and the number of periods.

6. To accumulate a large future amount, an investor may make a periodic series of deposits. A periodic series of equal sized cash payments (or receipts) is called an *annuity*. Table FA-2 may be used to determine the future amount to which an annuity will accumulate. The future amount is determined by multiplying the factor from the table (corresponding to the appropriate interest rate and number of periods) by the amount of the periodic investments.

7. If the investor needs to determine the amount of the periodic investment needed to accumulate a specified future amount, the future amount is divided by the factor from Table FA-2.

8. The length of the period used to calculate the future value of an investment depends upon how often interest is earned (compounded). For example, if interest is earned monthly, a month is used as the period and the monthly interest rate is used.

9. The present value of an investment is the amount an investor would pay today for the right to receive an expected future amount of cash. The present value of a future amount depends upon (a) the estimated *amount* of the future cash receipt (or payment), (b) the *length of time* until the future amount will be received (or paid), and (c) the rate of return required by the investor. The required *rate of return* is called the discount rate and depends upon the amount of *risk* associated with the investment opportunity, and upon the return available from alternative investment opportunities.

10. Computing the present value of a future cash flow is called discounting the future amount. The easiest method of discounting a future amount is by the use of present value tables (Tables PV-1 and PV-2). Your textbook includes present value tables which show

247

(a) the present value of a single, lump sum, amount to be received at a future date and (b) the present value of a series of equal-sized periodic cash flows, called an *annuity*.

11. The use of present value tables can be demonstrated by finding the present value of $800 to be received annually for 10 years, discounted at an annual rate of 12%. Since this is a series of 10 *equal-sized* payments, Table PV-2 in the textbook is applicable. The present value of $1 received annually for 10 years, discounted at 12%, is 5.650, meaning $5.65. Therefore, the present value of the $800 annuity is $800 x 5.650, or *$4,520*.

12. The interval between regular periodic cash flows is termed the *discount period*. Annual cash flows involve discount periods of one year; in these situations, the annual rate of interest is used as the discount rate. When the periodic cash flows occur on a more frequent basis, such as monthly, the discount rate must be expressed as a monthly interest rate. For example, an annual rate of 18% must be expressed as a monthly rate of 1.5% when the cash flows occur monthly. The discount rate must relate to the time interval of the *discount period*.

13. The concept of present value has many applications in accounting, including the valuation of certain assets and liabilities, determining the portions of certain cash flows that represent payment or receipt of interest, and evaluating investment opportunities. Many of these applications are discussed below.

14. Accountants use the term *financial instruments* to describe cash, equity investments in another business, and any contracts calling for the receipt or payment of cash. Examples include cash, accounts receivable, investments in marketable securities, and all common liabilities except for unearned revenue and deferred income taxes.

15. Whenever the present value of a financial instrument *differs* significantly from the sum of the expected future cash flows, the financial instrument initially is recorded in the accounting records at its present value. Differences between this recorded present value and the actual future cash flows are accounted for as interest.

Assume, for example, a company borrows $10,000 for one year, signing a $10,000, 9%, note payable. The cash outlay at the maturity date will be $10,900. But the note originally is recorded as a *$10,000* liability—an amount equal to its present value at the date of issuance. The other $900 will be treated as interest expense.

16. In the preceding illustration, the terms of the note clearly distinguish between the principal amount (a present value) and interest. In other cases, however, the present value of the obligation must be *computed*.

17. Consider, for example, *capital lease agreements* (capital leases are discussed in Chapter 9). When an asset is "sold" under a capital lease, the lessor records a receivable equal to the present value of the future lease payments, and the lessee records this present value as a liability. The present value of the future lease payments is computed by discounting these payments at a realistic interest rate.

18. Companies sometimes issue notes payable which make no mention of an interest charge. The present value of such "non-interest-bearing" notes can be determined either by present value computations or, sometimes, by appraising the consideration received in exchange. If this present value is substantially *less* than the payments to be made on the note, the note should be recorded at its present value. The excess of the future payments over this *present value* will be treated as interest expense.

19. Present values increase over time toward the actual amount of the future cash flow. Also, present values may fluctuate because of changes in the market interest rate, which is used as the discount rate. The present value of a financial instrument at a particular date after its issuance is called its *current value*.

20. Some financial instruments (cash, investments in marketable securities, and postretirement obligations) *are adjusted to their current value* at the end of each accounting period. For other financial instruments, the current value should be *disclosed* if it differs significantly from the carrying value shown in the financial statements.

Obligations for postretirement benefits are shown at the *estimated present value* of the future benefit payments earned by employees during the current and prior accounting periods. Because these benefits will be paid many years in the future, their present value is *much less* than the expected future outlays. (Accounting for postretirement costs is discussed in Chapter 9.)

21. The only long-term liability *not* recorded in financial statements at its present value is deferred income taxes payable. This is because there is no "contract" determining the amount or payment date of deferred taxes. However, many accountants believe that deferred tax liabilities are overstated because they are not discounted to their present value.

22. Present value computations often are used in *capital budgeting* decisions. In this context, comparing the estimated present values of future cash receipts and payments indicates whether or not the proposed investment will earn a rate of return at least equal to the discount rate.

TEST YOURSELF ON APPLICATIONS OF FUTURE AMOUNTS AND PRESENT VALUES

True or False

For each of the following statements, circle the T or the F to indicate whether the statement is true or false.

T   F   1. The present value of an amount to be paid or received in the future is always less than the future amount.

T   F   2. The future amount of an investment depends upon the interest rate and the number of periods on which the interest accumulates.

T   F   3. Using a larger interest rate results in a larger future amount.

T   F   4. The table of the "future value of $1 paid periodically for n periods" is used to compute the future amount of equal-sized or unequal-sized payments.

T   F   5. As the number of periods increases the future value of an investment decreases.

T   F   6. If an investment fund pays 12% interest compounded monthly for 5 years, the future amount should be determined using the factor for 5 periods at 12% interest.

T   F   7. The discount rate used in computing the present value of a future cash receipt may be viewed as the investor's required rate of return.

T   F   8. Using a higher discount rate results in a higher present value.

T   F   9. The longer the length of time until a future amount will be received, the lower its present value.

T F   10. The concept of present value is applicable to future cash receipts, but not to future cash payments.

T F   11. All the factors in the table showing the present value of $1 to be received in n periods are less than 1.000.

T F   12. The interest rate shown in a present value table must be interpreted as an annual rate, even if the time interval of the discount period is only a month.

T F   13. Both accounts receivable and accounts payable are examples of financial instruments.

T F   14. Financial instruments initially are recorded in the accounting records at present values whenever these present values differ substantially from the expected future cash receipts or outlays.

T F   15. At every balance sheet date, the carrying values of all financial instruments are adjusted to their current values.

T F   16. When the net present value of a proposed capital expenditure is zero, the proposal provides no return on investment.

T F   17. When equipment is purchased in exchange for a "non-interest-bearing" installment note payable, the cost to be recorded is equal to the present value of the note.

T F   18. The market price of a bond may be regarded as a present value, whereas the maturity value of the bond is a future value.

Completion Statements

Fill in the necessary word to complete the following statements:

1.   The basic premise of the _____ _____ concept is that a dollar available today is worth (more, less) _____ than a dollar that will not be available until a future date.

2.   The future amount of an investment depends on the _____ rate, and the period of time over which the _____ _____.

3.   The _____ _____ of an amount of cash is always greater than its present value.

4.   The process of determining the present value of a future cash receipt or payment is termed _____ the future cash flow.

5.   The present value of a future cash flow depends upon three things: (a) the estimated _____ _____ of the future cash flow, (b) the _____ _____ _____ until the cash flow will occur, and (c) the _____ _____ used in computing the present value.

6.   An annuity is a series of periodic cash flows that are _____ in dollar amount.

7.   Present value tables may be used with discount periods of any length, but the _____ must apply to the period of time represented by one discount period.

8.   Super Store borrowed $30,000 from First Bank by issuing a six-month note payable in the face amount of $31,200. At the date the loan is made, the present value of Super Store's liability to the bank is $_____; the difference between this amount and $31,200 represents _____ included in the face amount of the note.

9.   The market price of bonds may be regarded as the present value to bondholders of the future _____ and _____ payments to be received.

Multiple Choice

Choose the best answer for each of the following questions and enter the identifying letter in the space provided.

___ 1.   The present value concept is based on the premise that:

     a.   A cash flow that will not occur until a future date is equivalent to a smaller amount of money receivable or payable today.

     b.   The present value of a future cash flow is greater than the actual amount of the future cash flow, because money on hand today is more valuable than money due at a future date.

     c.   Money invested today can be expected to become equivalent to a smaller amount at a future date.

     d.   The present value of a future cash flow may be greater or smaller than the future amount, depending upon the discount rate.

___ 2.   The future value of a $100 investment that earns a 10% annual return for three years is:

     a. $110.00.

     b. $121.20.

     c. $133.10.

     d. $136.50.

___ 3.   Cipher Data Systems is required to accumulate $5 million in a bond sinking fund to retire bonds payable 10 years from now. Cipher will make annual equal payments to the fund at the end of each of the next 10 years. If Cipher can earn 12% annual return on the bond sinking fund, the required annual payments will be $284,916.52. If the return on the sinking fund is 10% instead of 12%, the required annual payments will be:

a. $267,854.20.

b. $275,453.55.

c. $280,333.25.

d. $313,735.33.

___ 4.   Assume that an investor has decided to invest $20,000 at the end of each of the next 5 years in an investment fund. If the investment fund earns 8% it will accumulate to a total of $117,340. If the investment fund earns 10% instead of 8%, the accumulated total amount will be:

a. $111,430.

b. $115,634.

c. $116,450.

d. $122,100.

___ 5.   Which of the following factors does not affect computation of the present value of a future cash flow?

a.   The discount rate.

b.   The period of time until the future cash flow will occur.

c.   Whether the future cash flow will be a cash payment or a cash receipt.

d.   The dollar amount of future cash flow.

___ 6.   The present value of $121 due in two years, discounted at an annual rate of 10% is:

a. $91.90.

b. $96.80.

c. $100.

d. $110.

____ 7.   Wine Country Safari purchased a hot-air balloon on a contract requiring 24 monthly payments of $730, with no mention of interest. An appropriate annual rate of interest for financing the purchase of the balloon would be 12%. To determine the cost of the balloon and the present value of the contract payable, Wine Country Safari should discount:

   a. $730 for 24 periods at 12%.

   b. $17,520 for two periods at 12%.

   c. $730 for 24 periods at 1%.

   d. $17,520 for two periods at 6%.

____ 8.   The present value of $1,000 due in five years, discounted at an annual rate of 12%, is $567. If this $1,000 future amount had been discounted at an annual rate of 15%, the present value would have been:

   a. $497.

   b. $582.

   c. $621.

   d. $747.

____ 9.   The present value of $500 due in five years, discounted at an annual interest rate of 10% is $311. If the $500 is due in six years, rather than five, its present value would be approximately:

   a. $282.

   b. $311.

   c. $374.

   d. $500.

____ 10.   Present value techniques are not used to determine the financial statement valuation of:

   a.   Long-term notes payable with interest charges included in the face amount.

   b.   The long-term liability for deferred income taxes.

   c.   A long-term note payable with no stated interest rate.

   d.   The liability arising from entering into a long-term capital lease.

Exercises

   1.   Listed below are seven technical accounting terms emphasized in this appendix:

   Discount rate   *Present value table*
   Annuity   *Discount period*
   Present value   *Annuity table*
   Future amount

Each of the following statements may (or may not) describe one of these technical terms. In the space provided below each statement, indicate the accounting term described, or answer "None" if the statement does not correctly describe any of the terms.

a. The interval between regular periodic cash flows.

_____

b. A table that shows the present value of $1 to be received periodically for a given number of periods.

_____

c. An investor's required rate of return.

_____

d. The amount that a knowledgeable investor would pay today to receive a certain amount in the future.

_____

e. A series of equal-sized periodic cash flows.

_____

f. The amount to which an investment is expected to accumulate.

_____

2. Use the future value tables in your textbook to determine the future value of the following investments.

   a. $10,000 to be deposited today in a fund that earns 6% annually for 5 years.

   b. $1,000 deposited at the end of each of the next 3 years in a fund that earns a 8% annual return.

   c. $20,000 to be deposited today in a fund that earns 10% annual return for 4 years, compounded semiannually.

3. Use the present value table in your textbook to determine the present value of the following cash flows:

   a. $10,000 to be received annually for seven years, discounted at an annual rate of 15%.

   b. $4,250 to be received today, assuming that money can be invested to earn an annual return of 12%.

   c. $400 to be paid monthly for 24 months, with an additional "balloon payment" of $10,000 at the end of the 24th month, discounted at a monthly interest rate of 1½%.

4. On November 1, Airport Transport purchased a new van by making a cash down payment of $3,000 and issuing an installment note payable in the face amount of $12,000. The note is payable in 24 monthly installments of $500 each, beginning on December 1. The following statement appears at the bottom of the note payable: "The $12,000 face amount of this note includes interest charges computed at a rate of 1½% per month."
In the space provided below, prepare the journal entries needed on (a) November 1 to record the purchase of the van, and (b) December 1 to record the first $500 monthly payment and to recognize interest expense for one month by the effective interest method. (Round interest expense to the nearest dollar.)

General Journal				
Nov. 1	Vehicles			
Dec. 1				

SOLUTIONS TO APPENDIX B SELF-TEST

True or False

1. **T** The amount by which the future cash receipt exceeds its present value represents interest.

2. **T** The future amount depends on two factors (1) the interest rate and (2) the period of time.

3. **T** As the interest rate increases, the future amount increases.

4. **F** The table is used to find the future amount of a series of equal-sized payments only.

5. **F** As the number of periods increase, the future amount increases.

6. **F** The future amount should be determined by using the factor for 1% interest for 60 monthly periods.

7. **T** Factors affecting the investor's required rate of return are the degree of risk associated with a particular investment, the investor's cost of capital, and the returns available from other investment opportunities.

8. **F** The higher the discount rate used, the lower the present value.

9. **T** Cash of $100 to be received in three years has smaller value today than $100 to be received next week.

10. **F** The process of discounting cash flows applies to both cash receipts and cash payments.

11. **T** The present value of an amount is always less than the future amount.

12. **F** Present value tables can be used with discount periods of *any length*; the discount rate shown is the *rate per period*.

13. **T** The term *financial instruments* describes cash, equity investments in other businesses, and contracts calling for the receipt or payment of cash. This latter category includes both receivables and payables.

14. **T** The difference between this present value and the future cash flows is accounted for either as interest revenue or interest expense.

15. **F** The carrying values of *some* financial instruments (investments in marketable securities and liabilities for postretirement costs) are adjusted to their current values at each balance sheet date, but the carrying values of other financial instruments are not. For these other instruments, the current values usually are *disclosed* in notes accompanying the financial statements.

16. **F** When the net present value is zero, the proposed investment provides a rate of return equal to the rate used in discounting the cash flows.

17. **T** The negotiated purchase price is the present value of the note payable; part of each payment constitutes interest expense.

18. **T** The market price is the price investors are willing to pay today (present value) for the future *principal and interest payments*.

Completion Statements

1. Present value, more. 2. Interest, interest accumulates. 3. Future value. 4. Discounting. 5(a). Dollar amount, (b) length of time (or number of periods), (c) discount rate. 6. Uniform (or equal). 7. Discount rate. 8. $30,000; interest. 9. Principal (or maturity value), interest.

Multiple Choice

1. Answer **a**—a present value is always less than the future amount. Answers b and d are incorrect, because they both state that a present value is greater than the future amount. Answer c is incorrect because money invested today should earn interest and thereby become equivalent to a larger amount in the future.

2. Answer **c**—$100 x 1.10 x 1.10 x 1.10 = $133.10.

3. Answer **d**—$313,735.33. You need not compute this amount to answer the question. Use of a lower interest rate results in higher required payments. Only answer d is higher than the original required payments of $284,916.52.

4. Answer **d**—$122,100. You need not compute this amount to answer the question. The higher interest rate will result in a larger future amount. Only answer d is higher than the original future amount of $117,340.

5. Answer **c**—three factors involved in computing the present value of a future amount: (1) the size of the future amount, (2) the period of time until the future cash flow will occur, and (3) the discount rate. Whether the future amount is a cash receipt or a cash payment is not relevant.

6. Answer **c**—$121 ÷ 1.10 ÷ 1.10 = $100.

7. Answer **c**—the discount rate must relate to the discount period. As we are using *monthly* discount periods, we must state the interest rate as a monthly rate.

8. Answer **a**—$497. You need not compute this amount to answer the question. Use of a higher discount rate results in a lower present value. Only answer a is lower than the original present value of $567.

9. Answer **a**—$282. You need not compute this amount to answer the question. The longer the time until a future cash flow will occur, the smaller its present value. Only answer a is lower than the original present value of $311.

10. Answer **b**—The liability for deferred income taxes is the *only* long-term liability to which present value concepts are not applied. This obligation is not a *financial instrument*, because there is no "contract" for payment. Tax laws may change at any time. Because of the uncertainty as to future tax rates and payment dates, no effort is made to reduce the deferred tax obligation to its present value. Many accountants believe that current practices can cause this liability to be substantially *overstated*.

Solutions to Exercises

1.
a. Discount period
b. Annuity table
c. Discount rate
d. Present value
e. Annuity
f. Future amount

2.
a. $13,380 ($10,000 x 1.338)
b. $3,246 ($1,000 x 3.246)
c. $29,540 ($20,000 x 1.477) The appropriate factor is the one for eight 6-month periods at 5% interest.

3.
a. $41,600 ($10,000 x 4.160)
b. $4,250 (An amount received or paid today is stated at its present value.)
c. Present value of $400 per month for 24 months, discounted at 1½% per month
    ($400 x 20.030).. $ 8,012

    Present value of $10,000 due in 24 months, discounted at 1½% per month
    ($10,000 x .700).. $ 7,000

    Total.. $15,012

4.

General Journal		
Nov. 1	Vehicles	13,015	
	Notes Payable		10,015
	Cash		3,000
	Purchased van paying part cash and issuing an installment		
	note payable with a present value of $10,015 ($500 monthly		
	payment for 24 months discounted at 1 ½% per month;		
	$500 x 20.030 = 10,015)		
Dec. 1	Notes Payable	350	
	Interest Expense	150	
	Cash		500
	To record monthly payment on installment note payable:		
	Payment		
	Interest ($10,015 x 1 ½%)		
	Reduction on principle		

NOTES

NOTES

NOTES

NOTES

NOTES

NOTES